Volume XII

Medievalism in *A Song of Ice and Fire* and *Game of Thrones*

ISSN 2043–8230

Series Editors
Karl Fugelso
Chris Jones

Medievalism aims to provide a forum for monographs and collections devoted to the burgeoning and highly dynamic multi-disciplinary field of medievalism studies: that is, work investigating the influence and appearance of 'the medieval' in the society and culture of later ages. Titles within the series will investigate the post-medieval construction and manifestations of the Middle Ages – attitudes towards, and uses and meanings of, 'the medieval' – in all fields of culture, from politics and international relations, literature, history, architecture, and ceremonial ritual to film and the visual arts. It welcomes a wide range of topics, from historiographical subjects to revivalism, with the emphasis always firmly on what the idea of 'the medieval' has variously meant and continues to mean; it is founded on the belief that scholars interested in the Middle Ages can and should communicate their research both beyond and within the academic community of medievalists, and on the continuing relevance and presence of 'the medieval' in the contemporary world.

New proposals are welcomed. They may be sent directly to the editors or the publishers at the addresses given below.

Professor Karl Fugelso
Art Department
Towson University
3103 Center for the Arts
8000 York Road
Towson, MD 21252–0001
USA

Dr Chris Jones
School of English
University of St Andrews
St Andrews
Fife KY16 9AL
UK

Boydell & Brewer Ltd
PO Box 9
Woodbridge
Suffolk IP12 3DF
UK

Previous volumes in this series are printed at the back of this book

Medievalism in *A Song of Ice and Fire* and *Game of Thrones*

Shiloh Carroll

D. S. BREWER

First published 2018
D. S. Brewer, Cambridge

ISBN 978 1 84384 484 6

D. S. Brewer is an imprint of Boydell & Brewer Ltd
PO Box 9, Woodbridge, Suffolk IP12 3DF, UK
and of Boydell & Brewer Inc.
668 Mt Hope Avenue, Rochester, NY 14620–2731, USA
website: www.boydellandbrewer.com

A CIP catalogue record for this book is available
from the British Library

This publication is printed on acid-free paper

Contents

Acknowledgements

Completing a work of this size and complexity requires a robust support system for any author, and I am deeply appreciative of those who helped me reach completion on this book: Amy Kaufman, mentor and friend, who coached me through the process of writing and seeking publication; Rhonda Kavan, who allowed me to adjust my schedule and work responsibilities in order to complete the draft on time; my readers and cheerleaders, Helen Young, Geoffrey Elliott, Alexandra Garner, Emily Stewart, Janice Lupo, Kiriél Hammond, and Skyla Hammond. To those who provided support in other ways – Louise D'Arcens, Kevin Moberly, Sinéad Hanrahan, Michael Gower, Brent Moberly, Shane Stewart, Paul Sturtevant, Valerie O'Brien, Donald Hammond and the entire Tales after Tolkien Society – my deepest gratitude. And sincere thanks, of course, to my husband, Eric, who provided support, a listening ear, and thoughtful "hmm"s whenever I needed them.

Author's Note

Many academic books that analyze large and/or serialized works such as *A Song of Ice and Fire* and *Game of Thrones* include plot summaries or other appendixes to help the reader keep track of characters and plot. However, with the level of complexity and the sheer number of characters in *A Song of Ice and Fire*, that is not feasible for this book. Instead, readers are encouraged to visit *A Wiki of Ice and Fire* (awoiaf.westeros.org) and the *Game of Thrones* wiki (gameofthrones.wikia.com); they should be aware that this book assumes familiarity with the novels and the show, and "spoilers" abound. Since production on this volume began before season seven of *Game of Thrones* aired, no discussion of that season appears here.

Introduction: Martin and Medievalist Fantasy

George Raymond Richard Martin is well known among fantasy fans and in the greater pop-culture zeitgeist, primarily for his epic fantasy series *A Song of Ice and Fire* (1996–), which has been adapted as *Game of Thrones* (2011–), a TV series on HBO. However, *A Song of Ice and Fire* is hardly his only fiction, and *Game of Thrones* hardly his only foray into television writing and production. Martin began writing fiction at a young age, using his collection of Miller Aliens toys and pet turtles as inspiration for science-fiction stories.[1] When one of his college professors allowed him to write a historical-fiction story rather than a term paper, then submitted it to a magazine on Martin's behalf, Martin discovered that submitting and being rejected was not as bad as he had feared and began pursuing publication on his own.[2] His first professional publication was a science-fiction story in *Galaxy* magazine in 1971; since then he has published science fiction, fantasy, and horror. In 1983, he released *Armageddon Rag*, a novel about a rock band that was equal parts love letter to and chiding of the Baby Boomer generation. Unexpectedly, it failed on the market and, in his words, "essentially destroyed my career as a novelist at the time."[3] However, this failure led to opportunities in Hollywood; the screenwriter who attempted

[1] "George R.R. Martin and Robin Hobb – Exclusive Event," YouTube video, 1:27:05, posted by Blinkbox Books, August 26, 2014, https://www.youtube.com/watch?v=tXLYSnMIrXM&feature=youtu.be.

[2] Ibid., n.p.

[3] Isobel Berwick, "Lunch with the FT: George R.R. Martin," *Financial Times*, June 1, 2012, https://www.ft.com/content/bd1e2638-a8b7-11e1-a747-00144feabdc0#axzz1wYzURClo.

to turn *Armageddon Rag* into a movie hired Martin as a writer for *The Twilight Zone* (1985–9), and thereafter, he worked on other TV shows such as *Beauty and the Beast* (1987–90) and *The Outer Limits* (1995–2002). He has won four Hugo and two Locus awards for his short fiction, two Hugos for screenwriting for *Game of Thrones*, and an Emmy for *Game of Thrones*.[4]

Martin has expressed frustration with working in television, claiming that it was not as rewarding as writing prose fiction.[5] He was frequently asked to reduce the size of his cast, down-scale the effects, or cut back other aspects of his scripts that would render them too expensive to shoot. He also struggled with attempts to write and produce new shows that were not picked up by studios, saying that undertaking all that work without a reader or a viewer was "ultimately unsatisfying."[6] In 1991, he began work on *A Game of Thrones*, the first book in the *Song of Ice and Fire* series, which was initially conceived as a trilogy. His work in television and on other books, such as the *Wild Cards* series, delayed his writing, but *A Game of Thrones* was released in 1996, followed by *A Clash of Kings* in 1998, *A Storm of Swords* in 2000, *A Feast for Crows* in 2005, and *A Dance with Dragons* in 2011. At the time of this writing, *The Winds of Winter* is still forthcoming, with no confirmed publication date.

George R.R. Martin: The American Tolkien?

In his 2005 review of George R.R. Martin's *A Feast for Crows, Time* magazine's Lev Grossman referred to Martin as "the American Tolkien," and the appellation stuck – "as it was meant to," he remarked

[4] "Awards and Honors," *George R.R. Martin*, 2016, http://www.georgerrmartin.com/about-george/awards-honors/; "67th Emmy Awards Nominees and Winners," *Academy of Television Arts and Sciences*, 2015, http://www.emmys.com/awards/nominees-winners?page=2; "2013 Hugo Awards," *The Hugo Awards*, 2013, http://www.thehugoawards.org/hugo-history/2013-hugo-awards/.

[5] Linda Richards, "January Interview: George R.R. Martin," *January Magazine*, January 2001, http://www.januarymagazine.com/profiles/grrmartin.html.

[6] Ibid., n.p.

in 2011.[7] Like J.R.R. Tolkien's *The Lord of the Rings*, Martin's *A Song of Ice and Fire* is epic in scope and highly influential on both fantasy writers and the public perception of medievalism. On the surface, Martin and Tolkien have much in common. Both created epic fantasy worlds that rely heavily on medieval material – medieval history in Martin's case, medieval legend and romance in Tolkien's. Tolkien is widely credited with instigating popular interest in high fantasy, while Martin has popularized "grimdark"[8] fantasy.

Despite their similarities, in many ways Martin and Tolkien are quite different, especially in their beliefs about fantasy, reality, and escapism. Unlike Tolkien, Martin's series does not involve a battle between good and absolute evil and does not (yet) offer much hope for a neat, fulfilling ending (though Martin says it will be "bittersweet").[9] Grossman claims that Martin's work is "an epic for a more profane, more jaded, more ambivalent age than the one Tolkien lived in."[10] Tolkien is too simplistic, Grossman argues, for contemporary audiences, and Martin provides the kind of high fantasy these audiences want. Tolkien's ideas about escapism and fantasy literature, or "fairy-stories," are well documented in his essays "On Fairy-Stories" and "The Monsters and the Critics," as well as his letters. Tolkien vigorously defended fantasy against the prevailing theories of folklore of the time, especially those of Max Müller and Andrew Lang.[11] He

[7] Lev Grossman, "George R.R. Martin's *A Dance with Dragons*: A Masterpiece Worthy of Tolkien," *Time*, July 7, 2011, http://content.time.com/time/arts/article/0,8599,2081774,00.html.

[8] Helen Young defines "grimdark" as "a sub-genre created in the late twentieth and twenty-first centuries, [...] marked by low-levels of magic, high-levels of violence, in-depth character development and medievalist worlds that are 'if not realistic, at least have pretentions to realism' in their depictions of rain, mud and blood" (*Race and Popular Fantasy Literature: Habits of Whiteness* [New York: Routledge, 2016], 63; quoting Guy Haley, "Fantasy Family Tree," *SFX*, 2011).

[9] Sean T. Collins, "Exclusive: George R.R. Martin Says *Game of Thrones* Ending Will Be 'Bittersweet,'" *Observer*, August 11, 2015, http://observer.com/2015/08/george-r-r-martins-ending-for-game-of-thrones-will-not-be-as-brutal-as-you-think/

[10] Ibid., n.p.

[11] Max Müller referred to mythology as "a disease of language" in *Lectures on the Science of Language* (Oxford: Oxford University Press, 1861), 12; Andrew Lang argued that mythology was "the working of the human intellect in its

wholeheartedly rejected their ideas that mythology was a "disease of language" and that myths arose during the "childhood" of the human race and were thus only fit for children, while simultaneously upholding the "intrinsic value" of stories as against the anthropologic tendency to mine them for "extrinsic information."[12]

Like Tolkien, Martin acknowledges the power of the imagination and the necessity of cultural myths – which he refers to as "necessary lies" – arguing that "[s]ome of these lies allow us to live richer, happier lives, and when we lose the capacity to believe those lies [...] it harms us."[13] However, he also frequently criticizes the fantasy that has followed Tolkien as "clichéd" and "Disneyland," arguing that readers deserve more realism in their fiction. He says that *A Song of Ice and Fire* is "fantasy for people who hate fantasy," and expresses a hope that his work will appeal to non-fantasy readers because it is not as predictable as other mainstream fantasy works.[14] Martin's dismissal of much of post-Tolkien heroic fantasy is similar to that of critics contemporary to Tolkien who dismissed him – for example, Edmund Wilson's vicious review of *The Lord of the Rings* describes the work as "balderdash" and "juvenile trash."[15] While Martin's words are not quite as harsh as Wilson's, he does refer to other fantasists as "lesser hands" than Tolkien, their work "completely unreal."[16]

---

earlier or in its later childhood, in its distant hours of barbaric beginnings, or in the senility of its sacerdotage" in *Myth, Ritual, and Religion* (London: Longman's, Green, & Co., 1899), 207.

[12] Verlyn Flieger, "'There Would Always be a Fairy-Tale': J.R.R. Tolkien and the Folklore Controversy," in *Tolkien the Medievalist*, edited by Jane Chance (New York: Routledge, 2003), 33–4.

[13] "George R.R. Martin: Necessary Lies," *Locus* 45, no. 6 (2000), 7.

[14] Dave Itzkoff, "His Beautiful, Dark, Twisted Fantasy: George R.R. Martin Talks *Game of Thrones*," *New York Times*, April 1, 2011, http://artsbeat.blogs.nytimes.com/2011/04/01/his-beautiful-dark-twisted-fantasy-george-r-r-martin-talks-game-of-thrones/?_r=0; Michael Levy, "George R.R. Martin: Dreamer of Fantastic Worlds," *Publishers Weekly* 243, no. 35 (1996), 70.

[15] Edmund Wilson, "Oo, Those Awful Orcs!" Review of *The Fellowship of the Ring* by J.R.R. Tolkien, *The Nation*, April 14, 1956, http://www.jrrvf.com/sda/critiques/The_Nation.html.

[16] Dorman T. Schindler, "*PW* Talks with George R.R. Martin: Of Hybrids and Clichés," *Publisher's Weekly* 252, no. 33 (2005), 37; Gregory Kirschling, "George R.R. Martin Answers Your Questions," *Entertainment Weekly*, November 27, 2007, http://www.ew.com/article/2007/11/27/george-rr-martin-answers-your-questions.

Tolkien and Martin also appear to have diametrically opposed views on escapism and fantasy's role as escapist fiction. In "On Fairy-Stories," Tolkien defends the idea of escapism, arguing that "escape" is necessary for one's mental health; the "real" world is so terrible and hard to live in, he argues, that there is nothing wrong with wanting to ignore it for a time and go somewhere more pleasant.[17] Verilyn Flieger claims that Tolkien's approach to writing *The Lord of the Rings*, *The Silmarillion*, and "The Long Road" was one of escape into the past, where the trials he saw in his present – war, environmental damage, and the rise of destructive technologies – did not yet exist.[18] Tolkien romanticized the past, especially the Middle Ages, and used the tropes of medieval romance for *The Lord of the Rings*, even when, as Flieger puts it, the heroic elements were "scaled down" to hobbit size.[19] Martin, contrarily, opposes such romanticization and, despite his claims about society's "necessary lies," appears to generally distrust escapism. "Someone who loves books too much, or lives too much in the world of imagination, is going to have this faint sense of disappointment about what life actually brings them," he tells Michael Levy. His view that disappointment is a reaction to reality's failure to meet the standards of escapist fiction is in sharp contrast to Tolkien's belief that escapism is a reaction to the world as an intrinsically hard and disappointing place.[20] In the same interview, Martin says that his work is unusual in that it is partially inspired by historical fiction, "which I don't think is true for a lot of other fantasies that are coming out."[21] Martin thus separates his work from, and elevates it above, that

[17] J.R.R. Tolkien, "On Fairy-Stories," 1939, in *The Monsters and the Critics and Other Essays*, edited by Christopher Tolkien (New York: Harper Collins, 2006), 151.

[18] While this may have been Tolkien's intent in writing these works, it is debatable whether he managed it; here I am examining the critics' views of Tolkien rather than the text of *The Lord of the Rings*. Verlyn Flieger, *A Question of Time: J.R.R. Tolkien's Road to Faerie* (Kent, OH: Kent State University Press, 1997), 3.

[19] Verlyn Flieger, "Frodo and Aragorn: The Concept of the Hero," in *Understanding "The Lord of the Rings": The Best of Tolkien Criticism*, edited by Rose A. Zimbardo and Neil D. Isaacs (New York: Houghton Mifflin, 2004), 138.

[20] Levy, 71.

[21] Ibid., 71.

of other fantasists through claims that his is more realistic and less escapist than theirs.

Both Tolkien and Martin create a version of the Middle Ages (though Tolkien's Middle Earth is meant to be pre-historic rather than medieval, it bears many of the markers that associate it with the medievalist rather than the ancient). This is not an insignificant choice, for it reveals a great deal about the authors' intentions and politics. After all, as Rainer Emig has pointed out, setting fantasy in a pre-industrial, pre-feminist, feudal, patriarchal world is a political choice; the Middle Ages are not "timeless" so much as "regressive," Emig argues.[22] Tolkien looked backward for a simpler time, one before the two great wars of his lifetime, before the Industrial Revolution, a time when humankind was more connected to the land. Of course, this view of the Middle Ages is heavily influenced by the Victorians and the Romantics, but that does not alter Tolkien's reasons for creating Middle Earth the way he did. As Flieger puts it, Tolkien "had a nostalgic yearning for a lost past coupled with the knowledge that this was impossible save in the realm of imagination."[23] Eric Rabkin has called this sort of nostalgia "atavistic," claiming that it is "a reversion to a vision of an earlier humankind in closer and happier relation to necessity and nature and self."[24] Looking back toward a past disconnected from our present allows a writer to create a sort of utopia, "an appealing fictional indulgence of a normal nostalgia for that pre-sexual time when we were protected and provided for, when the demands of ourselves were less troubling and when we more willingly followed the patterns set down for us."[25] Alice Chandler refers to this Victorian view of the Middle Ages as "a dream of order," a wistful, idealized view of the past that allowed people to imagine a world more stable and predictable than their own.[26]

[22] Rainer Emig, "Fantasy as Politics: George R.R. Martin's *A Song of Ice and Fire*," in *Politics in Fantasy Media: Essays on Ideologies and Gender in Fiction, Film, Television, and Games,* edited by Gerold Sedlmayr and Nicole Waller (Jefferson, NC: McFarland, 2014), 87.

[23] Flieger, *A Question of Time*, 3.

[24] Eric Rabkin, "Atavism and Utopia," *Alternative Futures* 1, no. 1 (1972), 74.

[25] Ibid., 73–4.

[26] Alice Chandler, *A Dream of Order: TheMedieval Ideal in Nineteenth-Century English Literature* (Lincoln: University of Nebraska Press, 1970), 1.

Martin, on the other hand, has rejected the utopian, atavistic view of the Middle Ages, focusing his political motivations for choosing a medieval setting on his desire to show fantasy readers what the "real" Middle Ages looked like – and it generally looks nothing like Tolkien's world. However, like many fantasy works, including *The Lord of the Rings*, *A Song of Ice and Fire* examines contemporary concerns or anxieties while placing them in a far-distant past, allowing the reader to consider them at a distance. Emig argues that "*A Song of Ice and Fire*, despite its mock-medieval setting, responds to the political situation of the world at the start of the twenty-first century, where old Cold War powers are a thing of the past and new imperial ones are only gradually making their impact felt."[27] Likewise, Martin purposefully challenges typical fantasy politics, avoiding binaries of right and wrong, the idea of absolute power, and the portrayal of women as secondary players in a patriarchal society.[28] He even criticizes Tolkien for overly simplified politics, asking what Aragorn's "ruling wisely" meant:

> What were his tax policies? What did he do when two lords were making war on each other? Or barbarians were coming in from the North? What was his immigration policy? What about equal rights for Orcs? I mean did he just pursue a genocidal policy, "Let's kill all these fucking Orcs who are still left over"? Or did he try to redeem them? You never actually see the nitty-gritty of ruling.[29]

Unlike Tolkien, Martin rejects the "pre-sexual" version of the Middle Ages, a version so often created because the Middle Ages are frequently seen as mankind's infancy and because Tolkien's Catholicism and early- to mid-twentieth-century mores have such a profound influence on the genre. Instead, Martin seems to agree with Rabkin's other assertion regarding utopian fiction: "There was no Golden Age to those inhabiting it."[30] Martin attempts to close the gap between the

[27] Emig, 94.

[28] Ibid., 89–91.

[29] Charlie Jane Anders, "George R.R. Martin: The Complete Unedited Interview," *Observation Deck*, September 23, 2013, http://observationdeck.kinja.com/george-r-r-martin-the-complete-unedited-interview-886117845.

[30] Rabkin, 78.

modern and the medieval by showing that people then were not that different from people now.

In many ways, thinking of George R.R. Martin as "the American Tolkien" is appropriate; his influence on the fantasy genre, particularly neomedieval fantasy, is on a par with Tolkien's. Both authors are deeply indebted to medieval material, not just history, but romance and folk tales as well. Martin has overshadowed many of the fantasy authors who came after Tolkien, if not Tolkien himself, and he has done so partially because of his work's insistence on "realism," historical accuracy, and anti-romanticism.[31] He is, of course, not the only "grimdark" fantasy author, just as Tolkien was not unique in his time, but he is the most popular, just as Tolkien became the most popular fantasy author of his age. Yet it is telling that Grossman chose not to refer to Martin as the "new" Tolkien, but the "American" Tolkien, which suggests not only Martin's nationality, but a certain mindset too. "American" carries with it many connotations, among them power, imperialism, individualism, and a level of cynicism – all of which are readily apparent in *A Song of Ice and Fire*. Thus, it seems that referring to Martin as "the American Tolkien" is fair – as long as all the implications of that title are considered.

On Analysis and Theory

When examining and analyzing a work of medievalist fantasy like *A Song of Ice and Fire*, it is important to be aware of some theoretical terms and frameworks used to consider both works based on the Middle Ages and fantasy in general. First, one must differentiate between "medieval" and "medievalism." The former refers to the period of history usually considered to span from 500 to 1500 CE, and to all the culture, literature, and modes of thinking that characterized that era. The latter is an interpretation of this era and its culture, literature, and modes of thinking; these interpretations are inevitably colored by the culture, biases, and purposes of the interpreters.

[31] Despite his – and many of his readers' – insistence that *A Song of Ice and Fire* is more realist, accurate, and anti-romantic than other fantasies, this is demonstrably not the case, as will be discussed in subsequent chapters.

Contemporary understanding of the Middle Ages is heavily influenced both by Renaissance thinkers, particularly Petrarch, who referred to the period as the "Dark Ages" and saw it as a regression from the Classical era,[32] and by the Victorians, who romanticized the Middle Ages as a time of unity and chivalry and saw in it the roots of their contemporary culture.[33] Thus, medievalism is, to quote Tison Pugh and Angela Jane Weisl, "the art, literature, scholarship, avocational pastimes, and sundry forms of entertainment and culture that turn to the Middle Ages for their subject matter or inspiration, and in doing so, explicitly or implicitly, by comparison or by contrast, comment on the artist's contemporary sociocultural milieu."[34] Medievalism is based on the historically medieval, but is not, itself, medieval.

Likewise, "neomedievalism" refers to yet another remove of medievalism; neomedieval texts use the trappings of the medieval as filtered through a "medievalist intermediary."[35] Most fantasy literature is neomedieval, having a vision of the Middle Ages based on the work of medieval scholars such as Tolkien or the medievalist work of Victorian artists such as the Pre-Raphaelite Brotherhood or Romantic artists such as Sir Walter Scott.[36] The term can also apply to purposefully inaccurate portrayals of the Middle Ages or reflections of popular beliefs about the Middle Ages, usually for satire, such as *Monty Python and the Holy Grail* (1975) or ABC's *Galavant* (2015–16). Neomedievalism is frequently referred to as "postmodern," as it may

[32] Theodore E. Mommsen, "Petrarch's Conception of the 'Dark Ages,'" *Speculum* 17, no. 2 (1942), 226–42.

[33] Walter Kudrycz, *The Historical Present: Medievalism and Modernity* (New York: Continuum, 2011), 57–8.

[34] Tison Pugh and Angela Jane Weisl, *Medievalisms: Making the Past in the Present* (New York: Routledge, 2013), 1.

[35] Amy Kaufman, "Medieval Unmoored," *Studies in Medievalism* XIX (2010), 4.

[36] All these terms are still largely debatable and in flux, but I have attempted to keep them as simple as possible here. Readers interested in these terms, the differences between them, and their application to texts are encouraged to consult issues of *Studies in Medievalism*, Pugh and Weisl's *Medievalisms: Making the Past in the Present*, David Matthews' *Medievalism: A Critical History* (Cambridge: D. S. Brewer, 2014), and Elizabeth Emory and Richard Utz's edited collection *Medievalism: Key Critical Terms* (Cambridge: D. S. Brewer, 2014).

comment on itself or the genre in which it is constructed – fantasy, fairy tale, faux history – and sometimes the anachronisms are deliberate and playful.[37]

These terms are neither negative nor judgmental, but are merely ways of designating the level of separation between the historical medieval and the text in question. Nor are they meant to imply how "accurate" a particular text is in its portrayal of the Middle Ages, as "accuracy" is a red herring in this type of study. Insistence on "authenticity" in fantasy literature is particularly fallacious, as fantasy is by nature transformative. While the facts of history regarding the Middle Ages can be reconstructed, knowledge and understanding are very different. Frederic Jameson has referred to the past as an "absent cause [...] inaccessible to us except in textual form";[38] the layers of interpreting, redefining, recasting, and mythologizing history and attitudes between the Middle Ages and now renders a true understanding of the medieval world and the medieval mindset practically impossible. Indeed, historical accuracy and authenticity only arise in this study because of Martin's (and his readers') frequent insistence that *A Song of Ice and Fire* adheres to some level of realism in its portrayal of the Middle Ages, and such a claim cannot go unexamined.

The "Real" Middle Ages?

A Song of Ice and Fire is frequently praised – and defended – for its "historical accuracy," with fans arguing that the quality of the novels lies primarily in their authenticity. Fans also defend the novels from critics who decry the series' violence, frequent rape, slavery, and other such offenses by saying that Martin is just portraying the Middle Ages the way they "really were." But what exactly do these supporters, and Martin himself, mean by "accurate" and "authentic"? For that matter, what do they mean by "medieval" or "the Middle Ages"? The claims that potentially problematic elements in the novels are acceptable because

[37] Carol L. Robinson and Pamela Clements, "Living with Neomedievalism," *Studies in Medievalism* XVIII (2009), 62–3.

[38] Frederic Jameson, *The Political Unconscious: Narrative as a Socially Symbolic Act* (Ithaca, NY: Cornell University Press, 1981), 20.

they "really happened" at a certain point in history, and that the novels are better than other fantasies because they faithfully recreate that historical period, need to be carefully and critically examined.

The assertion that Martin's "realism" creates a better story than other fantasists have managed in the last fifty or so years requires examination of the attitudes towards those other fantasy works. Fantasy literature has suffered from accusations of "escapism" and rotting the minds of children almost since its advent. Early critics such as Joseph Addison ("The Fairy Way of Writing," 1712), Anna Laetitia Barbauld ("On the Pleasure Derived from Objects of Terror," 1773), and Anthony Nesbit (*Introduction to English Parsing*, 1817) criticized imaginative literature as dangerous, especially to young minds. This gave rise to a tendency for fantasy writers and critics who enjoy such works to vigorously defend the fantastic: writers such as George MacDonald ("The Fantastic Imagination," 1893), J.R.R. Tolkien ("On Fairy-Stories," 1939), and G.K. Chesterton (*All Things Considered*, 1956) argued strenuously that fantasy is inherently moral, deeply creative, and supportive of – even necessary to – one's mental health. Academic theorists and critics continued this argument, leading to a number of books and essays on the inherent value of the fantastic in literature, as well as many that attempted to define fantasy and the fantastic (with mixed results).

Despite these defenses, literary critics in the mid- to late-twentieth century continued generally to deride fantasy, though Tolkien's *The Lord of the Rings* is often cited as an exception to the rule and a yardstick by which to measure other examples of the genre. In 1995, P.J. Webster attempted to differentiate between "creative" fantasy and "escapist" or "derivative" fantasy in order to reinforce the idea of Tolkien as a paragon of fantasists and those who came after him as wanting. Mirroring Renaissance attitudes about the dangers of escapism and fantasy's contributions to imagination, Webster argues that "intrinsically all escapism is detrimental because by its very nature it seeks to avoid reality, it is determined to distract the mind from the reality of life."[39] Martin has likewise shown himself to be

[39] P.J. Webster, "Tolkien and Escapist Fantasy Literature," *Amon Hen* 133 (1995), 12.

critical of escapism (as seen above), while maintaining a deep regard for Tolkien. Martin's focus, however, is in general less on "escapism" and more on what he sees as flimsy constructions of the Middle Ages and poor imitations of the power of Tolkien's worldbuilding, plotting, and prose. He never provides specific examples of the works he means, probably assuming that readers will recognize the trends to which he is referring.

In an interview with John Hodgeman, Martin claims that realism is a major goal for *A Song of Ice and Fire*:

> I sort of had a problem with a lot of the fantasy I was reading, because it seemed to me that the Middle Ages or some version of the quasi Middle Ages was the preferred setting of a vast majority of the fantasy novels I was reading by Tolkien imitators and other fantasists, yet they were getting it all wrong. It was a sort of Disneyland Middle Ages, where they had castles and princesses and all that. The trappings of a class system, but they didn't seem to understand what a class system actually meant. [...] It was like a Ren Fair Middle Ages. Even though you had castles and princesses and walled cities and all that, the sensibilities were those of twentieth-century Americans.[40]

Martin goes on to say that part of his goal is to "write an epic fantasy that had the imagination and the sense of wonder that you get in the best fantasy, but the gritty realism of the best historical fiction."[41]

By referring to the fantasy stories that he dislikes for their lack of authenticity as "Disneyland," Martin implies that neomedievalism is for children, and that his own works, with their attempts at realism, are for adults. In an email correspondence with a fan, Martin goes further; he states outright that his works are "a more complex, adult, and realistic flavor of fantasy."[42] In an interview with George Stroumboulopoulos, Martin said that Tolkien's imitators created clichéd

[40] John Hodgeman, "George R.R. Martin, Author of *A Song of Ice and Fire*," *Bullseye*, September 19, 2011. http://www.maximumfun.org/sound-young-america/george-r-r-martin-author-song-ice-and-fire-series-interview-sound-young-america.

[41] Ibid., n.p.

[42] "Readers and Realism," *The Citadel: So Spake Martin*, June 28, 2001, http://www.westeros.org/Citadel/SSM/Entry/1176.

characters and plots "that have ultimately harmed the genre and made people think that it's for children or particularly slow adults."[43] However, these claims are somewhat problematic – dubious at best and elitist at worst. Implicitly they castigate authors who wrote many years after fantasy began to be considered appropriate only "for children," and who thus worked within an established tradition. Also, echoing Webster's attempt to separate "escapist" fantasy from "creative" fantasy, Martin then defines his work as superior to such lesser neomedievalist offerings (despite obvious neomedievalisms in his own output). At the same time, he fetishizes his own version of fantastic realism, which requires contrast with the "Disneyland," neomedieval Middle Ages, a contrast that he establishes and exploits within the novels.

Several issues surround claims to realism, accuracy, or authenticity when discussing fantasy literature in general and *A Song of Ice and Fire* in particular. Fantasy literature is, by its nature, speculative. It rarely takes place in the historical Middle Ages as they existed on Earth, but instead in a fictional world that borrows the flavor of our Middle Ages, often neomedievally. Thus, there is no actual historical era for the author to emulate. Likewise, the layers of interpretation between the contemporary reader or author and the medieval past make it nearly impossible to recreate a truly "realistic" Middle Ages – a fact Martin has himself acknowledged, saying, "I can't say I've done a complete medieval mindset. I haven't. In fact, I think if I had, it would be too alien. But I've tried to convey some of it."[44] The impact of Renaissance and Victorian scholars and artists on the way the contemporary popular zeitgeist understands the Middle Ages is inescapable. As Veronica Ortenberg puts it:

> Accuracy cannot exist even when most of the factual information is as appropriate as it is possible to make it. This is because generally the writers' perception of the period is overruled, indeed has to be left

[43] "George R.R. Martin on Strombo: Full Extended Interview," *YouTube,* 21:49, posted by "Strombo," March 14, 2012, https://www.youtube.com/watch?v=fHfip4DefG4.

[44] Wayne MacLaurin, "A Conversation with George R.R. Martin," *SF Site,* November 2000, http://www.sfsite.com/01a/gm95.htm.

> out, in order to make the book palatable and interesting to readers. It almost inevitably means projecting twentieth-century attitudes and moral issues onto medieval characters.[45]

The problem of history is not unique to the study of the Middle Ages; Keith Jenkins explains at length the issues with historiography, pointing out that the past itself is "inaccessible simply by virtue of it no longer existing."[46] Historians by nature create narrative and meaning in the way they curate and catalogue the past; there is always some sort of agenda, however subconscious, in portraying the events of the past and writing them into history. Jenkins explains that historians create stories, but people do not live stories, and thus historians "give [the past] an imaginary series of narrative structures and coherences it never actually had."[47] Even working with primary sources from the era one is studying has its pitfalls; Michael Oakeshott has claimed that even records written during the period in question must be treated as secondary, because "a record is a *res gesta* and its authentic utterance is nothing but the performance it constitutes."[48] Like Ortenberg, he claims that authenticity with regards to the past does not exist, because "there is nothing that may be properly called 'direct' evidence of a past that has not survived."[49] Thus, recreating the Middle Ages (or any historical period) in a way that could be called "realistic," "authentic," or "accurate," is impossible. Rather, what is created is one's *idea* of what the Middle Ages were, based on one's exposure to the past as filtered through historians, whether contemporary or from the era, and medievalist intermediaries.

Another issue is the tendency of readers and authors to view the Middle Ages as monolithic, rather than recognizing that the era spanned nearly 1,000 years and dozens of countries, each of which had its own culture. Thus, one must ask to which Middle Ages one

[45] Veronica Ortenberg, *In Search of the Holy Grail: The Quest for the Middle Ages* (London: Hambledon Continuum, 2006), 192.

[46] Keith Jenkins, *On "What is History?": From Carr and Elton to Rorty and White* (New York: Routledge, 1995), 16.

[47] Ibid., 20.

[48] Michael Oakeshott, *On History and Other Essays* (Totowa, NJ: Barnes and Noble, 1983), 55.

[49] Ibid., 56.

intends to be faithful when demanding accuracy in one's work. What was true of France in 1300 CE will not be true of England in 900 CE, or Germany in 1200 CE. However, few contemporary readers consider these vast differences in time, geography, and culture; instead they have a basic set of preconceived notions of the Middle Ages, usually falling into the "Dark Ages" model and the "Chivalric Age" model. Umberto Eco delineated ten "little Middle Ages" that describe how he saw these medievalist and neomedieval models; of these ten, three are most applicable to fantasy medievalism. These three are "pretext," in which "the Middle Ages are taken as a sort of mythological stage on which to place contemporary characters"; "Barbaric Age" medievalism, which focuses on the lack of technology and in which everything is dirty, "shaggy," and primitive; and "Romanticism," in which castles, knights, and princesses are the main motifs.[50] *A Song of Ice and Fire* contains elements of all three of these, though it primarily uses "Barbaric Age" medievalism to contrast and undercut the "Romantic" medievalism of other works of fantasy. In this way, it epitomizes David Matthews' discussion of two branches of medievalism – "gothic" and "romantic" – and the tension between these two views often seen in medievalist literature and film.[51]

Finally, one must consider that "authenticity" is frequently used as a defense against critics who denounce the violence of *A Song of Ice and Fire*, particularly violence against women. That rape, child marriage, inequality, and war were hallmarks of the era is presented as an explanation and excuse for the same in the novels and HBO series. However, these beliefs are frequently based on "Barbaric Age" medievalism and do not take into account medieval laws, class systems, religious edicts, or gender roles – or, again, the vast differences in these between countries and spans of time within the 1,000 years covered by the term "Middle Ages."

Interestingly, Martin's insistence on a "realistic" medieval setting creates its own kind of neomedievalism among the fans of the books and show. Helen Young has studied the fan culture for several years,

[50] Umberto Eco, *Travels in Hyperreality*, translated by William Weaver (San Diego: Harcourt, 1986), 68–9.

[51] Matthews, *Medievalism: A Critical History*, 15.

primarily by reading the *Westeros.org* forums and the discussions of books and TV series in that arena, and has presented her findings in several conference talks and an article in *Year's Work in Medievalism*. Young differentiates between "fans" and casual readers by describing the former as those who have an affective relationship with the text or franchise, who emotionally connect to the story. Young argues that a cognitive dissonance exists in fans; they understand that the world Martin has created is fictional, and yet it is important to them that the world is "authentic," or just like the "real" Middle Ages. She claims that "there is a very strong desire amongst fantasy fans [...] for imagined worlds to reflect historical realities of the Middle Ages," adding that "[t]he point that a fantasy world is, by definition, not historically accurate, however, does not derail the demand for historical authenticity."[52] Young believes that what these fans really want is a sense of verisimilitude, a "feeling" of authenticity but not necessarily true realism. After all, these fans do not seem to understand that the Middle Ages were not homogeneous in terms of culture, laws, traditions, customs, and religious beliefs. They do not back up their "truth claims," because they are not historians; rather, they have combined Martin's "grittiness" with preconceived ideas about the Middle Ages that they have gleaned from other neomedievalist material. Martin's world "feels" more real to them than the "Disneyfied" Middle Ages Martin himself has dismissed, and thus Martin's work must be based on the Middle Ages as they "really" were.[53] To the fans, an authentic representation of the Middle Ages is of paramount importance, but "authenticity" depends on the individual's preconceived beliefs.[54] Young believes that readers are caught in a "feedback loop" in which Martin's work helps to create a neomedieval idea of the Middle Ages, which then becomes their idea of what the Middle Ages "really" looked like, which is then used to defend Martin's work as "realistic"

[52] Helen Young, "'It's the Middle Ages, Yo!': Race, Neo/medievalisms, and the World of *Dragon Age*," *Year's Work in Medievalism* 27 (2012), 6.

[53] Helen Young, "Authenticity and *Game of Thrones*," presented at the 48th Annual International Congress on Medieval Studies, Kalamazoo, Michigan, May 10, 2013.

[54] Young, "'It's the Middle Ages, Yo!,'" 7.

because it matches their idea of the real Middle Ages.[55] Thus, Martin becomes the conduit through which fans understand the Middle Ages, much as Tolkien has been since *The Lord of the Rings*.

One could argue that Martin's frequent complaints about the romantic fantasy Middle Ages found in so much literature do not help dispel the perception of Westeros as representing the "authentic" version. Indeed, he claims the "real" Middle Ages as the basis of his own work: "The impetus here is to keep the story more realistic," he says in a *Game of Thrones* DVD special feature.[56] He has used the "real" medieval to justify his treatment of the children in the series; in an interview with Christina Radish, he claims, "If you read about the real Middle Ages, as I do all the time, it was a brutal time for everybody – for men, women and children. Children weren't sentimentalized, the way they are today."[57] Medieval and ancient precedents are also used as justification for Targaryen and Lannister incest, arranged marriages for girls as young as thirteen, sexual assault and rape, and the overall violence in the series.[58] While Martin has only named a few of his sources in interviews and correspondence, he has stated a preference for "popular" histories and historical fiction. "I am not looking for academic tomes about changing patterns of land use," he tells a fan in an email, "but anecdotal history rich in details of battles, betrayals, love affairs, murders, and similar juicy stuff."[59] He has also admitted to preferring immersion to specific research, reading everything on the history of the Middle Ages, particularly in England, that he can, in order to create "verisimilitude" rather

[55] Helen Young, "The Pleasure of Neo/medievalist Fantasy," presented at the International Conference on Medievalism, De Pere, Wisconsin, July 2013.

[56] "Religions of Westeros," *Game of Thrones: The Complete Second Season* (HBO, 2012).

[57] Christina Radish, "George R.R. Martin Interview: *Game of Thrones*," *Collider*, April 20, 2011, http://collider.com/george-r-r-martin-interview-game-of-thrones/.

[58] James Poniewozik, "George R.R. Martin Interview, Part 1: *Game of Thrones*, from Book to TV," *Time*, April 15, 2011, http://entertainment.time.com/2011/04/15/george-r-r-martin-on-game-of-thrones-from-book-to-tv/; Itzkoff, n.p.

[59] "Historical Influences," *The Citadel: So Spake Martin*, January 20, 2001, http://www.westeros.org/Citadel/SSM/Entry/1170.

than any sort of one-to-one historical correspondence between Westeros and England.[60] He claims that even with this immersion, he allows himself to be "unfaithful to the facts" when it serves the story.[61] In another *Game of Thrones* DVD special feature, he says, "I take [history], and I file off the serial numbers, and I turn it up to eleven, and I change the color from red to purple, and I have a great incident for the books."[62] None of this is bad; rather, it is a very sensible approach that has helped Martin produce the story he wants to write. The trouble comes with insisting that *A Song of Ice and Fire* reflects an accurate, objectively true version of the Middle Ages. At times, Martin even appears to say that medieval history constrains his choices despite the fact that he is writing fantasy: "Just because you put in dragons doesn't mean you can put in anything you want. If pigs could fly, that's your book. But that doesn't mean you also want people walking on their hands instead of their feet. [...] I wanted my books to be strongly grounded in history and to show what medieval society was like."[63] So although Martin is aware that he is writing fantasy and thus has complete control over his world and setting, he still relies heavily on his background reading of history and historical fiction to lend credibility to his work, and sometimes to "pass the buck" to the Middle Ages regarding its more controversial aspects.[64]

Martin is aware that many of his readers come to his work from the fantasy novels of Tolkien imitators with their "Ren Faire Middle

[60] Ron Hogan, "The Beatrice Interview: George R.R. Martin (2000)," *Ron Hogan's Beatrice*, 2000, http://www.beatrice.com/interviews/martin/.

[61] Roz Kaveney, "A Storm Coming," *Amazon.co.uk*, July 2000, http://www.amazon.co.uk/exec/obidos/tg/feature/-/49161/026-1281322-7450821?tag=westeros-21.

[62] "The Real History Behind *Game of Thrones*," *Game of Thrones: The Complete Fifth Season* (HBO, 2016).

[63] James Hibberd, "George R.R. Martin Explains Why There's Violence Against Women on *Game of Thrones*," *Entertainment Weekly*, June 3, 2015, http://www.ew.com/article/2015/06/03/george-rr-martin-thrones-violence-women.

[64] Generally speaking, his response type seems to depend on the tone of the interview; when amiably discussing his writing process and thoughts about medievalism and fantasy, he is more likely to talk about changing medieval traditions to fit the story. When defending these choices against accusations of sexism or glorifying violence against women and children or rape, I suggest that he is more likely to lean on the "historical realism" defense.

Ages." He therefore sets up situations and characters to show that his books will not follow the tropes and structure of the fantasies to which he believes those readers may be accustomed. Martin's disdain for the "Disney" Middle Ages comes through in *A Song of Ice and Fire* as he rejects several tropes of the medieval, medievalist, and neomedieval. While Martin's desire to move past the Romantic archetypes of neomedievalist fantasy can be understood, his insistence that his portrayal of the Middle Ages conforms to an objective historical reality rather than representing another (neo)medievalist interpretation can be problematic. Not only does this insistence suggest that an objective historical reality exists, it also implies that his narrative choices and character arcs are based not on his own viewpoint and understanding of history or humanity, but on an external, inevitable truth that validates his treatment of women, people of color, and those with non-normative sexualities. Once again, it is important to remember that the novels represent an invented world, one that bears similarities to the culture and history of our Middle Ages, but whose culture and characters are entirely constructed by the author. Despite Martin's frequent claims that he is attempting to show the Middle Ages as they "really" were, and his insistence that fantasy does not give a writer leeway to "put in whatever you want," *A Song of Ice and Fire* is not historical fiction that must conform to a series of recorded incidents in order to tell a story. Notwithstanding the historical influence from the Wars of the Roses and the Hundred Years' War, Martin has pointed out that his work is inspired by history, not bound to it, and readers will not be able to guess the ending of *A Song of Ice and Fire* by studying the Wars of the Roses.[65] Martin has the ultimate freedom to create his world the way he wishes to; his argument that he is somehow constrained by history is therefore somewhat flawed. A willingness on the part of the audience to accept fantastical elements such as dragons, wights, and magic, while yet insisting on "realism" in the treatment of women, slaves, the poor, people of color, or people with disabilities raises questions regarding the nature and veracity of authenticity claims. That these groups are almost always treated poorly, and that this poor treatment is deemed necessary to create

[65] Hogan, n.p.

realism in the text, raises further questions regarding audience beliefs about social constructs and systems, and about minorities, the less fortunate, and the otherwise marginalized.

If fantasy neomedievalism is an insulating layer between contemporary concerns and a contemporary audience, creating a safe distance from which these concerns can be examined, then Martin's insistence on realism is an attempt to bridge that gap. His expressed disdain for the Victorian medievalism as expressed in other neomedieval fantasy texts indicates a disdain for escapism in general. However, his insistence that his version of the Middle Ages is the "right" one creates its own problems and neomedievalism. Since he claims that his Middle Ages are based on research and history, he indirectly argues that the "Barbaric Age" model of the Middle Ages is the correct one. In this way, he conforms to a Rationalist view of the Middle Ages, in which, according to Kevin Morris, "[m]edieval ignorance, barbarism and superstition became a byword, it being assumed that such qualities were the moral defects of a corrupt system."[66] Morris argues that this view of the Middle Ages has persisted, and that the Middle Ages continue to be seen as a time of "barbarism, delusion, profligacy, and oppression."[67] Thus, Martin legitimizes Rationalist ideas about the Middle Ages through his choice to dismiss "Disney" neomedievalism as childish, even feminine, and privilege a harsh "realism" in which women are brutalized, commoners are exploited, and power for its own sake is a reasonable goal. Yet the text itself often works against these stated goals, as will be shown throughout this book.

Like most examples of medievalism and neomedievalism, Martin's construction of Westeros reveals more about his *beliefs* about the historical Middle Ages and the human condition than it does about the Middle Ages themselves. It is a bleak and potentially depressing view. If Martin sees the tendencies of his characters to engage in wanton brutality for the sake of power as realistic portrayals of human beings, then his view of the world would seem to be similarly dark. On the *Game of Thrones* season one DVD special features, Martin

[66] Kevin L. Morris, *The Image of the Middle Ages in Romantic and Victorian Literature* (Dover: Croom Helm, 1984), 71.

[67] Ibid., 92.

says: "When I look around at the real world, it's a world full of greys. Even the greatest heroes have weaknesses, and even the blackest villains are capable of the greatest acts of compassion and humanity. People are complicated, and I want my characters to be complicated, too."[68] Martin casts this approach to his characters as another way of avoiding fantasy clichés, explaining to Dorman T. Schindler, "I wanted [...] to get away from the traditional good guys and bad guys clichés of so much of contemporary fantasy."[69] He further claims that:

> The struggle between good and evil is certainly a legitimate topic; but that struggle is not waged against dark lords with evil minions. It's waged against the individual human heart. All of us have good and evil in us; the question is, what choices will we make when we're confronted difficult and dangerous situations? That's the approach [to fantasy] that I wanted to take.[70]

Essentially, Martin's central conceit in writing *A Song of Ice and Fire* is purposeful avoidance of the tropes of medieval romance, medievalist romance, and fantasy literature – all of which are connected, as will be discussed in later chapters. However, his understanding of these tropes, and of medieval culture, is an amalgamation of information gleaned from history, historical fiction, fantasy, and possibly medieval romance; this leads to an inconsistent approach to rejecting and undercutting those established patterns.

Chapter 1 will explore the relationship of Martin's works to medieval romances, and the ways in which he acknowledges and rejects the motifs of both medieval texts and contemporary beliefs about medieval romance, as well as the ways in which his work reflects historians' tendencies toward the narratization of the past. Chapter 2 will examine in detail Martin's treatment of masculinity, femininity, and non-normative gender performance with an eye to how these treatments subvert or uphold traditional medievalist views of women in the Middle Ages, as well as contemporary ideas about gender roles.

[68] "From the Book to Screen," *Game of Thrones: The Complete First Season* (HBO, 2011).

[69] Schindler, 37.

[70] Ibid., 37.

Chapter 3 carries these ideas into a discussion of sexuality, examining Martin's approach to masculine and feminine sexualities, homosexuality, homoeroticism, and other queer sexualities, especially in light of how his medievalist world shapes his narrative decisions regarding his characters and their encounters. Chapter 4 moves into postcolonial theory, considering non-European cultures, non-white people, and imperialism, particularly in the history of Westeros and the movements of Daenerys Targaryen. Finally, Chapter 5 steps outside the text itself to examine fandom and adaptation, focusing primarily on the HBO series *Game of Thrones* and the choices made in adapting the books to the screen, as well as the fandom's reaction to these choices and the showrunners' defenses of their choices.

Verlyn Fleiger claims that one should read and re-read *The Lord of the Rings* "[f]or refreshment and entertainment and, even more important, for a deeper understanding of the ambiguities of good and evil and of ethical and moral dilemmas of a world constantly embroiled in wars with itself."[71] The same can be said of *A Song of Ice and Fire*, which is a multilayered, deep series that invites reading, re-reading, and careful analysis to tease out its subtleties. The novels address good and evil, exploring how these are defined by perception, how people are frequently their own worst enemies without the need for an outside evil force, and how war impacts every level of society. While not without its flaws, the series is an impressive, influential work of medievalist fantasy that has made a deep and lasting mark on the fantasy genre.

[71] Verlyn Flieger, *Splintered Light: Logos and Language in Tolkien's World*, 2nd edition (Kent, OH: Kent State University Press, 2002), viii.

1

Chivalric Romance and Anti-Romance

FANTASY LITERATURE IS in some ways a direct descendent of medieval romance, though it picked up influences from various genres and ideologies on its way to the late twentieth century, when George R.R. Martin began writing *A Song of Ice and Fire*. Authors such as William Morris, Lord Dunsany, and E.R. Eddison purposefully reached back for romance influences, especially "saga literature, Arthurian legend, Old French romances, Anglo-Saxon philology, utopian visions, and vigorous medieval and gothic scholarship."[1] These influences help to explain why fantasy is so often set in a medievalist or neomedieval world. Also, as Kim Selling points out, the Middle Ages are "comfortable" for readers; myth and fairy tale have had a profound enough influence on Western culture that the neomedieval vision of the Middle Ages is familiar, yet different enough and far enough away for readers to believe that fantastic things could happen there and then.[2] In Raymond Thompson's comparative study of medieval romance and fantasy literature, he points out several clear parallels between the genres: both highlight the chivalric virtues of the heroes; both have adventures meant to encourage the hero to discover his own inner strength; both require the hero's virtues – "prowess, courage, loyalty, courtesy, and wisdom" – to be proven; and both set their stories in the past or a secondary world that is "representative

[1] Richard Mathews, *Fantasy: The Liberation of Imagination* (New York: Twayne, 1997), 21.

[2] Kim Selling, "'Fantastic Neomedievalism': The Image of the Middle Ages in Popular Fantasy," in *Flashes of the Fantastic: Selected Essays from the War of the Worlds Centennial: Nineteenth International Conference on the Fantastic in the Arts*, edited by David Ketterer (Westport: Praeger, 2004), 212.

rather than realistic."[3] Perhaps it is because of this link between fantasy and romance that some today think of medieval romance as shallow and escapist, full of knights in shining armor who always live up to the greatest ideals of chivalry and protect women, children, and the innocent. This viewpoint is not limited to non-academic readers, either; W.R.J. Barron claims that romance is idealistic, portraying the world as it could be if people would strive to their highest potential. He also points out the link between fantasy and romance, especially in plot structure and motif; fantasy, he argues, contains such romance motifs as:

> [T]he court gathered around an archetypal feudal monarch in embodiment of chivalric values, the challenge to those values which its reputation provoked, the solitary quest of its representative along forest pathways to answer that challenge, the temptations which beset him in welcoming wayside castles, the lovely woman wooed and won among a maze of adventures, the eventual victory in combat against the challenger and eventual return to court.[4]

Yet closer examinations of medieval romance show much deeper, more complicated issues at work. Joanne Charbonneau and Desiree Cromwell point out that the modern public's ideas about medieval romance tend to be based on eighteenth- and nineteenth-century critics' work on and understanding of the texts, leading to a view of romance as "idealized knights whose adventures include rescuing damsels in distress or succumbing to romantic love."[5]

However, while some romances did portray an idealized version of reality, they did so in reaction to the violence of the era, as clerics and other leaders attempted to build a more ordered society. Romances wrestle with issues such as the effects of unrestrained violence on the

[3] Raymond H. Thompson, "Modern Fantasy and Medieval Romance: A Comparative Study," in *The Aesthetics of Fantasy Literature and Art*, edited by Roger C. Schlobin (Notre Dame: University of Notre Dame Press, 1982), 212–23.

[4] W.R.J. Barron, *English Medieval Romance* (Harlow: Longman, 1987), 4–8.

[5] Joanne Charbonneau and Desiree Cromwell, "Gender and Identity in the Popular Romance," in *A Companion to Medieval Popular Romance*, edited by Raluca L. Radulescu and Cory James Rushton (Cambridge: D.S. Brewer, 2009), 98.

land and people, licit versus illicit violence, gender roles, the stability of bloodlines, and the structure of society as a whole. As Roberta L. Krueger puts it, "Courtly literature flourished as emerging elites attempted to construct an ethos of moral superiority, grounded simultaneously in sanctioned violence by men against outsiders or transgressors and in sentimental refinement toward members of the group, especially women."[6] Likewise, Richard Kaueper and others have provided strong evidence that romance influenced the real lives and behaviors of medieval kings, lords, and knights, and thus was not simply shallow, escapist literature.[7]

Martin has referred to himself as a romantic "in the classical sense," and claims that he finds the conflict between romantic ideals and reality fascinating.[8] As this conflict is one of the central motifs of medieval romance, it is no surprise that *A Song of Ice and Fire* bears many similarities to that genre, especially romance as it was, not as medievalism has defined it. Gail Ashton's description of medieval romance calls to mind many aspects of Martin's novels:

> These set pieces and motifs probably offered a safe space in which to play out contemporaneous issues such as dynastic inheritance and marriage, social ties and identities, and noble birth versus personal merit. Many romances turn upon clashes of consent and desire, on questions of succession, *gentillesse* or kinship, on incest or rape averted and failures of dynasty like adulterous or childless marriages.[9]

At the same time, Martin also includes plotlines and motifs that work against or undercut the themes and motifs of medieval romance and

[6] Roberta L. Krueger, "Questions of Gender in Old French Courtly Romance," in *The Cambridge Companion to Medieval Romance*, edited by Roberta L. Krueger (Cambridge: Cambridge University Press, 2000), 132.

[7] See Richard Kaeuper, *Chivalry and Violence in Medieval Europe* (Oxford: Oxford University Press, 1999), and "The Societal Role of Chivalry in Romance: Northwestern Europe," in *The Cambridge Companion to Medieval Romance*, edited by Roberta L. Krueger (Cambridge: Cambridge University Press, 2000), 97–114.

[8] "U.S. Signing Tour (Seattle, WA)," *The Citadel: So Spake Martin*, November 21, 2005, http://www.westeros.org/Citadel/SSM/Entry/1391.

[9] Gail Ashton, *Medieval English Romance in Context* (London: Continuum, 2010), 14–15.

its neomedieval descendants, creating a fascinating tension between medievalism and cynical modernism.

"They are boys drunk on song and story": Chivalric Romance

Parallels between medieval romance and Martin's fantasy appear in both the structure and plot of the novels. Plot similarities especially tend to lie in pre-novel events and people, such as the Great Tourney at Harrenhal and the Kingswood Brotherhood, while Martin's counter-romance plots affect the characters in the primary timeline. Structural similarities include interlacement, episodic organization, interpretation of events by a narrative voice, and the use of legend as lesson for the present, while plot similarities include the primacy of the nobility, the "fair-unknown" motif, the focus on the prowess and honor of knights, the tension between expectations of honor, law, religion, and dynastic stability, and the role of kings in maintaining peace and stability in the realm.

Interlacement in medieval romance involves several storylines that "echo each other through analogies and the interplay of repetition and variation."[10] In Sir Thomas Malory's *Le Morte Darthur*, for example, the stories found in several other French romances are woven together into one larger story, while Malory leaves out available stories that do not support his overall narrative, message, and theme.[11] Interlacement developed as literacy rose, allowing for more complicated plotlines than would be possible for a story that was entirely oral in its transmission. In *A Song of Ice and Fire*, Martin uses interlacement to great effect, contrasting characters' approaches to leadership, knowledge of past events, and beliefs about current events, leaving it to the reader to connect the various threads and put together the truth of the narrative. Bartołomiej Błaszkiewicz argues that the contrasting and interlaced stories of House Stark and House Lannister form the primary diptych of the series, with the destruction

[10] Matilda Tomaryn Bruckner, "The Shape of Romance in Medieval France," in *The Cambridge Companion to Medieval Romance*, edited by Roberta L. Krueger (Cambridge: Cambridge University Press, 2000), 23.

[11] Ashton, 37.

of House Stark making up the first major storyline and the destruction of House Lannister the second, the two mirroring each other closely. Błaszkiewicz points out that this pattern of transgression and punishment is found in medieval romances such as *Morte Arthur* or *Amis and Amilioun.*[12] Błaszkiewicz also sees parallels between the narrative arcs of Daenerys and Jon Snow, their stories thematically linked while contrasting with the stories occurring in Westeros proper.[13] He claims that the story is made up of "a multitude of voices with the *trouvère* [minstrel] silently pulling the narrative strings playing one voice against another by means of the implicit relations of correspondence and contrast emerging in the juxtaposition of the individual points of view."[14] Joanna Korkot, meanwhile, draws attention to the interlacement of the natural and the supernatural in the text, which allows (and requires) the reader to construct the geography and metaphysical rules of Westeros for him- or herself.[15]

Perhaps the clearest and most obvious plot interlacement occurs near the end of *A Clash of Kings*, in the chapters that describe the Battle of the Blackwater as Stannis' forces attack King's Landing. Martin writes the battle over the course of six chapters, from three different viewpoints, each of which provides a different angle. Sansa's chapters describe the fear of the cloistered women and children waiting to hear the news of the outcome of the fighting, Tyrion's chapters describe the defense of the city, and Davos' chapter describes the attack. The sequence begins with Sansa preparing to go into the Red Keep with the rest of the noble ladies and their children to wait out the battle; she bids Joffrey and Tyrion farewell as they ride out to the walls. As Sansa is locked in a tower during the fight, all she knows about the battle she gets secondhand and through rumor and speculation. The

[12] Bartołomiej Błaszkiewicz, "George R.R. Martin's *A Song of Ice and Fire* and the Narrative Conventions of the Interlaced Romance," in *George R.R. Martin's "A Song of Ice and Fire" and the Medieval Literary Tradition*, edited by Bartołomiej Błaszkiewicz (Warsaw: University Press of Warsaw, 2014), 27–9.

[13] Ibid., 29–30.

[14] Ibid., 34.

[15] Joanna Kokot, "The Text and the World: Convention and Interlacement in George R.R. Martin's *A Game of Thrones*," in *George R.R. Martin's "A Song of Ice and Fire" and the Medieval Literary Tradition*, edited by Bartołomiej Błaszkiewicz (Warsaw: University Press of Warsaw, 2014), 57.

reader, however, is provided with a firsthand view through Davos and Tyrion. The full extent of the defense Tyrion has been building becomes apparent when Stannis' fleet is trapped in the Blackwater and attacked with wildfire. The reader experiences the horror of this trap through Davos' point of view, which is quickly lost when his ship explodes under him and he is swept out to sea. From then on, the firsthand view of the battle comes solely through Tyrion, who helps command the defenses and leads a sortie out of the Mud Gate. When Tyrion is wounded and knocked unconscious, the reader is left with the reports Sansa overhears as they are brought to Cersei before Cersei leaves the great hall, then the bells ringing victory and Dontos' wild report about the ghost of Renly riding in to break the siege. In these chapters, Martin not only depicts the terror and excitement of a battle, but also the plight of those who cannot fight as they wait for the fighting to be over and to learn their fate. These three points of view weave together to provide the reader with a comprehensive view of the most detailed battle in the series up to this point.

In order to create this structure of interlacement, Martin also relies heavily on episodic organization and interpretive narrative voice. Similar to interlacement, episodic organization structures the narrative in individual episodes that share similar motifs but build on each other toward completion of the plot.[16] In the case of the Battle of the Blackwater, the fight is described in five relatively short chapters, each of which ends with a cliffhanger. Without this episodic, interlaced structure, the reader would not have a complete view of the battle and its effects on people with different roles. While the Battle of the Blackwater is, again, one of the most tightly interwoven episodes in *A Song of Ice and Fire*, the episodic structure is the foundation of the series, as each chapter is narrated by a different character, each with a distinct voice and way of looking at the world, each of whom interprets the events in which he or she is involved. Martin leaves it up to the reader to decide whether the character's interpretation is valid; there is no interference from the authorial voice within the text. None of Martin's narrators is particularly reliable, and some even conceal information from the reader by refusing to think about it directly; Jon Snow's true

[16] Bruckner, 24.

parentage is a major example of this, but there are dozens of smaller instances scattered throughout the series. Martin emphasizes the unreliability of his narrators through misremembered episodes that the reader has witnessed. For example, Sansa and Sandor have an encounter as the Battle of the Blackwater winds down, and later Sansa remembers Sandor kissing her, though he did not.[17]

Likewise, as Jonathan Evans points out, the episodic plots of medieval romance, in which the ultimate goal of the main character often is not disclosed to the reader, creates the sense that the protagonist is "rid[ing] interminably from place to place beset by an unending string of foes, challenges, tests, and other obstacles."[18] As Martin avoids traditional fantasy plotlines, leaving the reader with no real idea of where characters might end up, *A Song of Ice and Fire* also creates this sense of interminable wandering. Readers have complained about Brienne of Tarth's plot in *A Feast for Crows*, for example, during which Brienne travels the countryside looking for Sansa Stark – whom the reader knows to be nowhere near the area where Brienne is looking – encountering any number of threats in the process. Martin has rejected the idea that "nothing" happens during Brienne's chapters, arguing instead that character development is happening, and that is just as important as "battles, sword fights and assassinations."[19] Frequently in romance, the structure of the narrative is a series of tests for the protagonist, and sometimes the outcome of these tests is not entirely clear. In Brienne's case, the "interminable" traveling and "foes, challenges, tests, and other obstacles" not only develop her character in preparation for whatever Martin has in store for her in *The Winds of Winter* and *A Dream of Spring*, but also show how the common folk

[17] Martin has expressed frustration with mistakes in his continuity, believing it makes incidents like this look like accidents rather than purposeful choices ("To Be Continued [Chicago, IL; May 6–8]," *The Citadel: So Spake Martin*, May 6, 2005, http://www.westeros.org/Citadel/SSM/Entry/To_Be_Continued_Chicago_IL_May_6_82); George R.R. Martin, *A Clash of Kings* (New York: Bantam Spectra, 1999; mass market reissue 2005), 866–7; *A Feast for Crows* (New York: Bantam Spectra, 2005; mass market edition, 2006), 870.

[18] Jonathan D. Evans, "Episodes in Analysis of Medieval Narrative," *Style* 20, no. 2 (1986), 126.

[19] Anders, n.p.

are affected by the War of the Five Kings and what is being done to restore order in the countryside.

The episodic, interlaced structure of the first three books creates a problem in *A Feast for Crows* and *A Dance with Dragons*. Martin decided that the best way to split *A Dance with Dragons*, which grew too long in manuscript for a single book, was geographically rather than chronologically. Thus, many characters who serve as foils or contrasts for each other do not appear in the same book, and opportunities for ironic contrast – for example, Cersei's constant terror that Tyrion is lurking in the walls of the Red Keep and might murder her at any moment, while in fact he is hundreds of miles away in Essos – are lost. While several guides for reading the two books side-by-side in order to preserve the chronology, and thus the interlacement, exist online, a casual reader would be unlikely to encounter them or seek them out.[20] Thus, these two books are not as structurally sound as the first three and have garnered a great deal of criticism regarding pace, narrative choices, and lack of action.

Martin's use of Westeros' past to illustrate of provide lessons for its present is particularly interesting because, as Carol Jamison has argued, he mirrors the medievalist tendencies of the medieval people in "creat[ing] a medieval past for self-understanding."[21] Like medieval authors such as the *Gawain* poet and Malory, Martin uses the oral history of Westeros to provide characters and society with models: Sansa uses her romances to help her create a persona that will allow her to survive King's Landing, Jaime uses his memories of Ser Arthur Dayne and the stories in the White Book to help him decide who he wants to be after losing his hand, and Daenerys uses the stories of her brother Rhaegar and father Aerys as exemplars of how to and how not to rule. Likewise, the characters themselves engage in a sort of medievalism by rejecting the idea of the supernatural as something that happened "back then" or "over there" (primarily in Yi Ti or

[20] For example, *All Leather Must be Boiled*, http://boiledleather.com/post/24543217702/a-proposed-a-feast-for-crowsa-dance-with-dragons; and *A Feast of Dragons*, http://afeastwithdragons.com/.

[21] Carol Jamison, "Reading Westeros: George R.R. Martin's Multi-Layered Medievalisms," *Studies in Medievalism* XXVI (2017), 132.

Asshai).[22] The difference between today's relegation of certain ideas and behavior to the Middle Ages and that performed by Martin's characters, of course, is that in his world, magic does exist, and such medievalizing patterns of thought will probably get the character killed.

Besides the structural similarities, Martin also borrows heavily from medieval romance for his thematic material. One of the most notable is the primacy of the nobility's viewpoint. According to Jeff Rider, the nobility is the central focus of chivalric romance, and anyone outside the courtly culture is cast as "other."[23] Besides entertainment, the purpose of romances appears to have been advancing an ideology to show nobility, especially knights, how they should act both in battle and toward women, and to reinforce the social order. However, the common folk were not a major consideration in these texts, or, as Kaeuper points out, for the actual nobility.[24] This does not mean, however, that class was not a consideration; especially as the middle class rose and the standing of at least the lower nobility fell, romances began to examine issues of class, economics, and politics. Chrétien's *Le Chevalier au Lion*, for example, explores the idea of economic debt through metaphor, with Yvain owing Laudine his time and struggling to repay it through adventures that restore his good name.[25] The common people appear in Malory's *Le Morte Darthur*, usually referred to as "all the people" and treated as a monolithic group who need something from, swear fealty to, or are slaughtered by one of the knights, but they have a much more tangible presence than is usual. *A Song of Ice and Fire* also focuses on the nobility; other than in a few prologues or epilogues, every point-of-view character is nobility of some sort. Narratively, this makes sense, as the nobility will be the ones closest to the action, but, unlike in romances, Martin

[22] Ibid., 141.

[23] Jeff Rider, "The Other Worlds of Romance," in *The Cambridge Companion to Medieval Romance*, edited by Roberta L. Krueger (Cambridge: Cambridge University Press, 2000), 115.

[24] Kaeuper, *Chivalry and Violence*, 185.

[25] Judith Kellogg, "Economic and Social Tensions Reflected in the Romance of Chrétien de Troyes," *Romance Philology* 39, no. 1 (1985), 16–17.

spends some time detailing the plight of the smallfolk as the nobles fight among themselves.

Identity is a major concern in both medieval romance and *A Song of Ice and Fire*. Anxiety about one's identity and place in a feudal society manifests in a trope known as "the fair unknown," in which a young man of uncertain parentage engages in acts of valor, often joining Arthur's court, and is eventually discovered to be of noble birth. Examples from romance include Chrétien de Troyes' *Perceval, le Conte du Graal* and the numerous tales about Sir Gingalain. Sometimes, a knight will disguise himself for a tournament, as do Lancelot in Malory's *Le Morte Darthur* and Chrétien's Cligès. Several instances of identity loss or concealment occur in *A Song of Ice and Fire*, but only one truly mirrors medieval romance: Meera Reed's story of the Knight of the Laughing Tree, a tale that takes place before the time of the novels, at the Great Tourney of Harrenhal. Meera even tells the tale in a grand romance style, heavy with metaphor, referring to the lords and knights by their house sigils rather than by name. In the story, Howland Reed, a young innocent crannogman, decides to visit Harrenhal for the tourney. When he gets there, he is harassed by three squires and rescued by Lyanna Stark, who recognizes him as one of her father's bannermen. The next day, a mysterious knight appears in the lists, carrying a sigil of a weirwood tree with a laughing face, and vanquishes the knights who mentor the squires in question. Rather than taking the usual winner's bounty, the unknown knight orders the knights to teach their squires honor. The next day, the unknown knight is gone, only his shield left hanging on a tree.[26]

Like most romances, the story of the Knight of the Laughing Tree takes place in the past, though in this case not long in the past. The idealism and grand spectacle of the story puts it on par with the Arthurian cycles, while Howland Reed's status as a minor, unknown noble at a narratively important tourney, and as the unknown knight who protects the weak and demands honor from other knights, matches the fair-unknown motif. Two possibilities for the knight's identity exist: Howland Reed himself and Lyanna Stark. Reed being

[26] George R.R. Martin, *A Storm of Swords* (New York: Bantam Spectra, 2000; mass market reissue 2005), 339–42.

the knight would be romantically consistent; the fair unknown often has no training but does well at martial arts because of his noble blood. However, Lyanna shows martial skill when she defends Reed from the squires, the weirwood tree indicates a tie to the Old Gods and the North, and Meera stops the story several times to ask if Bran is *sure* he has never heard this story before, indicating that it should be a Stark family story. In this case, the identity of the "fair unknown" is never made entirely clear, either to characters or reader, but it is obvious that the knight was a person of noble blood who would otherwise not have been allowed to fight in the tourney.

Jon Snow could also be considered a fair unknown, since his true identity is a mystery to the audience and himself. He believes he is the bastard son of Ned Stark, barely tolerated in the court at Winterfell and with no real standing in society. However, many fans suspect that he is actually of royal blood, the son of Rhaegar Targaryen and Lyanna Stark (this would not change his status as bastard, however, as Rhaegar and Lyanna were unmarried).[27] However, he subverts the trope, as he possesses no martial or social skills that could be attributed to his breeding; all of his fighting and leadership abilities come from hard work and painful character development. He begins as a semi-noble young man with a slight sense of entitlement, disillusioned by the realities of the Night's Watch, and yet grows into a leader, though still not without flaws. While the revelation of his true parentage may allow him to have more power and potentially help Daenerys Targaryen protect Westeros from the Others, this is an effect of the patriarchal, feudal society Martin has built – a society that values one's bloodline above one's character – not the result of Jon's blood itself.

The question of identity also arises in issues of dynastic stability, both in romance and in *A Song of Ice and Fire*. Medieval romances were deeply concerned with maintaining the stability of the bloodline and often dealt with anxieties that the heir was not truly of his

[27] While the HBO series *Game of Thrones* establishes in season seven that Rhaegar had his marriage to Elia Martell annulled and married Lyanna before Jon's birth, the book series has not yet shown a formal relationship between them.

father's blood; *Sir Gowther*, in which a childless queen (knowingly or otherwise) has sex with a fiend disguised as her husband in order to conceive, is a strong example of this concern. Alcuin Blamires claims that, despite scientific knowledge of reproductive systems, medieval thought tended to attribute a male child's nature to its father and considered fertility to relate entirely to the mother. Romances also have a tendency to equate "successful" procreation with "strong male issue," and if a child "fail[ed] to conform to elite social expectations, medieval society [was] prepared to allege contamination in the succession" – always blamed on the mother, of course.[28] Concerns about dynastic stability and the true heritage of children, especially heirs, run deeply through *A Song of Ice and Fire*. The Targaryens practiced inbreeding for generations to keep their bloodline pure. Robert was placed on the throne after the Rebellion not only because of his military prowess, but also because of a thin blood connection to the Targaryens.[29] The War of the Five Kings begins primarily because of Ned's assertion that Joffrey is not Robert's issue, and therefore has no claim to the throne.

For the nobility, a child's status as a bastard is important enough for the child to be given a surname that denotes it – Flowers, Rivers, Storm, or Snow, depending on which kingdom the child is born in. Jon's status as a bastard is a major issue that runs through his story; Catelyn resents his presence, partly because he is a constant reminder of Ned's infidelity, and partly because he is a danger to Robb's claim to the lordship of Winterfell. By joining the Night's Watch, Jon removes himself as a danger, and he holds to his vows even after all the male heirs to Winterfell are dead or presumed dead. Cersei has several of Robert's bastards murdered after his death, partly because their dark hair is evidence that Joffrey, Tommen, and Myrcella are not Robert's, and partly to protect her own children's claim to the throne. Ramsay Snow/Bolton shows anxiety that his succession to his father's title will be taken away even after he is legitimized; Roose Bolton suspects him

[28] Alcuin Blamires, "The Twin Demons of Aristocratic Society in *Sir Gowther*," in *Pulp Fictions of Medieval England: Essays in Popular Romance*, edited by Nicola McDonald (Manchester: Manchester University Press, 2004), 47–50.

[29] Martin, *A Clash of Kings*, 352; *A Feast for Crows*, 744.

of murdering all his trueborn brothers and expects that should any sons be born of his wife, Walda Frey, those too will be killed.[30]

Since identity and its link to one's place in society are so important in romance, a loss of identity or status often causes madness, as seen in Chrétien's *Le Chevalier au Lion*, Malory's *Morte Darthur*, and the prose *Tristan*. Romance heroes, when stripped of their titles, riches, or ladies, have a tendency to literally run mad until they regain their sense of self and chivalry. In *Le Chevalier au Lion*, Yvain's madness and relationship with the lion provide, as Sylvia Huot argues, "an exploration between the underlying violence of the warrior life and the overlaying gloss of chivalry and love that is supposed to give it meaning: the ideology of courtliness that redefines rape, pillage, and plunder as sublime love and chivalric glory."[31] Similarly, in *A Song of Ice and Fire*, Martin explores the toxic masculinity of Westerosi society that rarely allows for male roles beyond the martial (see Chapter 2).

While a loss of status in *A Song of Ice and Fire* rarely results in a literal, running-naked-in-the-woods madness as it does in *Le Chevalier au Lion* and *Le Morte Darthur*, men who are faced with such loss inevitably sink into despair and even wish for death before managing to find a new way of being that does not necessarily include martial prowess. Bran Stark's early plans include being a knight, a member of the Kingsguard, and one of his brother Robb's sworn bannermen. When Jaime pushes him from the tower and he loses the use of his legs, for a long time, all Bran can think about is what he has lost. He cries, snaps at Old Nan, and even tries to argue that with his new saddle, he could still learn to fight, citing a legend from the Age of Heroes to make his claim.[32] Even when he decides to go north and accept the Three-Eyed Crow's training, part of him hopes that the Three-Eyed Crow will be able to fix his legs.[33]

When Jaime Lannister loses his hand, he goes through a similar

[30] George R.R. Martin, *A Dance with Dragons* (New York: Bantam Spectra, 2011; mass market edition, 2013), 472–3.

[31] Sylvia Huot, *Madness in Medieval French Literature: Identities Found and Lost* (Oxford: Oxford University Press, 2003), 30.

[32] George R.R. Martin, *A Game of Thrones* (New York: Bantam Spectra, 1996; mass market reissue 2005), 237–8, 730.

[33] Martin, *A Dance with Dragons*, 202.

process, even willing himself to die until Brienne calls him a coward. Even after he begins fighting to live again, he struggles with questions over his identity now that he no longer has his martial prowess: "*They took my sword hand*," he thinks, "*Was that all I was, a sword hand*?"[34] Later, he contemplates that the hand he lost was not only his sword hand, but the hand he used to kill King Aerys, to throw Bran from the window, and to make love to Cersei; without that hand, he has lost his identity.[35] Slowly, over the course of the next two books, Jaime refashions himself into a new man, though he also attempts to regain his martial prowess by learning to fight (poorly) with his left hand. He strives to find a new way of being a man in a feudal society that defines "manliness" through violence, instead working for peace, though he still ultimately thinks first of his own glory: "*Make a habit of it, Lannister, and one day men might call you Goldenhand after all. Goldenhand the Just*."[36] He also endeavors to rebuild his reputation, pointedly keeping his oaths, even to people who are now dead.

Interestingly, despite his motivations, Jaime takes on the traditional romance role of the king who serves as arbiter of justice and keeper of the peace, preventing lesser lords from fighting among themselves and thus causing chaos in the realm. In romance, when a king is bad, sick, dead, or otherwise neglectful, the feudal structure ceases to function.[37] At several points in Malory's *Le Morte Darthur*, Britain collapses into infighting because of the absence or incompetence of the king, whether that king is Uther Pendragon or Arthur. The central plot of *A Song of Ice and Fire* is of a kingdom in disarray due to trouble with the monarchy, trouble stretching back to Mad King Aerys, before the events of the book. Robert's inability to stand up to his father-in-law, Tywin Lannister, leads to Gregor Clegane's rampage through the Riverlands; Joffrey's contested paternity leads to the War of the Five Kings; Joffrey's cruelty leads to riots in King's Landing; Cersei's attempt to rule for Tommen leads to the rise of the Faith Militant, which destabilizes all of King's Landing and a good

[34] Martin, *A Storm of Swords*, 415.
[35] Ibid., 507.
[36] Martin, *A Feast for Crows*, 571.
[37] Kaeuper, *Chivalry and Violence*, 93–7.

portion of the countryside. Power vacuums at the levels of both monarch and higher lord cause untold chaos all through Westeros. Jaime's intervention in the Riverlands helps to put the kingdom back in order, though between Brienne kidnapping him for Lady Stoneheart and Varys murdering Kevan Lannister, it seems unlikely that this stability will continue into *The Winds of Winter*.

"Life is not a song": Anti-Romance

While *A Song of Ice and Fire* has many clear similarities with medieval chivalric romance, Martin makes a point rejecting what he sees as the tropes of fantasy, many of which have been borrowed from the Victorian understanding of medieval chivalric romance. Some of these rejections are clear in the text, while other references are more subtle and gently poke fun at traditional motifs.

Westeros is a feudal society with a thin veneer of chivalric courtesy overlying brutal violence, which, as has been discussed above, is not very different from the sociological content of medieval chivalric romance and accords with Matthews' view of the two major categories of medievalist thought, gothic and romantic.[38] The "romance" Martin rejects is that of the Victorian era, which codified the Middle Ages as a "Golden Age" for social structure, environmentalism, and religion.[39] The Pre-Raphaelites in particular saw the Middle Ages in the light of idealized Arthurian romance and themselves as a sort of brotherhood of the Round Table.[40] The Victorians cast the Middle Ages in their entirety, not just the literature, as a time when "such patriarchal ideals as chivalry, manliness, selflessness, gallantry, nobility, honor, duty, and fidelity (to the crown as well as to a beloved)" were at their height.[41] Victorian medievalism has been one of the greatest influences on

[38] Matthews, 15.

[39] Alice Chandler, *A Dream of Order: The Medieval Ideal in Nineteenth-Century English Literature* (Lincoln: University of Nebraska Press, 1970), 4–6.

[40] Alicia Faxton, "The Pre-Raphaelite Brotherhood as Knights of the Round Table," in *Pre-Raphaelitism and Medievalism in the Arts*, edited by Liana de Girolami Cheney (New York: Edwin Mellen, 1992), 53–5.

[41] Antony H. Harrison, *Victorian Poets and the Politics of Culture: Discourse and Ideologies* (Charlottesville: University Press of Virginia, 1998), 18.

contemporary understanding of the Middle Ages, especially through its influence on Disney, with its "inherently flexible reinterpretation of history guided not by dates and facts but by an asynchronous nostalgia for fairy tales and fantasies set in the past, while inspired by an American view of the future."[42] Since Martin has dismissed much of today's fantasy as "Disneyland," it's fair to think that his rejection of "romance" is primarily a rejection of the idealized, romanticized reinterpretation of the chivalric romance rather than the romance itself.

The Victorian romance motif most pointedly excluded from Martin's text is the idea of chivalry and all the associated trappings – the knight in shining armor rescuing the damsel in distress, the ultimate goodness and prowess of the nobility, the strict yet mutually beneficial gender roles and social structure. Instead, Martin argues – both diegetically and extradiegetically – that these are faulty ideas of the "real" Middle Ages, unfit for "adult" entertainment. Indeed, within the novels, the only people who truly believe in all of the chivalric ideals are children, especially Sansa Stark. Martin attacks these ideals in two ways: by playing on readers' expectations for a novel of this type by setting up Ned Stark as the romance hero, and by disabusing Sansa of her romantic ideas of the world and nobility.

Ned Stark appears, at first reading, to be the hero of the story. He is honorable and honest, and he attempts to use his influence to make Westeros a more honorable kingdom. The first time the reader encounters Ned, he is imparting wisdom to his young son, Bran, about the duty of a lord in passing judgment on his people: "[T]he man who passes the sentence should swing the sword. If you would take a man's life, you owe it to him to look in his eyes and hear his final words. And if you cannot bear to do that, then perhaps the man does not deserve to die."[43] Ned agrees to travel south to King's Landing with King Robert not only because they are friends, or because he owes Robert fealty and cannot refuse him, but because he recognizes the treachery in King's Landing – illustrated by the murder of his old friend Jon

[42] Tison Pugh and Susan Aronstein, "Introduction: Disney's Retroprogressive Medievalisms: Where Yesterday is Tomorrow's Today," in *The Disney Middle Ages: A Fairy-Tale and Fantasy Past*, edited by Tison Pugh and Susan Aronstein (New York: Palgrave Macmillan, 2012), 5.

[43] Martin, *A Game of Thrones*, 16.

Arryn – and wants to make it right.[44] Once in King's Landing, he consistently does what he thinks is right, regardless of how politically inexpedient it might be; he does not flinch from angering the Lannisters, the richest and most powerful family in the kingdom, or Robert himself.

This honorability is the reason Robert wants Ned for Hand of the King to begin with; Robert has grown tired of politics and ruling, and he wants to "eat and drink and wench [himself] into an early grave."[45] Rebekah Fowler notes that Robert recruits Ned "in the hope of reclaiming some of the idealism of the honorable warrior for the corrupt King's Landing."[46] Robert turns to Ned to rule the kingdom in his stead because Ned is the most honorable man he knows, and he believes honor is what is needed to curb the cutthroat politics of the city. Unfortunately for everyone involved, Robert is wrong, and both he and Ned are dead by the end of *A Game of Thrones*, victims of the Lannisters' (specifically Cersei's) ambition.

The indications that Ned's story will not end well appear early on, foreshadowed in a myriad of ways. Fowler mentions that Northrop Frye's conception of the enemy of the romance hero is associated with "winter, darkness, confusion, sterility, moribund life, and old age," whereas the hero is associated with light and summer.[47] Thus, Ned's association with winter – the Stark house words are "Winter is Coming"; the hold is named "Winterfell"; and the hold is located so far north that summer never really reaches it – places him at odds with the usual associations for a romance hero. Likewise, Ned is associated with, and frequently invokes, the First Men and the Old Gods, indicators both of age and a lost past, suggesting early on that Ned and his unswerving honor are doomed. There is diegetic foreshadowing, too, in Ned's sense of foreboding when he considers taking Robert's offer, in their visit to Winterfell's crypts, and in Ned's memory of his father,

[44] Ibid., 63.

[45] Ibid., 47.

[46] Rebekah M. Fowler, "Sansa's Songs: The Allegory of Medieval Romance in George R.R. Martin's *A Song of Ice and Fire* Series," in *George R.R. Martin's "A Song of Ice and Fire" and the Medieval Literary Tradition*, edited by Bartołomiej Błaszkiewicz (Warsaw: University Press of Warsaw, 2014), 87.

[47] Ibid., 90.

who "went south once, to answer the summons of a king. He never came home again."[48] Yet a first-time reader who is unfamiliar with the themes of medieval romance might easily overlook these signs and expect Ned to be the fantasy hero who brings order to Westeros.

In many ways, Ned's character arc follows that of a traditional romance hero, until the end, that is. He experiences the call to action that, when answered, removes him from his home and thrusts him into a strange land with strange customs. He has quests, both given and assumed: Catelyn charges him with discovering who killed Jon Arryn; Ned takes it upon himself to discover the meaning of Arryn's cryptic last words; and when Robert dies, Ned works to place Stannis Baratheon on the throne. Like many romance heroes – Fowler compares him to Sir Gawain in *Sir Gawain and the Green Knight* – Ned ultimately falls short of his own ideals and fails in all but one of his quests.[49] Unlike other romance heroes, however, Ned is not given the chance to redeem himself or correct his errors; instead, he is beheaded as a traitor.

Ned's story is one of Martin's examples of what happens when romance ideals meet the "real world" – in this case, the politics and cunning of those who intend to remain in power. Rather than the nobility being inherently gracious and honorable, Ned faces Cersei Lannister, who will do anything to preserve her legacy and her children's claim to the throne. Ned, perhaps naively, expects her to act with honor when he confronts her with the truth of her children's parentage: they are the result of her union with her brother, Jaime, not Robert. He gives her the opportunity to leave the kingdom before he tells Robert of her treason, and she refuses, instead orchestrating Robert's death and having Ned arrested for treason. Even then, Ned might have managed to escape with his life, as Cersei plans to send him to the Wall, where many criminals are sent to defend the realm against the monsters of Winter. Instead, Joffrey, king after Robert's death, orders Ned beheaded, and the headsman obeys before any protest can be made. This is the first of many such shocks for a new

48 Martin, *A Game of Thrones*, 63.
49 Fowler, 90.

reader, as Martin is not afraid to kill off his central characters, no matter how heroic or beloved they are.[50]

Belief in honor and an idyllic vision of the nobility does not always lead to the death of a character, however. Of all the characters in the first book, Sansa Stark is the most romantically minded, and over the course of *A Game of Thrones* and *A Clash of Kings* she has that romantic-mindedness brutalized out of her. Sansa's character arc is the most heavy-handed example of Martin's rejection of the "Disneyland" Middle Ages; Fowler claims that Sansa's storyline "presents medieval romance as superficial fluff – as a genre of appearances devoid of serious content."[51] Sansa begins as an innocent (if slightly spoiled), naïve girl, eleven years old at the beginning of *A Game of Thrones*. She loves the Westerosi version of romance tales and embraces her role as lady and future queen of Westeros wholeheartedly. Her mother, Catelyn, recalls Sansa's early years to Brienne in *A Clash of Kings*: "Sansa was a lady at three, always so courteous and eager to please. She loved nothing so well as tales of knightly valor."[52] On being introduced to Joffrey, the prince to whom she has been promised as part of Robert and Ned's agreement, she thinks he is like a prince out of a story, everything she has ever wanted from a prince and a suitor.[53] Her direwolf is named Lady, which reflects her desire to be a lady herself. Nothing excites her more than the tourney in King's Landing, which appears to conform to all her ideas of what chivalry and nobility are about.

Of course, the reader learns that the glory is all an illusion; the knight Sansa sees as a paragon, Loras Tyrell, cheats in the joust, riding

[50] Despite Martin's message that romantic heroism will not save someone in a "realistic" political climate, one could argue that characters such as Ned die because they have failed to hold to their own standards of honor. After all, Ned is on the steps of the Great Sept of Baelor before his beheading to confess to a treason he did not commit. That he is trying to protect his family does not change the fact that he is lying and allowing a bastard to take the throne. His son Robb, who rallies the lords of the north and incites them to secede from the southern kingdoms, is cut from the same cloth, but dies just as brutally because he broke an oath and shamed another lord.

[51] Fowler, 80.

[52] Martin, *A Clash of Kings*, 783.

[53] Martin, *A Game of Thrones*, 140.

a mare in season against a knight known for his tendency to ride ill-tempered stallions.[54] Later, it is revealed that he is in a sexual relationship with Renly Baratheon, taking the usual homosocial relationships of the chivalric romances a stage further and complicating his status as a perfect knight (see Chapter 3). Though Sansa is also faced with some truths about Joffrey and chivalry, she willfully chooses not to see the lessons. Despite Joffrey's instrumental role in Lady's execution, Sansa chooses to believe that the incident was not Joffrey's fault, but Cersei's and Arya's.[55] Likewise, when Sandor Clegane walks her from the feast back to the keep, he tells her of the true nature of knights, especially his brother, Gregor Clegane (known as the Mountain who Rides), who purposefully killed one of the knights he jousted against and burned Sandor's face as a boy. Sansa proclaims that Gregor is "no true knight," removing Gregor from the definition of knighthood while preserving that definition and its attendant expectations for all other knights.[56]

Despite Sandor's warnings and Petyr Baelish's admonition that "life is not a song, sweetling. You may learn that one day to your sorrow," Sansa continues to hold onto the idea that knights and members of the nobility are inherently better and more honorable than the common folk.[57] Only when Cersei imprisons Ned and tells Sansa that he is guilty of treason does Sansa begin to doubt her own beliefs; she cannot believe that her father is a traitor, but she also cannot believe that Cersei would lie to her. The cognitive dissonance cripples her until Joffrey orders Ned's death, at which point Sansa accepts that the Lannisters do not have her best interests at heart and that Cersei does not live up to the model of queenhood Sansa holds in her mind.

Martin does not leave Sansa's re-education at that. Following Ned's death, Joffrey begins his psychological and physical abuse of Sansa, using his Kingsguard knights as weapons against her. Cersei, having been beaten by Robert many times, attempts to teach Joffrey not to hit women, but Joffrey takes the wrong lesson away. Acknowledging

[54] Martin, *A Game of Thrones*, 316.
[55] Ibid., 298.
[56] Ibid., 303.
[57] Ibid., 473.

Cersei's lesson that a king should not strike his queen, Joffrey turns to Ser Meryn, who prevents her from shielding her face and strikes her backhanded.[58] This is only the first of several such beatings, which get worse over time, culminating in Joffrey ordering his knights to "make her naked."[59] Only the intercession of Tyrion Lannister, Joffrey's uncle and acting Hand of the King, prevents Sansa from being subjected to worse treatment, perhaps even rape.

These beatings drive home to Sansa that chivalry is a myth and an illusion, and that she cannot expect others to behave like her heroes in stories and songs. She is forced to reconsider her beliefs about knighthood, realizing that none of the knights in the garden had attempted to stop Joffrey or the Kingsguard. The only people who stepped in were Dontos, a drunken, disgraced former knight reduced to court jester; Sandor Clegane, Joffrey's "Hound," who has never been a knight and hates knighthood on principle; and Tyrion, a dwarf generally hated by the populace. She decides that the Kingsguard "are no true knights, not one of them," which indicates that though she has acknowledged that life is not a song, she still retains an ideal of "true" knighthood, even if no real knights live up to it.[60]

Sansa's lessons about knighthood and knights are reflected throughout *A Song of Ice and Fire*, in which only a handful of knights attempt to keep their oaths. Jaime Lannister tells Catelyn Stark that keeping all the oaths a knight is expected to swear is "too much," and that the oaths contradict and frequently conflict with each other.[61] Sansa's attackers might be (partially) excused on the grounds that they have sworn to obey the king, but they have also sworn to protect women, children, and the weak. That they do not even hesitate to beat Sansa bloody when ordered speaks volumes about their internal character. Knights such as these and Gregor Clegane reflect Martin's belief that medieval knights were never the paragons of virtue and honor that medievalist and neomedieval fantasy makes them out to be: "[T]he way it often worked out is the people the peasants most

[58] Martin, *A Game of Thrones*, 744.
[59] Martin, *A Clash of Kings*, 488.
[60] Ibid., 490.
[61] Ibid., 796.

often needed protection from were their own protectors. The ideals of knighthood embody some of the finest ideals the human race has ever come up with. The reality is somewhat less than that, and often horribly so."[62] So few of Martin's knights are redeemable characters that their brutality is practically its own trope, an anti-trope to the grand, honorable knight in shining armor of the "Disneyland" Middle Ages Martin so despises.

Yet Sansa does not completely give up on her ideals, though she does stop expecting others to live up to them. Instead, she internalizes them, striving to live up to her own expectations, and finds in them a useful tool for navigating life at court. Her mantra becomes "a lady's armor is courtesy," and she repeats this mantra to herself frequently. She still strives to be a lady, but she recognizes that she cannot rely on the protection of knights, and thus must protect herself. She likewise recognizes that Cersei Lannister does not live up to her idealized version of a queen, and vows to do better; when Cersei informs her that the best way to keep the people's loyalty is through fear, Sansa thinks, "When I'm queen, I'll make them love me."[63] When Joffrey breaks off their betrothal, it is even more important for Sansa to be able to protect herself and build alliances with other nobles in the Red Keep, and she does so with a finesse that impresses Tyrion. Watching her in action at Joffrey's wedding to Margaery Tyrell, he thinks, "She would have made Joffrey a good wife and a better queen if he'd had the sense to love her."[64] So while Sansa's initial expectations for chivalry – that it is a universal constant to which all nobility will conform – are defeated, her belief in the concepts of honor and chivalry are not (yet) completely annihilated.

Jaime Lannister provides an example of a man who has grown out of his previous romantic ideas, and allows Martin to question the notion of the past as a Golden Age. When the reader first meets Jaime, he seems a monster – he pushes Bran Stark out of a high window because the boy sees Jaime having sex with Cersei; Ned tells Robert not to trust Jaime because he killed the last king; and Jaime orders

[62] MacLaurin, n.p.
[63] Martin, *A Clash of Kings*, 848.
[64] Martin, *A Storm of Swords*, 816.

Ned's men killed as a warning to Catelyn, who holds Tyrion hostage.[65] When Catelyn confronts him about the fate of her daughters after Ned's death, claiming that his honor is worth less than nothing, Jaime does not seem to care about her verdict. Rather, he willingly and unabashedly admits to killing King Aerys, laughing about the circumstances surrounding that decision, his own capture, and Ned Stark's death.[66] Only when Jaime's internal life is revealed does the reader understand that he is a broken man in much the way Sansa was broken; he grew up with the knights out of legend, only to have those legends destroyed.

Jaime's backstory and adolescence are revealed piecemeal throughout *A Storm of Swords* and *A Feast for Crows*. Jaime began his career as a knight younger than most, squiring under Ser Sumner Crakehall from the ages of twelve to sixteen, then riding with Ser Arthur Dayne against the Kingswood Brotherhood, whereupon Dayne knighted him on the battlefield.[67] At sixteen, he was appointed to the Kingsguard, a ploy on his and Cersei's part to keep him from a marriage he did not want and to allow him to be near Cersei, whom their father hoped to marry to one of the princes.[68] The plan backfired, and Jaime found himself in service of a cruel, capricious king who had named Jaime to the Kingsguard only "to rob Tywin Lannister of his heir."[69] His time serving and protecting King Aerys was a nightmare; Jaime witnessed men burned alive, Queen Rhaella raped and abused, and Aerys growing ever more paranoid about the possibility of treason.[70] When the houses of Arryn, Stark, and Baratheon rose against him, Aerys ordered King's Landing burned to the ground, with all the people still inside. He also ordered Jaime to go to the gate where Tywin was waiting and kill him. Jaime chose not to obey this order, instead slaying Aerys' pyromancer and then Aerys himself.[71]

Once branded "Kingslayer," Jaime's outlook on life radically

[65] Martin, *A Game of Thrones*, 383.
[66] Martin, *A Clash of Kings*, 796–9.
[67] Martin, *A Storm of Swords*, 157–8.
[68] Ibid., 156.
[69] Ibid., 605.
[70] Martin, *A Feast for Crows*, 330; *A Clash of Kings*, 797–8.
[71] Martin, *A Storm of Swords*, 507.

changes; he no longer sees himself as a hero or believes in the tenets of chivalry. He has experienced the impossibility of holding to a chivalric code, as he expresses to Catelyn Stark:

> So many vows … they make you swear and swear. Defend the king. Obey the king. Keep his secrets. Do his bidding. Your life for his. But obey your father. Love your sister. Protect the innocent. Defend the weak. Respect the gods. Obey the laws. It's all too much. No matter what you do, you're forsaking one vow or the other.[72]

Through Jaime, Martin offers one reason why knighthood and chivalric oaths would not work in a realistic setting; in a world populated by people of less-than-noble intentions, vows will conflict. Jaime found himself trapped between the orders of his king and the life of his father – not to mention all the innocents in King's Landing – and was forced to choose between two oaths. The reader might believe that he ultimately made the right decision, but those characters who still believe in an objective right and wrong (such as Ned and Catelyn) despise Jaime. Ned even admits that Aerys needed killing, but does not think that Jaime should have done it. Robert, on the other hand, has a more pragmatic view, claiming that the Targaryens never showed honor or mercy, so they deserved none in return.[73] His response to Jaime's murder of King Aerys is a joke: "I hear they've named you Kingslayer […] Just don't think to make it a habit."[74]

Jaime remembers his childhood and adolescence as Westeros' Golden Age. It contained heroes such as Ser Arthur Dayne, "the Sword of the Morning", remembered as one of the greatest knights who ever lived and admired by Ned and Jaime both.[75] He bears marked similarities to King Arthur, and his sword, Dawn, is similar to Excalibur; Dawn was "pale as milkglass, alive with light,"[76] while Malory describes Excalibur as "so bright in his enemy's eyes that it gave off

[72] Martin, *A Clash of Kings*, 796.
[73] Martin, *A Game of Thrones*, 115.
[74] Martin, *A Storm of Swords*, 405.
[75] Martin, *A Game of Thrones*, 332; *A Storm of Swords*, 932.
[76] Martin, *A Game of Thrones*, 425.

light like thirty torches,"[77] and in the Middle English Prose *Merlin* it is described as "so clear and shining so brightly that it seemed to those who saw it that it glowed as if it had the brightness of twenty candles burning."[78] Dayne, like Arthur, died during a violent revolution, at the hands of a close friend rather than a son, though the details of his death are unclear.[79] Interestingly, Martin here presents the ideal Arthur as found in Victorian texts rather than the flawed Arthur of the medieval romances, echoing Pre-Raphaelite tendencies to see Arthur and his court as "a model of chivalry, courage, loyalty, and mutual support."[80] Despite Dayne's celebrated courage and nobility, he is a member of Mad King Aerys' Kingsguard, and he remains loyal to Aerys until his death, yet he remains a role model and larger-than-life memory for both Jaime and Ned.

Similarly, the Kingswood Brotherhood reflects Robin Hood and his merry men, and the tales about them are many and varied. Led by Simon Toyne, the Brotherhood terrorized nobles from the Kingswood, prompting King Aerys to send Dayne to destroy them. While little is specifically revealed about the Brotherhood in the novels, what information is available creates clear parallels with the Victorian portrayal of Robin Hood; the Victorian-era tales of Robin Hood, such as Howard Pyle's *The Merry Adventures of Robin Hood* (1883), are an example of the sort of idealized medievalism Martin claims to revise. This portrayal is at odds with the early ballads about Robin Hood, who, according to Stephen Knight, "robs the rich to give to himself and his friends, not to be generally charitable to the poor."[81] The Brotherhood operated out of the Kingswood, much as Robin Hood's men operated out of Sherwood Forest. Like Robin Hood's merry

[77] "[…] so breyght in his enemyes eyen that it gaf light lyke thirty torchys," Thomas Malory, *Le Morte Darthur*, edited by Stephen H.A. Shepherd (New York: Norton, 2004), 14.

[78] "[…] so cler and bright shynynge as thei semed that it be helden that it glistred as it hadde be the brightnesse of xx tapres brennynge," *Merlin, or the Early History of King Arthur*, edited by Henry B. Wheatley (Ann Arbor: University of Michigan Early English Text Initiative, 1997), 118.

[79] Martin, *A Game of Thrones*, 425.

[80] Faxton, 55.

[81] Stephen Knight, *Robin Hood: A Mythic Biography* (Ithaca: Cornell University Press, 2003), 2.

men, the Brotherhood was an ensemble of colorfully-named men and women: Wenda the White Fawn, Oswyn Longneck, Big Belly Ben, Fletcher Dick, and the Smiling Knight.[82] Finally, the Brotherhood earned the loyalty of the smallfolk of the Kingswood; in order to find them, Dayne had to win it back by championing the rights and needs of the smallfolk to King Aerys, using his position to give them more than Toyne could.[83] However, Martin again undercuts the simplicity of the Robin Hood tales in his depiction of the Brotherhood; the only member described at any length is the Smiling Knight, whom Jaime recalls as "a madman, cruelty and chivalry all jumbled up together."[84] Far from the more simple morality of the later tales of Robin Hood, who stole from the rich in order to feed the poor, Martin depicts the Kingswood Brotherhood as a gang of bandits, a scourge that needed to be removed.[85]

While Martin's subversion of romance tropes, or at least their neomedieval equivalents, most often contributes to his "grimdark" world of violence and backstabbing, occasionally he uses it ironically, for comic relief, or to make a point about the sexism or ableism inherent in medieval romance. For example, Tyrion Lannister's character arc both utilizes and subverts the tropes of the romantic hero, though in quite different ways from Ned Stark's. Tyrion is a dwarf, a figure common in medieval romance as an extension of the knight, much as his lady is. In Chrétien's *Érec et Énide*, for example, the two dwarves in the story act as symbols of their respective knights' aggression, driving the knights into the adventure of the plot.[86] In

[82] Martin, *A Storm of Swords*, 446; *A Dance with Dragons*, 714–15.

[83] Martin, *A Feast for Crows*, 646.

[84] Martin, *A Storm of Swords*, 916.

[85] Justyna Brzezińska continues the Robin Hood parallels by reading Beric Dondarrion's Brotherhood without Banners as another reflection of the Robin Hood legend, albeit even more brutal and less clear-cut than the Kingswood Brotherhood, as the Brotherhood without Banners exists in Westeros' present rather than its idealized past. See "Reading Beric Dondarrion in the Light of the Robin Hood Legend," in *George R.R. Martin's "A Song of Ice and Fire" and the Medieval Literary Tradition*, edited by Bartołomiej Błaszkiewicz (Warsaw: University Press of Warsaw, 2014), 231–45.

[86] Joan Brumlik, "The Knight, the Lady, and the Dwarf in Chrétien's *Erec*," *Quondam et Futurus* 2, no. 2 (1992), 69.

Malory's *Book of Gareth*, the dwarf is "one of the accoutrements of knighthood," like Gareth's sword, horse, and armor, and his inability to protect himself is played for comedy.[87] Tyrion, on the other hand, is a character in his own right rather than a symbol or an extension of another character, a person with a disability rather than a mysterious and supernatural creature. Further, Tyrion's arc bears many similarities to that of knights of medieval romance, though Martin gives these a slight twist, either for humor or to remind the reader that Tyrion is not a knight or a hero.

Tyrion does not initially appear to have any particularly heroic qualities about him, let alone romance-hero qualities. Besides being a dwarf, he is more intellectual than physical, keeps company with prostitutes, and is not above using less-than-honorable political methods to get what he wants. However, despite his disability, he fights in two battles, taking the front line in both. He recognizes that he has no place in either battle, but also that his participation is necessary for his side's success, and so he fights despite his certain belief that he will die in the attempt.

At the Battle of the Green Fork, Martin includes an arming scene that gently mocks both Tyrion and arming scenes from medieval and fantasy literature such as *Sir Gawain and the Green Knight* and *The Two Towers*. In *Sir Gawain and the Green Knight*, Gawain's fellow knights help to arm him in a scene that describes in detail each piece of armor and in what order it is placed on Gawain's body, how he mounts his horse, and the detail of his shield. All told, the arming of Gawain takes three stanzas, which indicates its importance and ritual significance to the poem.[88] Similarly, in *The Two Towers*, Aragorn, Legolas, and Gimli are armed just before the Battle of Helm's Deep, and while their armor is not described in as much detail as Gawain's, the ritual significance of preparing for battle still shows in this passage.[89] Arming scenes such as these tend to be solemn events, knights (or

[87] Emily Rebekah Huber, "'Delyver Me My Dwarff!': Gareth's Dwarf and Chivalric Identity," *Arthuriana* 16, no. 2 (2006), 50.

[88] *Sir Gawain and the Green Knight*, translated by J.R.R. Tolkien (New York: Ballantine, 1975), 23–121.

[89] J.R.R. Tolkien, *The Lord of the Rings: The Two Towers* (New York: Ballantine, 1965), 135–6.

other warriors) donning the accoutrements that help constitute their identity – armor, swords, shields – and mounting their horses.

Tyrion's arming scene, on the other hand, satirizes these scenes and reads much more like Bilbo's scene just before the Battle of the Five Armies in *The Hobbit*. Tyrion's squire, Podrick Payne, and Tyrion's paid companion, Shae, help to armor him in bits of found armor, since his custom-fitted suit is back at Casterly Rock. These pieces are described in some detail (not as much as Gawain's, but more than Legolas', Aragorn's, and Gimli's):

> [M]ail hauberk and coif, a dead knight's gorget, lobstered greaves and gauntlets and pointed steel boots. Some of it was ornate, some plain; not a bit of it matched, or fit as it should. His breastplate was meant for a bigger man; for his oversize head, they found a huge bucket-shaped greathelm topped with a foot-long triangular spike.[90]

Tyrion then struggles up onto his horse; the shield Podrick hands him is immensely heavy. Shae tells him he looks "fearsome," but Tyrion replies that he looks like "a dwarf in mismatched armor."[91] This remark echoes Bilbo's "I expect I look rather absurd" after Thorin outfits him with a mithril shirt and a helm.[92] Although Tyrion is acting as a knight, wearing armor, riding a horse, carrying a weapon, and leading the vanguard, he is not a knight, and neither Martin nor Tyrion pretends that Tyrion's situation is anything but absurd.

Tyrion also has certain romantic notions about his relationships with prostitutes, especially Shae and Tysha.[93] While he constantly reminds himself that Shae has no actual love for him, he treats her like a lady, protecting her from those who would harm her and lavishing her with gifts. Tyrion's relationship with Shae is quite typical of medieval romance; he steals her from another knight, which in medieval romance is not only allowed, but encouraged.[94] He sees

[90] Martin, *A Game of Thrones*, 683.

[91] Ibid., 683.

[92] J.R.R. Tolkien, *The Hobbit* (New York: Ballantine, 1965), 240.

[93] Tysha's status as a prostitute is questionable, but for most of the series Tyrion believes she was a prostitute.

[94] Roberta L. Krueger, *Women Readers and the Ideology of Gender in Old French Verse Romance* (Cambridge: Cambridge University Press, 1993), 39–40.

her as an extension of himself, as women in medieval romances are nearly always defined by their relationships with the male hero.[95] At one point, he thinks that Shae has helped him to heal from Tysha's rape and banishment, reflecting the tendency in medieval romance for the hero to move from one woman to another – usually from his mother to his lover, but Tyrion's mother is dead, and his marriage to Tysha shaped his youthful development.[96] Tyrion believes in Shae's faithfulness up until the moment she betrays him, testifying against him during his murder trial and publically airing their pillow talk.[97] Later, the reader learns Cersei promised Shae a manse in the city and a knight to marry in exchange for this testimony, which was more than Tyrion had managed to give her.[98] When Tyrion discovers Shae in his father's bed, he murders her, which can be seen as a punishment for her failing to act as a passive object and instead seeking to better her own position.[99] As David Salter says, "the particular form of femininity that the romance idealizes is the undemanding, self-denying kind that presents absolutely no challenge to masculine authority."[100] Shae is anything but undemanding or self-denying, and when Tyrion finally understands that she does not love him and never did, he punishes her for this transgression.

After losing his "lady," his status, and all his riches, Tyrion follows the path typical of medieval romance heroes after such losses – he leaves behind his home and descends into madness. In Tyrion's case, this madness consists of a spate of drunkenness as Varys smuggles him across the Narrow Sea to Pentos. He is unshaven and covered in his own vomit, urine, and blood, too drunk even to use his wits and book-learned knowledge.[101] Yet once again, there is an element of humor, as the final leg of his trip takes place in a barrel, echoing the

[95] David Salter, "'Born to Thralldom and Penance': Wives and Mothers in Middle English Romance," in *Writing Gender and Genre in Medieval Literature: Approaches to Old and Middle English Texts*, edited by Elaine Treharne (Cambridge: D.S. Brewer, 2002), 43.

[96] Martin, *A Clash of Kings*, 452; Salter, 43.

[97] Martin, *A Storm of Swords*, 961–3.

[98] Martin, *A Feast for Crows*, 74.

[99] Martin, *A Storm of Swords*, 1071.

[100] Salter, 58.

[101] Martin, *A Dance with Dragons*, 18–21.

dwarves' escape from the Mirkwood elves in *The Hobbit*. As he travels toward Volantis in hopes of meeting Daenerys before she invades Westeros, he encounters a potential fair unknown – Aegon Targaryen, masquerading as a boy called "Young Griff" and planning to marry Daenerys when they reach her.[102] In a way, Tyrion even becomes a fair unknown himself, as he goes by the names "Yollo" and "Hugor Hill" while traveling. Tyrion's status reaches its lowest point when he is sold into slavery, but he regains his wits and uses his true name and the promise of gold to join a mercenary company with the intention of putting them in Daenerys' service and ultimately regaining his birthright – the lordship of Casterly Rock. How closely the remainder of Tyrion's tale will accord with a romance hero's, namely in his regaining his title, station, property, and lover, remains to be seen.

As Martin has never discussed his influences from medieval literature, it is difficult to know to what extent he is aware of these parallels. It is possible that the romance elements in his work come from Tolkien and other such medievalist fantasists; Tolkien's influence is clear in *A Song of Ice and Fire*, after all. Perhaps Martin's ideas about medieval romance come entirely from the Victorians and early critics who saw them as escapist and idealistic rather than addressing the social and political issues of their time. In that case, it would be truly ironic that his strategy of undercutting the tropes of medievalist fantasy in order to show how the Middle Ages "really" were result in such close alignment with the structure, tropes, and motifs of medieval romance.

Regardless of Martin's conscious intentions, these similarities are clearly apparent in the novels (indeed, there are many more similarities that could be explored, and explored in greater detail, than there was space for here). In this sense, he might be considered to have succeeded in his stated intention to return to a more "real" Middle Ages; *A Song of Ice and Fire* has much more in common with medieval romance than many contemporary, "Disneyland" fantasies. Martin shows the same concerns about the unrestrained use of violence, especially by the knightly class, about the effects of this violence on

[102] Whether Young Griff truly is Aegon Targaryen or a pretender, the "mummer's dragon" Daenerys sees in her vision in the House of the Undying and whom Quaithe warns her about, is yet to be revealed.

the kingdom, about gender roles and the effects of a hyper-masculinist patriarchy on both men and women, and about the impossibility of living up to chivalric ideals that appear in medieval romance.

2

Masculinity, Femininity, and Gender Relations

TODAY, AN UNDERSTANDING of the gender dynamics and gender roles of the Middle Ages generally stems from a confluence of several literary and historical streams: anti-feminist treatises from the Middle Ages, medieval romance, medievalist fiction from writers such as Tolkien and Tennyson, and even scholarship on the Middle Ages and medieval romance. As discussed in the introduction, whether the perception of gender in the Middle Ages as portrayed in medievalist fantasy is "correct" or not is secondary to understanding what that perception is and how it developed, as well as how writers such as Martin approach, use, and/or reject that perception.

Various uses of medievalism – both social and literary – indicate that the general beliefs about gender roles in the Middle Ages favor strong, warrior men and submissive, chaste women, with the occasional warrior woman allowed. Michael Drout believes some of this impression may have been inspired by Tolkien, whose Middle-Earth includes very few women and largely eschews all forms of reproduction. Drout claims that students new to medieval studies might be surprised by the visibility of women in medieval literature and history, even viewing the idea of gender as an "intrusion" on their preconceived notions of the Middle Ages.[1] This observation generalizes to a larger point about the role of men in constructing the Middle Ages – for the most part, medieval writers were men, medieval historians were men, and early medieval scholars were men – in that the portrayal and construction of gender is one-sided. Nancy Partner

[1] Michael Drout, "The Influence of J.R.R. Tolkien's Masculinist Medievalism," *Medieval Feminist Newsletter* 22 (1996), 26–7.

reminds us that many of the medieval women available for study are fictitious, invented by men for male interests, and that medieval studies has traditionally been "men studying men."[2]

Since Martin is writing epic fantasy set in a medievalist world, especially one that is strongly influenced by medieval romance and attempts to avoid high fantasy's tendency toward simple morality and an innocent Middle Ages, gender issues are, of course, complicated in *A Song of Ice and Fire*. As with the structures and narrative discussed in the previous chapter, Martin's handling of gender issues also shows strong influences from medieval romance – again, the original romances and not the Victorian or Pre-Raphaelite reconstruction of them. Moreover, Martin not only reconstructs the gender dynamics of medieval romance, but also considers the implications of these dynamics on society in general and his characters in particular – men as well as women.

"Sharp steel and strong arms rule this world": Chivalry and Toxic Masculinity in Westeros

As Richard Kaueper and others have discussed, the idea of chivalry was not primarily about courtesy or protecting women, but about when, against whom, and at whose orders violence was permissible. He claims that "[c]hivalry was a code of violence in defense of a prickly set of honor [...] just as thoroughly as it was a code of restraint."[3] Chivalric codes also served to place male violence in service to the State and the Church by appealing to an idea of honor, though, as Leo Braudy points out, that idea is often vague, individualized, and internal, and thus is difficult to codify, let alone follow.[4] Chivalry and honor are, like so many medievalist ideas, nostalgic; those who successfully practiced them are always in the past, just as the mythical Golden Age when everyone had a place and was happy is always in

[2] Nancy F. Partner, "No Sex, No Gender," *Speculum* 68, no. 2 (1993), 423.

[3] Kaeuper, "The Societal Role of Chivalry in Romance: Northern Europe," 99–100.

[4] Leo Braudy, *From Chivalry to Terrorism: War and the Changing Nature of Masculinity* (New York: Alfred Knopf, 2003), 51–2.

the past (usually in the Middle Ages or the Roman Empire).[5] Braudy argues that chivalric ideals also help to idealize the past and past wars as somehow "more honorable and perhaps more humane than the grand slaughters of the twentieth century,"[6] though, as has been shown, these simplified and romanticized ideas about the Middle Ages have little basis in history and more basis in people's need for such stories.

As he does with most romantic, idealized perceptions of the Middle Ages, Martin rejects the idea that chivalry created an ideal society where men fought only to protect their women or in grand, bloodless tournaments, instead creating a society in which chivalry is a thin veneer over a violent, toxic masculinity that victimizes men, women, and children alike. Martin's Westeros does not reward chivalry, does not even really believe in chivalry as more than a masquerade behind which "true" masculinity – violent, aggressive, and misogynist – hides. In this way, Martin interrogates the patriarchal society of the Middle Ages – turning history "up to eleven," as he has described his worldbuilding[7] – and shows how poisonous a society that devalues women and glorifies strength of arms can be. It is in this that *A Song of Ice and Fire* most closely exemplifies Matthews' view of popular medievalism as "a fundamental tension between the gothic-grotesque and the romantic."[8] Martin acknowledges romantic medievalism, which assures the reader that while violence exists, rescue is available from knights in shining armor, but denies that there is any truth in it through his use of gothic medievalism, which assumes that "anything medieval will involve threat, violence, and warped sexuality."[9] His work bears out Amy Kaufman's theory of "muscular medievalism," which she argues "imagines the past as a man's world in which masculinity was powerful, impenetrable, and uniquely privileged."[10] A "real" Middle Ages must, then, include violence and rape or else

[5] Ibid., 6.

[6] Ibid., 83.

[7] "The Real History Behind *Game of Thrones*: Part I."

[8] Matthews, 15.

[9] Ibid., 15.

[10] Amy Kaufman, "Muscular Medievalism," *The Year's Work in Medievalism* 31 (2016), 58.

risk becoming "Disneyfied." Much attention is paid to the treatment of women in the books (discussed below), but the idea that the patriarchy is as damaging for men as it is for women, even in Westeros, is rarely explored.

Perhaps the clearest example of toxic masculinity in *A Song of Ice and Fire* can be found in Randyll Tarly and his treatment of both his son, Samwell, and Brienne of Tarth. Sam Tarly describes his upbringing to Jon Snow fairly soon after their first meeting in *A Game of Thrones*, describing how he was born into "a family old in honor," heir to "rich lands, a strong keep, and a storied two-handed greatsword named Heartsbane."[11] However, Sam proves to be an unfit heir in his father's eyes, more interested in books, food, and music than knighthood and killing. Randyll tries everything to make his son more "manly," including various forms of abuse and shaming, even witchcraft and blood magic.[12] When Sam suggests that he might like to study to be a maester, Randyll chains him up and leaves him in a room; though the duration of the ordeal is not specified, the experience is traumatic enough that Jon's later orders for Sam to travel to and study at the Citadel nearly cause a panic attack.[13] Finally, Randyll gives his son an ultimatum: renounce his birthright in favor of his younger brother and join the Night's Watch, or suffer a "hunting accident" out in the woods. Randyll clearly believes there is one model for manhood and refuses to accept anything different. His treatment of Sam leads to Sam becoming a timid, anxiety-ridden young man who cannot see his talents as worthwhile and cannot even admit that killing an Other was his doing, instead giving all the credit to the obsidian dagger with which he stabbed the creature.

The reader first encounters Randyll Tarly in person in *A Clash of Kings*, through Catelyn's point of view, and he is every bit as hard as Sam painted him. He sits in Renly Baratheon's council and constantly urges violence. He criticizes Robb Stark for not killing Jaime Lannister, whom he is holding as a prisoner of war, and for not coming to see Renly himself, rather than "hiding behind his mother's skirts," clearly

[11] Martin, *A Game of Thrones*, 267.
[12] Ibid., 268.
[13] Martin, *A Feast for Crows*, 117–18.

not recognizing Catelyn's authority as an ambassador.[14] He also urges Renly to attack Stannis' encampment before dawn – the agreed-upon time for the battle to begin – a move that Renly decries as "treachery" and "unchivalrous."[15] Tarly appears again in *A Feast for Crows*, where his misogyny is on full display as he chastises Brienne for acting like a knight and warns her that if she is raped, it will be her own fault and she will get no justice from him.[16] This encounter triggers a memory for Brienne: at Renly's camp, the men made a wager on who would claim her maidenhead and aggressively courted her to win the ever-growing pot. Randyll blamed Brienne entirely, claiming that the knights were "honorable men" and that if she "behave[d] like a camp follower, she cannot object to being treated like one." Brienne protested that she wants to fight, and Randyll said that "the gods made men to fight, and women to bear children."[17] This strictly dichotomous view of gender roles is not unusual for Westeros, though Randyll's attitude is extreme even there.

The prowess-focused masculinity of Westeros is also obvious in the culture's treatment of men and boys with disabilities. This is apparent in Bran Stark's depression after the accident that leaves him paralyzed, as well as the way people talk about his chances of surviving. Sandor Clegane remarks that Bran is taking a long time to die and he wishes it would go faster.[18] Jaime claims that if Bran were his son, he would give the boy the mercy of a swift death: "Even if the boy does live, he will be a cripple. Worse than a cripple. A grotesque. Give me a good clean death."[19] Eddard Karstark remarks that he'd rather be dead than "live like that," and his brother Torrhen speculates that the fall broke Bran's spirit as well, leaving him too much of a coward to kill himself.[20] Because Bran has lost his physical abilities, many now consider him less than a man – less than human, even – and worthless, not fit to live. Bran does not see his own worth, either; he had planned to be

14 Martin, *A Clash of Kings*, 346.
15 Ibid., 499–500.
16 Martin, *A Feast for Crows*, 295.
17 Ibid., 301.
18 Martin, *A Game of Thrones*, 87.
19 Ibid., 91.
20 Ibid., 580.

a knight, possibly a knight of the Kingsguard, and keeps trying to find ways to be a warrior even with his disability. Even his decision to seek the Three-Eyed Crow is an attempt to regain his physical abilities rather than hone his mental ones.[21] Bran believes in knighthood above all else, despite Luwin's lessons about the nature of knighthood and how "A man's worth is not marked by a *ser* before his name."[22] In Westeros, the only acceptable role for a man or boy, particularly one of noble birth, is as a fighter.[23]

Tyrion suffers similar indignities, but accentuated, partly because he spends much more time around people than Bran does, and partly because he was born disabled. He suffers from dwarfism, probably achondroplasia, along with heterochromia.[24] This leads not only to a fearsome appearance which earns him the enmity of nearly everyone, including his own family, but also constant pain. He claims that if he had not been born noble, he probably would have been killed at birth or sold to slavers for a "grotesquerie."[25] Despite his disability, Tywin Lannister constantly compares him – physically – to Jaime, of course finding Tyrion lacking. Tyrion attempts to make up for his physical shortcomings by learning everything he can and becoming remarkably good at politics and government. However, he has very little support from anyone, least of all his own family, and is routinely denied rights that should be his. Tywin refuses to name Tyrion his heir, at least partly because of his disability:

> You are an ill-made, devious, disobedient, spiteful little creature full of envy, lust, and low cunning. Men's laws give you the right to bear my name and display my colors, since I cannot prove that you are not mine. To teach me humility, the gods have condemned me to watch you waddle about wearing that proud lion that was my father's

[21] Martin, *A Dance with Dragons*, 202.

[22] Martin, *A Game of Thrones*, 570.

[23] Lower-born boys have more choice: Gendry is a blacksmith, Hot Pie a baker, and bards abound. Nobody shames them for holding these roles in the way Sam is shamed for being interested in becoming a maester.

[24] Achondroplasia is a form of dwarfism causing shortened limbs and a larger head on an average-sized torso; heterochromia is a genetic mutation causing mismatched eyes.

[25] Martin, *A Game of Thrones*, 123.

> sigil and his father's before him. But neither gods nor men shall ever compel me to let you turn Casterly Rock into your whorehouse.[26]

Further subtext underlies Tywin's claims; Tyrion is often blamed for Joanna Lannister's death, and Tywin loved his wife deeply.[27] Likewise, Tyrion himself has noted that "all dwarfs are bastards in their father's eyes,"[28] and it may be that Tywin believes Tyrion's disability reflects badly on his own masculinity. While Tyrion does have some character defects, they are nothing worse than many of those demonstrated by other high lords; Tywin himself has sex with Shae after she betrays Tyrion. The true issue is that Tywin believes Tyrion's disability shames him and the family name. Tywin wants Jaime to inherit, failing to recognize that while Jaime more closely matches the Westerosi ideal of masculinity, Tyrion is better suited both mentally and temperamentally to carry on Tywin's legacy.

The books also contain many statements about war and the inherently violent nature of man that contribute to the atmosphere of violence and toxic masculinity in Westeros. Jorah Mormont tells Daenerys, "There is a savage beast in every man, and when you hand that man a sword or spear and send him forth to war, the beast stirs."[29] Jaime has a similar sentiment, claiming that "[m]en [...] would kill at their lord's command, rape when their blood was up after battle, and plunder wherever they could, but once the war was done they would go back to their homes, trade their spears for hoes, wed their neighbors' daughters, and raise a pack of squalling children."[30] Frequently, the suggestion that a man should show mercy or avoid a fight is described as womanish, and those who suggest it as having "the soft hearts of women."[31] The capacity and willingness to do violence is expected of the noblemen of Westeros, and any suggestion that they are incapable or unwilling is an affront to their honor. These expectations can leave men deeply damaged in ways that they may not even

[26] Martin, *A Storm of Swords*, 65.
[27] Ibid., 968.
[28] Martin, *A Game of Thrones*, 57.
[29] Ibid., 328.
[30] Ibid., 603.
[31] Martin, *A Game of Thrones*, 726.

recognize, and cannot admit if they do. Jaime, for example, has no mechanism for coping with emotional stress except dissociation, and he teaches Tommen to do the same. Sandor Clegane struggles with pyrophobia from his brother holding his face to the fire when he was a child, leaving horrible scars, but whenever it becomes a problem, he is called a coward despite his otherwise loyal service to the Lannisters, in which he does everything asked of him (except strike Sansa).

In this way, Martin takes the culture portrayed in the romances and considers what living in such a culture would be like for those who are not, like Gregor Clegane, mindless killing machines. He rejects the idea that chivalry leads to an idealistic and idyllic culture and instead demonstrates that violence is inherent to this form of masculinity, and chivalry cannot curb that violence. Again, Martin's ideas show in his interview with Wayne MacLaurin, in which he claims that the "class of protectors" was often the group from whom the lower classes most needed protection.[32] While his assertion that the ideals of knighthood are grand and idealistic betrays some influence from romance and Victorian ideas about chivalry, it still informs the way he has written expectations for men in Westeros.

"A lady's armor is courtesy": Women in Westeros

Just as Martin rejects the "knight in shining armor" model of chivalry, so does he reject the "damsel in distress" and "Madonna/Whore" portrayals of women so often found in romance and fantasy. Dozens of books and articles examine the portrayals of women in both genres, and the conclusions rarely commend the writers of these works. Jessica Salmonson claims that women in fantasy fall into a few archetypes:

> [A] series of contradictory images of demonic rage and angelic passivity; virtuous ethereal lady, or frigid hen; noble prostitute, or vicious whore; beauty/princess, hag/witch; languid sex symbol, or the dominatrix of the more masochistic side of male imaginings; the feline child protector who fights only from maternal instinct, or the

[32] MacLaurin, n.p.

> Medean baby killer; evil sorceress (if powerful), or helpless prize (if meek); incompetent burden, or, at best, the spunky "girl" who guards her man's back by day and warms his bed by night.[33]

Generally speaking, romances and fantasy focus primarily on men, usually men's coming-of-age or other chivalric development. Throughout the Middle Ages and much of the twentieth century, the primary writers of romance and fantasy, respectively, were men, and even when the stories were female-focused, as romances could be, they were still constructed by a male author through a male point of view with male ideologies.[34] In medieval and medievalist fiction, women are usually constructed as objects of exchange between men, objects on which to build a knight's chivalric identity, disruptive or unifying social forces, and otherwise extensions of men and men's homosocial relationships. Passive women are venerated, and active women (especially sexually active women) are demonized. For the most part, Martin has avoided portraying his women as objects of any kind, instead aiming to grant them the same independence and personality as he does his male characters. While some female characters seem to exist solely to further the plotlines of their attached male characters, many male characters serve female ones in the same way. While Westerosi society's expectations for women still fall into this woman-as-object model, and men in the series frequently attempt to put women "in their place," Martin explores this dynamic from the internal view of women, allowing them a narrative voice to express their frustration and desires even when social pressures prevent them from speaking these aloud.[35]

[33] Jessica Amanda Salmonson, "Introduction: Our Amazon Heritage," in *Amazons!*, edited by Jessica Amanda Salmonson (New York: DAW, 1979), 14.

[34] Simon Gaunt, *Gender and Genre in Medieval French Literature* (Cambridge: Cambridge University Press, 1995), 71.

[35] In a conversation with fans in 2005, Martin strongly rejected the idea that Sansa Stark and Catelyn Stark in particular – two of the longest-running female POV characters – "whine" too much; he claims that whining is by definition a physical act, speaking one's troubles aloud and burdening others with them, which neither Sansa nor Catelyn does very often. They keep most of their darker thoughts inside ("Interaction [Glasgow, Scotland, UK: August 4–8], *The Citadel: So Spake Martin*, August 4, 2005, http://www.westeros.org/Citadel/SSM/Entry/1348).

Martin's handling of his point-of-view (POV) women is remarkable in its depth; his women do not passively accept their roles in this patriarchal, hyper-masculine world, but fight for their own interests and recognize that the definitions of womanhood placed on them by society are faulty and need not necessarily be conformed to. Nor does Martin force his POV women into typical literary stereotypes – the Madonna or the whore, the Earth mother, the damsel in distress, etc. Even when the women seem at first to fall into these stereotypes – as Cersei appears to be an Evil Queen archetype early on – once Martin admits the reader into her inner narration, the character's complications emerge. As with most of Martin's characters, his women are neither entirely virtuous nor entirely debauched, but rich, complicated characters with full backstories and strong personalities. However, while he avoids some of the worst clichés in writing women in romance and fantasy, his use of several other contemporary popular-culture conceptions and characterizations can tend to weaken his overall portrayal.

Martin considers himself a feminist, claiming that "I've always considered women to be people."[36] He says he approaches writing women – and anyone different from himself in any way – from a place of empathy and respect.[37] "I regard men and women as all human – yes, there are differences, but many of those differences are created by the culture that we live in, whether it's the medieval culture of Westeros or twenty-first-century Western culture," he claims.[38] Thus, Martin works against a traditional attitude toward writing women in historical settings; as Nira Yuval-Davis has pointed out, the creation of history and knowledge is frequently androcentric, ignoring the contributions of women or the private sphere in general, dismissing the private sphere (and by extension, women) as politically (and

[36] "George R.R. Martin on Strombo."

[37] Ibid., n.p.

[38] Jessica Salter, "*Game of Thrones*' George R.R. Martin: 'I'm a Feminist at Heart,'" *The Telegraph*, April 1, 2013, http://www.telegraph.co.uk/women/womens-life/9959063/Game-of-Throness-George-RR-Martin-Im-a-feminist.html.

historically) irrelevant.[39] Martin does not (generally) dismiss women as non-influential in his society; indeed, his women are demonstrably influential to the plot and the societies of the novels.

The structure of Westeros' society forces women to find power in one of two ways: they are either politicians or fighters. While the men can be both – for example, Barristan Selmy is a formidable fighter who also provides advice to Daenerys Targaryen and runs Meereen in her absence – the women tend to be one or the other, with varying levels of success. Frequently, their failures as warriors or politicians are caused by the feudal, patriarchal society in which Martin has placed them, though their own character flaws are just as likely to be the cause of their downfalls.

Westeros is made up of several different regions, each with its own ideas about a woman's place and abilities. The south, where the capital, King's Landing, sits, has the most in common with the traditional medievalist conception of the Middle Ages in its rigid feudalistic power structure and strictly defined gender roles. This is the society that produces Cersei Lannister, Brienne of Tarth, and Catelyn Stark *née* Tully, and to which Sansa Stark aspires. The north is far more like the Anglo-Saxon or Viking era, and at least one of the Stark banner houses, the Mormonts, boasts several warrior women. Arya Stark comes out of this society and aspires to the physical arts, despite her mother, Catelyn, trying to press her into the southern mold of a "proper" young lady. Further north, beyond the Wall, the culture is tribal, and women like Ygritte are expected to fight alongside the men. The Iron Isles are home to Asha Greyjoy, a formidable seawoman and fighter, who is still not quite equal to her male peers, as she has little to no chance of being elected queen by the Kingsmoot due to the Isles' patriarchal power structure. Likewise, in the far southern kingdom of Dorne, the bastard daughters of Prince Oberyn are fighters, though Princess Arianne is still expected to marry for the good of the kingdom.

Due to the differences in expectations, women from different regions have different approaches to gaining and keeping power.

[39] Nira Yuval-Davis, *Gender and Nation* (Thousand Oaks, CA: Sage Publications, 1997), 2.

Those from King's Landing and the surrounding areas are much more likely to seek political power and wield it with some subtlety, as society does not technically allow them to be much more than wives, mothers, and trophies used for alliances and furthering the status of the house. One of the most successful examples of women's political power in King's Landing is Olenna Tyrell, the matriarch of House Tyrell. When she first appears in *A Storm of Swords*, she is portrayed as an opinionated old lady whose family is deeply embarrassed by her tendency to speak her mind, regardless of who is listening and to whom she's speaking. This tendency makes her seem eccentric and harmless, convincing Sansa to trust her enough to discuss Joffrey's abuse.[40] Yet this persona also covers a shrewd planner who murders King Joffrey at his wedding.[41] Thus, Olenna ensures that her granddaughter, Margaery, marries into the royal family but removes the monstrous Joffrey so that the younger and more biddable Tommen will replace him.

In contrast to Olenna, Cersei has a very different approach to politics. Essentially, Cersei attempts to rule like a man – or her perception of how a man rules – which does not endear her to the people, Joffrey's (later Tommen's) Small Council, or her own family. Jaime is Cersei's twin brother, and thus Cersei grew up intensely aware of the differences in social status between men and women, as Jaime was granted much more privilege than she was. "When we were little, Jaime and I were so much alike that even our lord father could not tell us apart," she tells Sansa:

> Sometimes as a lark we would dress in each other's clothes and spend a whole day each as the other. Yet even so, when Jaime was given his first sword, there was none for me. 'What do *I* get?' I remember asking. We were so much alike, I could never understand why they treated us so *differently*.[42]

More than anything, Cersei wants to be respected like Jaime and the other men in her life; she does not rebel against the patriarchy

[40] Martin, *A Storm of Swords*, 81–7.
[41] Ibid., 829–30, 935.
[42] Martin, *A Clash of Kings*, 848–9.

so much as internalize the misogyny of it, believing that she should have been born a man so that she would be given the respect she feels she deserves. In many ways, she lives vicariously through Jaime, claiming that they are "one person in two bodies" and taking pride in his accomplishments.[43] Lena Headey, who plays Cersei in *Game of Thrones*, claims that her rejection of Jaime when he returns without a hand is deeply tied to that hand being the way in which she wielded power, a power now denied her.[44] Her internalized misogyny also aligns her with the expectations of the toxic masculinity of Westerosi society, and so she cannot accept Jaime's loss of status after his injury. Having completely absorbed her society's beliefs about women's weaknesses, Cersei attempts to prove that she is different, that she is more masculine and therefore less irrational than other women, but this leads her to overcompensate; her methods backfire and reinforce the stereotypes of women as emotional, irrational, and unstable.

Cersei's understanding of how to get and keep power is based on watching her husband, King Robert, and her father, Tywin Lannister. Tywin is a brutal man, given to harsh and pointed punishments. One of these punishments, against a rogue vassal's house, was so brutal and thorough that it inspired a song, "The Rains of Castamere," which serves as a warning to any other rebellious vassals.[45] Nor does he spare his own family when he believes they need correcting; when Tyrion married a commoner, he forced Tyrion to watch as the entire company of Lannister soldiers raped her, ordered Tyrion to rape her as well, then sent her away.[46] Tywin's belief that his family's reputation and power supersede all – even his family, if necessary – causes him to be an authoritarian leader. Robert is quite the opposite. He is hedonistic, using his power to further his own enjoyment, but he has no real interest in ruling. His pleasures include sex, alcohol, tourneys, and hunting, and he pursues these regardless of the consequences. Though Cersei finds his single-mindedness abhorrent, she accepts his

[43] Martin, *Game of Thrones*, 485.

[44] C.E. Taylor, *Inside HBO's "Game of Thrones": Seasons Three and Four* (San Francisco: Chronicle Books, 2014), 135.

[45] Martin, *A Storm of Swords*, 272.

[46] Martin, *A Game of Thrones*, 458.

behavior as the mark of a strong leader and imitates it when she feels she is not being given the respect she is due.

Unfortunately for Cersei, Westerosi society does not respect a woman's authority. Her reaction is to go on the offensive, threatening violence against any who oppose her. However, she was never trained to be a leader, and thus has no sense of proportion or idea of when her threats will be most effective; she responds to every threat against her power, no matter how trivial, with violence. For example, when rumors about her children's true parentage are sweeping the kingdom, she orders the Small Council to issue an edict that "[a]ny man heard speaking of incest or calling Joff[rey] a bastard should lose his tongue for it," failing to realize that such an act will only validate the rumors and further turn the smallfolk against her and Joffrey.[47] Yet she also uses her womanhood as a way of consolidating power; she tells Sansa that tears and sex are a woman's best weapons, and she uses veiled and not-so-veiled promises of sex to pay men for their loyalty.[48] Sex is also a weapon in the more traditional sense; Robert raped her when he was drunk, and Cersei in turn assaults her bedmate, Taena, in an attempt to feel as powerful as she thinks Robert did when he assaulted her.[49] Cersei has internalized the violence-oriented masculine culture of Westeros and attempts to act as a man is expected to, but violence does not earn her the same respect that it would a man.

Eventually, Cersei's schemes unravel, and she is caught in the trap she set for Margaery, standing trial in the Sept for treason, regicide, deicide, and incest.[50] Her pre-trial atonement – walking, shaved and naked, from the Great Sept of Baelor to the Red Keep – strips away any semblance of power she had left; she is aware that the people will never be able to take her seriously as a leader again.[51] She appears to accept her place as a woman and a Lannister, becoming more subdued and quiet while waiting for her trial by combat. She tells her uncle Kevan that "[i]t is a wise woman who knows her place," and he

[47] Martin, *A Clash of Kings*, 229.
[48] Ibid., 847.
[49] Martin, *A Feast for Crows*, 692.
[50] Martin, *A Dance with Dragons*, 796.
[51] Ibid., 939–40.

reflects that she is much less fiery than he remembers her.[52] Whether this new attitude is honest or a careful façade remains to be seen, as the reader encounters post-walk Cersei only through Kevan's point of view.

In contrast to Cersei, Catelyn Stark works within the patriarchal power structure, supporting her husband, Ned, then her son Robb, offering advice but never seeking to lead on her own. Yet she faces some of the same frustrations Cersei does: she struggles to make her voice heard and heeded among the men of the north and their Tully allies. Despite Maege Mormont's battle prowess and willingness to talk back to Robb – she "told [him] bluntly that he was young enough to be her grandson, and had no business giving her commands … but as it happened, she had a granddaughter she would be willing to have him marry" – even the men of the north do not necessarily respect a woman politically.[53] When Catelyn tries to talk the men out of declaring war on the south, one of Robb's bannermen tells her, "You are a woman, my lady […] Women do not understand these things."[54] She attempts to negotiate Arya and Sansa's return from King's Landing in exchange for Jaime Lannister, who is the Starks' prisoner, but Robb will not agree to such terms – because, as Catelyn accuses him of calculating, girls are not important enough to trade for such a high-value hostage as Jaime.[55] Robb sends her to negotiate with Renly, one of the contenders for the throne, only because he has no one else to send, and the only time he admits that he should have heeded her council is after he has made the blunder that ultimately leads to his death – breaking a betrothal and thus a vow to another lord.[56] His failure to heed Catelyn's advice results not only in his death, but hers as well.

In further contrast, Daenerys Targaryen uses men's assumptions about her intelligence and cunning against them. She frequently claims, "I am just a young girl and know little" – of men, or war, or love. In order to obtain an army to help her invade and conquer Westeros,

52 Ibid., 1046.
53 Martin, *A Game of Thrones*, 574.
54 Ibid., 795.
55 Martin, *A Clash of Kings*, 114.
56 Martin, *A Clash of Kings*, 336; *A Storm of Swords*, 196.

she allows the Astapori slaver with whom she must deal to believe that she does not understand Valeryian and is willing to trade one of her dragons for the slave army; she then turns that dragon on him, turns the slaves on their masters, frees the slave army, and leads them out of Astapor.[57] Once Daenerys is queen of Meereen, she continues to serve as a foil to Cersei, as her primary concern is to serve and protect her people from the nobles of Slavers Bay, while returning to Westeros and reclaiming the throne becomes a secondary concern.[58] Unlike Cersei, Daenerys is focused more on being a strong leader, not on consolidating and keeping her personal power.[59]

While these women may wield considerable political power, they wield little to no physical power, instead relying on the men around them to do so. An episode of *Game of Thrones* makes this point, albeit obliquely: during a conversation between Petyr Baelish and Cersei, he says, "Knowledge is power." Her response is to order the members of the Lannister guard surrounding her to "seize him. Cut his throat. Stop. Wait. I've changed my mind; let him go. Step back three paces. Turn around. Close your eyes." The soldiers follow her every instruction, and she tells a now-flustered Petyr that "Power is power."[60] Yet her power relies on others to carry out the threat of force behind it, as she cannot do so herself, and when the ability to command knights is taken away, Cersei's power disappears with it. Similarly, much of Daenerys' power rests on her possession of three dragons, and when one escapes and she locks the others away for the safety of her people, her power likewise dwindles. Even Catelyn must remind the bannermen present in the Inn at the Crossroads of their loyalty to her father before calling on them to arrest Tyrion Lannister.

In these women, we see Adrienne Rich's point about women's power made clear: that it is, and has been, inextricably linked with men's power. History has shown "the hatred of overt strength in women, the definition of strong independent women as freaks of

[57] Martin, *A Storm of Swords*, 367–81.

[58] Her reasoning for this shift in priorities is disturbing, and will be discussed in more detail in Chapter 4.

[59] Daenerys' leadership style will be examined more closely in Chapter 4.

[60] "The North Remembers," *Game of Thrones*, written by David Benioff and D.B. Weiss, directed by Alan Taylor (HBO, 2012).

nature, as unsexed, frigid, castrating, perverted, dangerous; the fear of the maternal woman as 'controlling,' the preference for dependent, malleable, 'feminine' women."[61] Catelyn's power comes from being Ned Stark's widow and Robb Stark's mother, and she is heeded to an extent (though not as thoroughly as she believes she should be); she is shown respect for her position and her willingness to stay mostly within the boundaries that Westerosi society has decreed for a woman of her standing. Only just before her death does she violate a feminine code and kill an innocent, helpless boy, and the only reason she finds herself in that position is that Robb has failed to heed her advice and counsel. Cersei and Daenerys refuse to conform to the expectations for women, and both are feared and hated by other characters. They also bear troubling narrative arcs and characterizations (which will be discussed later in this chapter) that indicate that even Martin may sometimes struggle to negotiate the power of the women he has created.

Although physical power is generally less available to women, a few of Martin's POV women do manage to wield it. However, in these women – most notably Brienne of Tarth – Martin falls into a fairly typical fantasy trope, that of the "exceptional woman." In a society that has specific expectations for women and women's roles, those who step outside of them – and are not immediately shamed, beaten, or otherwise forced back into line – are exceptions to society's rules. Exceptional women are isolated due to the liminal space they inhabit, not part of a community of women nor truly accepted into the company of men. Mary D. Sheriff claims that the term "refers to the woman who, owing to some particular circumstance […] has been exempted from rules or laws […] prescribing the behavior of the female sex."[62] Their very existence is problematic, for, as Sheriff explains, "aspiring to her position implies collusion with the general subjugation of women. Separation from other women is the price a woman pays for her exceptionalness, and she pays it doubly, since the

[61] Adrienne Rich, *Of Woman Born: Motherhood as Experience and Institution*, 2nd edition (New York: W.W. Norton, 1986), 70–1.

[62] Mary Sheriff, *The Exceptional Woman* (Chicago: University of Chicago Press, 1996), 2.

exceptional woman was easily construed as the unnatural or unruleable (unruly) woman by men and women alike."[63] The exceptional woman trope also illustrates a common problem with neomedieval fantasy settings; fantasy heroines may speak out against the patriarchal social structures of their world, but they are often alone when doing it. As Jane Tolmie explains, "The emphasis remains on the individual woman rising above a system that keeps her down – triumphing over it, reversing expectations – rather than in cultural revolution or innovation, and oppressive structures continue to provide the basis for representation."[64]

Frequently, the fantasy heroine's quest is to overcome patriarchal structures: those structures, which are designed to oppress and limit her, are the "dragon" she must slay in order to be successful. But defeating this dragon often does not benefit anyone around her; the other women in the story – if indeed there are any – are just as trapped in the patriarchal structure as they were before the heroine embarked on her journey. Yuval-Davis argues that such women are not meant to redeem or free all women:

> Mythical or historical figures of women who led the men to battle, like Boadicea or Jeanne d'Arc, have existed for many centuries in the western collective imagination. However, like the Amazons, their main function has usually been not to point out that women are capable of warfare heroism like men, but rather to construct them as unnatural if romantic women.[65]

A few women – literary or historical – are allowed to take on masculine roles to serve as cathartic exceptions, but not as role models or examples to other women. In *A Song of Ice and Fire*, this trope appears in the characterization of Brienne of Tarth, Arya Stark, and Ygritte, though Arya and Ygritte complicate it more than Brienne.

Brienne's role as an exceptional woman places her outside traditional gender roles but does not extend to anyone around her. Brienne

[63] Ibid., 2.

[64] Jane Tolmie, "Medievalism and the Fantasy Heroine," *Journal of Gender Studies* 15.2 (2006), 147.

[65] Yuval-Davis, 95.

rejects womanly pastimes because she believes her physical appearance makes her unsuited to such activities, and other women's scorn of her due to her looks is hurtful.[66] When men came to seek an alliance with her father through marriage and courted her, Tarth's septa told her not to listen to them, warning her against listening to their flattery rather than relying on her own reflection.[67] Catelyn Stark provides the most thorough description of Brienne:

> Beauty, they called her … mocking. The hair beneath the visor was a squirrel's nest of dirty straw, and her face … Brienne's eyes were large and very blue, a young girl's eyes, trusting and guileless, but the rest … her features were broad and coarse, her teeth prominent and crooked, her mouth too wide, her lips so plump they seemed swollen. A thousand freckles sprinkled her cheeks and brow, and her nose had been broken more than once.[68]

Thus, Martin places Brienne outside the company of women, whom he portrays as elitist and superficial, with a tendency to judge other women by their looks alone; Brienne has no worth as a woman because she is not beautiful, and therefore neither decorative nor a sexual object. Other than passing encounters, Catelyn is the only woman with whom the reader sees Brienne interact in any meaningful way, and Catelyn pities Brienne for her looks. Brienne meets the criteria for the exceptional woman by having no community with other women, but Martin rarely creates communities of women at all. Nearly all of his women, especially his POV women, are profoundly isolated from others, Brienne especially due to her violation of feminine gender roles.

Brienne is also never fully accepted into the ranks of the male soldiers or knights, who either mock her or chastise her for not knowing her place. When Brienne joins Renly's camp, most of the men mock her, but a few begin courting her; Brienne is left "confused and vulnerable" by the attention, until Lord Randyll Tarly informs her that the men have a wager on which of them will claim her virginity,

66 Martin, *A Feast for Crows*, 286.
67 Ibid., 403.
68 Martin, *A Clash of Kings*, 344.

as discussed above.[69] Although Brienne acts outside of the traditional medievalist gender roles prescribed by the patriarchal, feudal society Martin has created, she is allowed to do so partly because she can defend herself and partly because, since the country is in the midst of a civil war, no one with the inclination to stop her has the time or manpower to follow through. Thus, she also meets the criteria for an exceptional woman in that she is exempt, however grudgingly, from the rules surrounding other women of her rank and position in Westeros. However, Martin indicates that her status as an exceptional woman makes her more vulnerable than other noblewomen to sexual assault and rape; while many of his common women are subjected to sexual assault, few of the noblewomen face more than the threat of violence. Brienne's choice to take on masculine power and act as a knight exposes her to physical violence, but unlike the men, Brienne is also subject to the threat of sexual violence because she is a woman acting outside of her gender role. Although none of the men who so threaten her are meant to be admirable or even likeable, the frequency with which she is faced with this threat implies that such treatment should be expected by a woman who fails to be "feminine."

Arya appears, early on, to be on her way to becoming another exceptional woman, but her storyline complicates the trope somewhat, partly because she leaves the patriarchal structure of Westeros entirely. She begins as a tomboy who is excused from her socialization as a noblewoman to study fencing instead; Ned provides her with a "dancing master" when he discovers her with Needle, her "bravo's blade."[70] Yet he still has some expectation that she will eventually settle down, marry, and have children.[71] Arya, like Brienne, has little to no interaction with communities of women, partly because she does not have the sort of interests that allow her to fit in with their society and partly because she spends most of the books alone or with groups of men like Yoren's recruits and the Brotherhood without Banners. When she does come in contact with another woman, a minor noble who gives Arya a dress and expects her to act like a lady, Arya is

69 Martin, *A Feast for Crows*, 299–300.
70 Martin, *A Game of Thrones*, 220.
71 Ibid., 256.

deeply uncomfortable both with the dress and with the now-visible class distinctions between her and Gendry.[72] Unlike Brienne, who takes on a different role within the patriarchal society of Westeros, Arya removes herself from it entirely, entering the much more egalitarian world of the Faceless Men in Braavos, across the Narrow Sea. While this removes her from Westeros' patriarchal society that would attempt to restrict her behavior and render her actions "exceptional," she does nothing to assist other women in escaping the strict gender roles of the patriarchy or to overturn the patriarchy itself. She is still an "individual woman rising above a system that keeps her down."

Ygritte also carries several signifiers of the exceptional woman despite being part of a society that expects and embraces "spearwives." Ygritte is one of the few named spearwives who appear, and the only one with whom the reader spends any significant time. The reader is told that Mance Rayder's army has many women among its ranks, but they remain an abstract concept, not made concrete with names and actions. Like Brienne and Arya, Ygritte has no visible community of women, spending her time with Jon and her raiding party. Several spearwives travel south with Mance to attempt to rescue Jeyne-as-Arya, but in order to do so, they must conform to Westerosi ideas of women's behavior – posing as camp followers and fighting only when they attempt to leave Winterfell. Ygritte is also different from Arya and Brienne because the reader only sees her through Jon's point of view, never from inside her own head. Thus, Jon's prejudices, fears, and expectations for women are projected onto Ygritte, and she falls into Salmonson's stereotype of "the spunky 'girl' who guards her man's back by day and warms his bed at night."[73]

Despite occasionally falling into these tropes and stereotypes, the evidence of Martin's own words and storytelling indicate that he actively tries to avoid the usual clichés of fantasy, especially the ways in which women are usually portrayed. However, the structures he builds with regards to society, both the larger Westerosi society and the smaller groups with which various characters interact and to which they belong, inevitably lead to women becoming "exceptional."

[72] Martin, *A Storm of Swords*, 304–10.

[73] Salmonson, 14.

As mentioned above, communities of women rarely exist in the narrative, with only passing mention made of the noblewomen at the court of King's Landing or the spearwives of Mance's army. Most large groups in *A Song of Ice and Fire* are primarily or entirely male – the Brotherhood without Banners, the Night's Watch, the maesters of the Citadel, the Kingsguard, etc. When Brienne and Arya come into contact with other women, they are deeply uncomfortable and disengage as soon as they can. Cersei avoids the company of other women because she believes women are silly and useless, owing to her internalized misogyny. Sansa has the most interaction with other women but is still outside the community because of her status as a "traitor's daughter" and later because of her marriage to Tyrion. None of the women who defy or break out of the patriarchal order of Westeros do so for the purpose or with the intent of helping other women to do the same. Whether any of them will attempt to do so in the last two books remains to be seen, but a full-scale overthrow of the patriarchal structures of Westeros would be an incredibly interesting and genre-defying coup for *A Song of Ice and Fire.*

Besides the exceptional woman, Martin's portrayal of women has other troubling aspects. Not least among these is the "monstrous woman" trope. While it can be argued that all of Martin's characters are monstrous in some way, and that his main characters are all "cripples, bastards, and broken things," the monstrosity of his women falls into very specific, recognizable patterns.[74] These patterns are those discussed in detail by Barbara Creed in her book *The Monstrous-Feminine*, which explores the ways in which women are portrayed in film and television as monsters rather than victims. The archetypes Creed describes that appear in *A Song of Ice and Fire* are the monstrous womb, the *femme castratrice*, and the witch. What all of these – indeed, all of the monstrous-feminine archetypes – have in common is depicting woman as abject, focusing on her sexuality and her reproductive abilities.[75] Rich has noticed this tendency, as well, commenting:

[74] Martin, *A Game of Thrones*, 244.

[75] Barbara Creed, *The Monstrous-Feminine: Film, Television, Psychoanalysis* (New York: Routledge, 1993), 3. Creed's theory of the abject draws on the work of Julia Kristeva, defining the abject as those things that break borders between "the symbolic order and that which threatens its stability"; Creed claims that

> Throughout patriarchal mythology, dream-symbolism, theology, language, two ideas flow side-by-side: one, that the female body is impure, corrupt, the site of discharges, bleedings, dangerous to masculinity, a source of moral and physical contamination, 'the devil's gateway.' On the other hand, as mother the woman is beneficent, sacred, pure, asexual, nourishing; and the physical potential for motherhood – that same body with its bleedings and mysteries – is her single destiny and justification in life.[76]

Jane Ussher further claims that women who do not perform femininity correctly according to their stage of life are "positioned as mad or bad, and subjected to discipline or punishment, which masquerades as treatment or rehabilitation to disguise its regulatory intent."[77] Martin's women primarily become monstrous when they refuse or fail to conform to society's expectations for their gender, even as Martin attempts to position these women as strong individuals battling the patriarchy. While the monstrosity of the men in *A Song of Ice and Fire* may manifest as a physical disability (Tyrion Lannister, Bran Stark, Varys), a tendency toward extreme violence (Joffrey Baratheon, Ramsay Bolton, Gregor Clegane), or underhanded manipulation (Petyr Baelish, Hizdahr zo Loraq), the monstrosity of the women is nearly exclusively based on sex and reproduction.

Perhaps the clearest example of the monstrous mother in *A Song of Ice and Fire* is Cersei Lannister, who fulfills the "monstrous womb" aspect of the monstrous feminine. Creed's discussion of the "monstrous womb" describes a woman or creature whose children are entirely her own creation – they are born from her body without the aid of a man and are often deformed or in other ways monstrous. All three of Cersei's children were fathered by her twin brother, Jaime, whom Cersei considers to be a part of her rather than a separate person, as mentioned above. Thus, while Cersei's monstrosity does

---

"Abject things are those that highlight the 'fragility of the law' and that exist on the other side of the border which separates out the living subject from that which threatens its extinction" (10–11).

[76] Rich, 34.

[77] Jane M. Ussher, *Managing the Monstrous Feminine: Regulating the Reproductive Body* (New York: Routledge, 2006), 4.

not extend to literal parthenogenesis, her view of Jaime as *her* rather than *other* indicates that, metaphorically, her children have no father. In a sense, they emotionally have no father, as Robert shows very little interest in them and Jaime cannot claim them. Throughout the series, insanity that manifests as cruelty is shown explicitly as an incest-caused birth defect – madness runs in the Targaryen family due to their generations-long habit of inbreeding, and Joffrey shows clear parallels to Aerys the Mad King. In this way, Joffrey's cruelty – even evil – is positioned as the fault of his mother for conceiving him in an incestuous relationship, as is typical for the offspring of the monstrous womb. As Rich mentions, defects or moral failings of a child (or even a grown man) are frequently seen as the fault of the mother in raising that child.[78]

Cersei's incest with Jaime also places her firmly in the realm of the abject, as she breaks the boundaries between "natural" and "unnatural," upsetting the socially established order of marriage and reproduction. Not only does she bear her brother's children, but she also actively refuses to bear her husband's, admitting to Ned Stark that she aborted the one pregnancy caused by Robert.[79] Further, when Robert does insist on sharing her bed, she makes sure his ejaculation occurs on the bed or her hands, then licks the semen off of her face and hands: "*You claimed your rights, my lord, but in the darkness I would eat your heirs.*"[80] Beyond refusing Robert the privilege of siring children on her, Cersei consumes his semen, which she thinks of as his "little princes," which not only (again) aligns her with the abject (as bodily fluids are symbols of the abject), but also with the *femme castratrice*, the castrating woman. By devouring the semen – inserting it into her mouth – rather than allowing it to be ejaculated into her vagina, Cersei invokes the *vagina dentata*, "a black hole which threatens to swallow [men] up and cut them into pieces."[81] Along with her use of sex as a weapon and a bribe and her sexual encounter with Lady

[78] Rich, 46.
[79] Martin, *A Game of Thrones*, 486.
[80] Martin, *A Feast for Crows*, 693.
[81] Creed, 106.

Taena (which will be discussed in the next chapter), many of Cersei's character flaws are based on her sexuality.

Daenerys, likewise, has much in common with the monstrous womb but is depicted with far less abject imagery and more sympathy. She is frequently associated with animals – her husband Drogo's wedding gift to her is a silver mare; her first child is referred to as "the Stallion who Mounts the World"; and after her dragons are born, she is called "the Mother of Dragons."[82] The child conceived with Drogo is born dead, and the woman who delivers him tells Daenerys that he was "monstrous […] Twisted. […] [S]caled like a lizard, blind, with the stub of a tail and small leather wings like the wings of a bat."[83] After this, Daenerys is barren, but though she is no longer able to have children of her own body, she refers to her dragons and the slaves she frees as her children. Daenerys hatches the dragons from fossilized eggs, placing them on Drogo's funeral pyre, to which she has also tied Mirri Maaz Duur, the witch-woman who failed to save Drogo's life. Daenerys herself also walks into the fire as the eggs begin to hatch, lactating in "streams"; when the fire dies, she is unharmed, and two of the dragons are nursing at her breasts.[84] After Daenerys has liberated Astapor, the slaves call her "*mhysa*," or "mother," and Daenerys begins referring to them as her children.[85] While Daenerys' insistence on referring to fully grown adults as children, and their insistence on referring to her as "mother," is troubling (and will be discussed further in Chapter 4), and while she shares characteristics with Cersei in having "unnatural" children in "unnatural" ways, the reader is encouraged to sympathize far more with Daenerys than Cersei.

Martin uses several narratological methods to achieve this sympathy; for example, Daenerys is a POV character from the beginning of the series, and all of her decisions are related through her own thoughts and motivations. The reader does not see Daenerys from an external POV until *A Dance with Dragons*, when Tyrion encounters

[82] Martin, *A Game of Thrones*, 105, 491; *A Clash of Kings*, 189.
[83] Martin, *A Game of Thrones*, 756.
[84] Ibid., 803–6.
[85] Martin, *A Clash of Kings*, 588; *A Storm of Swords*, 783.

her, and later in the same book, Ser Barristan becomes a POV character. Cersei, on the other hand, is portrayed entirely externally until *A Feast for Crows*, and by this time, she has been firmly established as a villain and monstrous feminine. Unlike Jaime, whose internal voice allows the reader to understand his motivations and come to sympathize with him, Cersei becomes more monstrous and more abject once the reader enters her point of view and is privy to her memories of having sex with Jaime and consuming Robert's semen.

Melisandre, also known as the Red Woman, is another example of the monstrous feminine; she represents the witch archetype. According to Creed, the witch "is defined as an abject figure in that she is represented within patriarchal discourses as an implacable enemy of the symbolic order."[86] Melisandre definitely threatens the symbolic order of Westeros; she is a priestess of R'hllor, a god new to Westeros, and actively works against the Seven and the Old Gods, burning their statues, trees, and relics and condemning their worship. She is clearly the power behind Stannis' bid for the Iron Throne – Jon notes that "every man there knew she was Stannis Baratheon's real queen, not the homely woman he had left to shiver at Eastwatch-by-the-Sea"[87] – and uses blood- and fire-magic to advance his cause. She frequently burns people alive to fuel her magic, and prefers royal blood when she can get it; for example, she keeps one of Robert Baratheon's bastards, Edric Storm, and leeches him, then burns the leeches to cause the deaths of some of Stannis' enemies – Joffrey Baratheon, Balon Greyjoy, and Robb Stark. All three of them die, though whether Melisandre's spell had anything to do with it is left to interpretation; Melisandre claims that "R'hllor chooses such instruments as he requires."[88] She has some limited powers of prophecy when she seeks visions in the fire, though her ability to interpret these visions is not always reliable.

Her most feminine monstrosity is shown when Stannis needs well-guarded targets assassinated; Melisandre is able to conceive and birth shadow monsters to send into keeps or guarded camps, and she arranges for the deaths of Renly Baratheon and Cortnay Penrose

[86] Creed, 76.

[87] Martin, *A Dance with Dragons*, 148.

[88] Martin, *A Storm of Swords*, 723.

using these shadow monsters. Davos witnesses the birth of the one that kills Penrose, and it pushes its way out of Melisandre's womb of its own volition, emerging as an enormous shadow that immediately dashes off to fulfill its purpose.[89] Thus, Melisandre represents both the witch and the monstrous womb, though she cannot conceive her shadow children without sexual intercourse with a man; she tries to seduce Davos so she can create another shadow-child, claiming that their creation requires the fires of life, and that she has drawn too often on Stannis.[90] Once again, Martin creates horror from childbirth, describing the process with words that invoke disgust and fear, both in the reader and in Davos:

> Swollen breasts hung heavy against her chest, and her belly bulged as if near to bursting. [...] Panting, she squatted and spread her legs. Blood ran down her thighs, black as ink. [...] And Davos saw the crown of the child's head push its way out of her. Two arms wriggled free, grasping, black fingers coiling around Melisandre's straining thighs, pushing, until the whole of the shadow slid out into the world [...][91]

Like Cersei, Melisandre is not given her own POV chapters until late in the books; only in *A Dance with Dragons* does the reader get inside her head. Before this, all observations of Melisandre are filtered through two men: Davos and Jon Snow. Davos sees Melisandre as a threat to Stannis and the social order, believing that Stannis relies too heavily on her and fearing her insistence on overturning worship of the Seven. All of his thoughts about and reactions to her are colored by his fear of the sort of change she represents, and while Davos wants Stannis to be king, he wants him to be a traditional Westerosi king, one who worships the Seven. Jon finds her beautiful but unsettling, and he does not trust her visions or her motivations for helping him. However, he does begin to internalize her warnings – perhaps too late, given his situation at the end of *A Dance with Dragons*. Thus, the reader is encouraged to find Melisandre frightening and horrifying, and even in her one POV chapter midway through *A Dance with*

[89] Martin, *A Clash of Kings*, 623.
[90] Martin, *A Storm of Swords*, 347.
[91] Martin, *A Clash of Kings*, 623.

Dragons, she continues to be linked to the abject: seeking visions in the fire causes vaginal bleeding, an abnormally high body temperature, and tears.[92] Neither does being in Melisandre's thoughts help the reader trust in her abilities, as she seems to miss or dismiss certain obvious interpretations of her visions.

Several other witches appear in *A Song of Ice and Fire*, frequently referred to as "*maegi*" and feared and distrusted. When characters do listen to them, misfortune follows: Daenerys trusts Mirri Maz Duur to save Drogo, but instead Drogo is reduced to a vegetative state and Daenerys loses her baby. Cersei listens to an old woman called "Maggy the Frog," who tells her fortune and warns her that she will rise to power but lose it to "another, younger and more beautiful."[93] Assuming that Maggy meant Margaery Tyrell, Cersei embarks on a crusade to discredit and destroy Margaery, only to discredit and destroy herself. The crones of Vaes Dothrak, whom Daenerys describes as "terrible old women," prophesy that her child will be "the Stallion who Mounts the World," leading Mirri Maz Duur to ensure the death of both Drogo and the child, so that the prophecy will never come true.[94]

The one literal female monster who appears in *A Song of Ice and Fire* is Lady Stoneheart, the resurrected Catelyn Stark. In death, she has become vengeance incarnate, murdering anyone associated with the Freys, Boltons, or Lannisters, even children and those who demonstrably had nothing to do with the Red Wedding. Her desire for vengeance recognizes no friend; she even attempts to have Brienne hanged, believing her to be allied with the Lannisters. Only an as-yet-unrevealed word saves Brienne's life.[95] Under her leadership, the Brotherhood without Banners, previously a ragtag guerilla band working to undermine Lannister rule in the Riverlands, becomes little more than a gang of outlaws. Even her appearance is monstrous; the resurrection spell does not mend the scratches on her face, the slice

92 Martin, *A Dance with Dragons*, 448.

93 Martin, *A Feast for Crows*, 254.

94 Martin, *A Game of Thrones*, 708, 491.

95 At Miscon in 2012, Martin revealed that the word was "sword," but that has not yet appeared in the books ("Miscon Report," *The Citadel: So Spake Martin*, June 3, 2012, http://www.westeros.org/Citadel/SSM/Month/2012/06).

across her throat that killed her, or the results of three days floating dead in a river:

> Her hair was dry and brittle, white as bone. Her brow was mottled green and grey, spotted with the brown blooms of decay. The flesh of her face hung in ragged strips from her eyes down to her jaw. Some of the rips were crusted with dried blood, but others gaped open to reveal the skull beneath.[96]

She wears grey, which Brienne notes is the color of the Silent Sisters, the Sept's handmaidens of death, and her eyes glow red, possibly a side-effect of the Red Priest's resurrection spell.

Lady Stoneheart is the ultimate failed mother – she died believing her sons all slain, her daughters missing or in enemy hands, and in undeath, attempts to avenge Robb by killing anyone remotely connected to the Houses involved in the Red Wedding. She is also a failed lady; she failed to keep the peace between the Freys and the Starks, all of her diplomatic abilities useless before the wrath and greed of the scorned Walder Frey. As Valerie Frankel puts it, she has "become her own shadow, a monster that lurks in the wild and subverts the patriarchy as a fearsome outlaw."[97] In life, her sole focus was her family, especially her children, and in death, that focus has been twisted and corrupted, making her a monster in spirit as well as body. Like Cersei, Lady Stoneheart represents the abject, breaking the boundary between life and death, and her physical presence as a reanimated corpse leaves the reader and characters no choice but to recognize and remember that she is dead and that her "life" is unnatural.

Although Martin can – and should – be commended for his commitment to writing his women as rounded people and including so many forceful personalities in his novels, some issues with his portrayal and characterization of women are still readily apparent. While nothing is particularly "wrong" or "problematic" about having monstrous or exceptional women in fiction, the issue arises when nearly all of the

[96] Martin, *A Feast for Crows*, 913–14.

[97] Valerie Estelle Frankel, *Women in "Game of Thrones": Power, Conformity, and Resistance* (Jefferson, NC: McFarland, 2014), 145.

major female characters can be read as falling into one or other of those categories. Likewise, the ways in which this monstrosity manifests are stereotypical rather than imaginative and fresh. These issues cannot be dismissed as "authenticity" in Martin's portrayal of the Middle Ages, as the primary problems do not come from the society Martin has built, the gender expectations that accompany that society, or even the ways in which the women rebel against said society and expectations; rather they lie in the women's personalities and characterizations themselves. Even if one were relieve Martin himself of responsibility for the feudal, patriarchal bent of Westeros, accounting for it entirely in the name of historical accuracy and authenticity, the problems with exceptional women and the monstrous feminine remain. These are not issues of setting and history, but of society's attitudes towards women (especially those who do not conform to traditional gender roles), and touch on masculine fear of, or disgust for, the female body and its reproductive function. That these issues probably entered the novels subconsciously as Martin was writing shows how deeply entrenched such tropes and tendencies are in the popular imagination.

Although medieval history and literature contain their fair share of warrior women, such as Joan of Arc or Boudicca; of cross-dressers of various genders, who cross-dress for various reasons, often in saints' lives and miracle tales; and people and characters of differing sexualities, as documented in Duberman, Vicinus, and Chauncey's *Hidden from History* (1990), popular understanding of the Middle Ages is of a homogeneous culture with religiously dictated gender roles.[98] In some ways, this view serves several cultural needs; for those who view non-normative gender roles as a threat to the cultural order, a past in which these did not exist proves that such things are new and thus unnatural, allowing them to yearn nostalgically for a time, however imaginary, when social roles were simpler. For fantasy writers, this perception of the Middle Ages provides the rigid society against which characters like Brienne can rebel, a society which young-adult fantasy

[98] Martin Duberman, Martha Vicinus, and George Chauncey, Jr., editors. *Hidden From History: Reclaiming the Gay and Lesbian Past* (New York: Penguin, 1990).

author Tamora Pierce refers to as "the default setting."[99] Rather than a time in which people "naturally" fell into gender and sexual binaries, these texts cast the Middle Ages as a time of repression, contrasting contemporary society with the Middle Ages in a call to move forward, away from a societal structure in which people are not free to express themselves or choose their own paths in life.

Yet the use of the medieval as an anti-feminist backdrop can result in the treatment of non-normative women becoming stagnant; as the culture in which fantasy writers place their rebellious characters does not change or move forward, neither can the characters themselves. They will always be fighting the same norms, the same expectations, and the same persecutions. Hence, the portrayals of, for example, Pierce's Alanna of Trebond (*The Song of the Lioness Quartet*, 1983–8)[100] and Brienne are not greatly different; despite the progress in contemporary society in its attitudes toward women and sexuality, the neomedieval societies of fantasy do not make the same progress. The powerful, influential women of the Middle Ages, of whom there are many, tend to be invisible to contemporary popular culture; only Joan of Arc, who fits the female warrior archetype, receives extensive attention in the media. Thus, the tropes of medievalist feminism or queerness will always decree that "strength" derives from masculinity; even when characters defy society's gender norms and disrupt stereotypes, they still must conform to masculine gender roles in order to be considered "strong." The mostly unspoken prejudice against the feminine continues to be perpetrated, and, regardless of the identity of the sword-bearer, the ubiquity of the sword remains.

[99] Tamora Pierce, "Girls Who Kick Butt," *Locus* 48, no. 5 (2002), 76.

[100] Tamora Pierce, *Alanna: The First Adventure* (New York: Atheneum, 1983); *In the Hand of the Goddess* (New York: Atheneum, 1984); *The Woman Who Rides Like a Man* (New York: Atheneum, 1986); *Lioness Rampant* (New York: Atheneum, 1988).

3

Sex and Sexuality

One of the reasons *A Song of Ice and Fire* gets so much attention, and draws so much criticism, is its portrayal of sex. Media critics have taken exception to the explicit and numerous descriptions of consensual and non-consensual sex, especially to how those descriptions frequently victimize women.[1] Martin has responded to these critics by pointing out that, for the most part, the violence in the books receives much less comment: "I can describe in exquisite detail an axe entering a man's skull, and splattering blood and brains – not a peep. I describe a penis entering a vagina in equivalent detail – the world is ending."[2] What these critics may miss is that, while at times Martin's approach to sex and sexuality can be unsettling, ultimately the texts make a point about sexuality, gender roles, societal expectations, and his belief that the people of the Middle Ages were not significantly different from people today. A side effect of amplifying the toxic masculinity and oppression of women, as discussed in the last chapter, along with Martin's "Barbaric Age" view of the Middle Ages, as discussed in the introduction, is the prevalence of rape. At the same time, Martin steps slightly outside the usual view of the Middle Ages by including portrayals of homosexuality in *A Song of Ice and Fire*, though these portrayals are often problematic in their own right. While his approach to rape and sexual violence has

[1] See, for example, Sady Doyle's piece "Enter Ye Myne Mystic World of Gayng-Raype: What the 'R' Stands for in George R.R. Martin," *Tiger Beatdown*, August 26, 2011, http://tigerbeatdown.com/2011/08/26/enter-ye-myne-mystic-world-of-gayng-raype-what-the-r-stands-for-in-george-r-r-martin/.

[2] Grace Dent, "George R.R. Martin Meets Grace Dent," *YouTube*, 21:11, posted by "Keet Bob," June 12, 2012, https://www.youtube.com/watch?v=MdSPFJcxCNM.

an anchor in chivalric romance, as so much of *A Song of Ice and Fire* does, his depictions of queer sexualities are entirely modern. Sex is a major part of *A Song of Ice and Fire*, both in politics and interpersonal relationships, and deserves to be examined closely and thoroughly.

"I had her before, a hunnerd times": Male Sexuality and Rape

In chivalric romance, male sexuality is generally portrayed as disruptive, if not explicitly violent. Several times, Martin has characters express sentiments that indicate a similar outlook: for example, Varys asks Tyrion whether a man has a choice between wit and a penis, and Cersei claims that Varys is dangerous because he is a eunuch and therefore does not have his thinking clouded by testosterone.[3] Tyrion's relationship with Shae is a major factor in his downfall in *A Storm of Swords*, and Jaime's relationship with Cersei is a major contributor to the fall of the kingdom. While female sexuality, whether transgressive or not, breaks relationships between men in chivalric romance, transgressive male sexuality has a far more destructive power.

Kristina Hildebrand claims in that the Arthurian romances, and Malory especially, male sexuality has a tendency to break relationships and even nations. She argues that chivalry in general and the Pentecost Oath in particular were meant to place restrictions and "controlling measures" on male sexuality so as to check its "potentially violent and disruptive" power.[4] The Pentecost Oath binds Arthur's knights to certain behavioral expectations, and while most of these upheld are on pain of exile, good treatment of women is enforceable on pain of death. Hildebrand speculates that Malory has nothing against love, but is concerned about the destructive possibilities of uncontrolled sexual desire.[5] Similarly, Martin uses transgressive sexuality – both male and female – to illustrate the problems in Westeros. In *A Clash of Kings*, he represents Westeros as a woman being savaged

[3] Martin, *A Storm of Swords*, 797; *A Clash of Kings*, 776.

[4] Kristen Hildebrand, "'Open Manslaugher and Bold Bawdry': Male Sexuality as a Cause of Disruption in Malory's *Morte Darthur*," in *Sexual Culture in the Literature of Medieval Britain*, edited by Amanda Hopkins, Robert Allen Rouse, and Cory James Rushton (Cambridge: D.S. Brewer, 2014), 13.

[5] Ibid., 14.

and raped by four rat-like men, representative of the four men who have declared themselves king – Joffrey, Stannis, Robb, and Balon. (By this point, Renly, one of the "five kings" in the "War of the Five Kings," is dead and thus is not represented.)[6] By projecting the land of Westeros onto a female body and showing the clash of kings not as the kings fighting each other but as men individually and collectively destroying the land, Martin makes a point about the nature of war as well as male sexuality.

As Martin frequently points out in interviews, sex is part of the human experience, and complications frequently arise from sexual relationships. When those who lead the nation are involved in transgressive sexual relationships, the effects are felt throughout the kingdoms. Love or desire that is not controlled by the tenets of so-called "courtly love," which helps to control a man's potentially dangerous sexuality by putting a woman in charge of it, is disruptive to the social order.[7] Just as Arthur's relationship with Morgawse and Lancelot's relationship with Guinevere lead to the downfall of Camelot, so Tyrion's relationship with Shae, Jaime's relationship with Cersei, and Robert's relationships with the many women who bore his bastards lead to the downfall of Robert's reign and the chaos of the War of the Five Kings. The chaos leads to unrestrained male aggression, as the lack of universally recognized central authority creates an unstable social order and the rules governing knightly behavior go unenforced.

One of the clearest ways that this social instability manifests in the novels is through rape. Sexual violence and the threat of sexual violence are rampant in Westeros. Martin has defended its inclusion in the novels by arguing for realism:

> I'm writing about war, which what [*sic*] almost all epic fantasy is about. But if you're going to write about war, and you just want to include all the cool battles and heroes killing a lot of orcs and things like that and you *don't* portray [sexual violence], then there's something fundamentally dishonest about that. Rape, unfortunately, is still a part of war

[6] Martin, *A Clash of Kings*, 700.
[7] Hildebrand, 18–19.

> today. It's not a strong testament to the human race, but I don't think we should pretend it doesn't exist.[8]

Martin's portrayal of rape also remains in line with the parallels between medieval chivalric romance and *A Song of Ice and Fire*; the women of most romances are systematically disenfranchised by the social construction of the story, and rape is far from unheard-of. Amy Vines argues that rape in chivalric romance is actually necessary to the plot, that the hero must engage in rape in order to be set on a redemptive quest, and that "a fundamental aspect of establishing chivalric identity is male sexual aggression against women."[9] In Chrétien, as well, rape is an archetypal story beat used to characterize men. Katheryn Gravdal points out that Chrétien's romances may "teach that rape is wrong," but they also "aestheticize rape as a formulaic challenge."[10] To Martin's credit, he does not portray rape as a necessary part of masculine identity formation, but as a way for men to assert their physical dominance over women. In only one case is a rapist in any way sympathetic, and his choice to rape is not condoned but used to show how far he has fallen (see further below).

The chivalric ideal, while appearing to provide protection to women, frequently does the opposite. In Chrétien's *Le Chevalier de la Charrette*, a social construction is set up in which a good knight will not harass a woman alone, but he is allowed to steal her from another knight, at which point he is within his rights to claim her sexually. This is yet another way that medieval romance portrays women as objects of exchange between men; Roberta Kreuger says:

> [T]he law inscribes a vicious circle that makes women dependent upon, and victims of, the chivalric system: the threat of rape, or more generally of male violence against women, makes women need the

[8] Hibberd, "George R.R. Martin Explains," n.p.

[9] Amy N. Vines, "Invisible Woman: Rape as a Chivalric Necessity in Medieval Romance," in *Sexual Culture in the Literature of Medieval Britain*, edited by Amanda Hopkins, Robert Allen Rouse, and Cory James Rushton (Cambridge: D.S. Brewer, 2014), 174.

[10] Katheryn Gravdal, *Ravishing Maidens: Writing Rape in Medieval French Literature and Law* (Philadelphia: University of Philadelphia Press, 1991), 50.

> protection of knights, and that protection makes them vulnerable to male aggression.[11]

This is one reason that Brienne is constantly threatened with rape while in the custody of the Bloody Mummers; by this reasoning, she "belonged" to Jaime, but Jaime has been defeated, and Brienne now "belongs" to them. Only Jaime's insistence that she is worth her weight in sapphires as a ransom, but only if she is still a virgin, keeps the threats from becoming reality.[12] Similarly, Cersei anticipates "a bit of rape" for her guests if Stannis takes King's Landing and is not the first man into Maegor's Holdfast, where the women are hiding;[13] rape in this case is another way for the men to secure their victory and express their masculinity, which, as discussed in Chapter 2, requires acts of violence.

While the noble women of Westeros have a layer of protection from sexual assault on account of their status and relationship to men who can protect them, the common folk have no such security. Martin reflects and subverts not only the tropes of chivalric romance in his portrayal of rape but also those of a medieval genre known as the *pastourelle*. The *pastourelle* involves a sexual encounter between a knight and a peasant woman, usually a shepherdess; frequently, this sexual encounter is rape. The songs, and modern analyses of them, tend to occlude the fact of the rape by writing it (or reading it) as slapstick humor. As Katherine Gravdal puts it, the songs "present rape as the inevitable encounter between the representatives of two different social classes."[14] One particular incident in *A Clash of Kings* takes this theme and shows it for the horror it actually is. Arya overhears Chiswyk telling a story about Gregor Clegane and his men molesting an innkeeper's daughter, whose age is put at either eighteen or thirteen. When the innkeeper requests that the men stop touching his daughter, declaring that she's not a whore, Gregor declares that she is, gives the innkeeper a silver piece, and rapes the girl on the table

[11] Krueger, *Women Readers*, 40.

[12] Martin, *A Storm of Swords*, 292, 417.

[13] Martin, *A Clash of Kings*, 846.

[14] Katherine Gravdal, "Camouflaging Rape: The Rhetoric of Sexual Violence in the Medieval *Pastourelle*," *Romanic Review* 76, no. 4 (1985), 365.

in front of her father. Gregor's men proceed to gang-rape her, and Chiswyk mentions that by the time he gets to her, "the girl was done fighting [...] maybe she'd decided she liked it after all."[15] Afterward, Gregor demands his "change," claiming that she "wasn't worth" the silver Gregor had given the innkeeper; the innkeeper proceeds to "fetch a fistful of coppers, beg m'lord's pardon, and *thank him for his custom!*"[16] Gravdal points out that in many of the *pastourelles*, the shepherdess fights initially, but then thanks the knight after the rape, or is shown to "have it coming" in some way due to a character flaw.[17] Both of these tropes are evident in the story, though here it is the father who thanks the knight rather than the girl. Martin undercuts these tropes, however, by making it absolutely clear that the girl is innocent, that the interaction is unequivocally rape, and that it happens because the knights are stronger than the innkeeper and his daughter, who are unable to defend themselves.

Class and sexual issues also intersect in matters of prostitution, sexual slavery, and the spoils of war. Women (and sometimes boys) in these positions are routinely raped and considered less than human. Lower-class women in Westeros who are caught in the upheaval in the Riverlands are also subject to this sort of treatment. When Arya is captured by Gregor Clegane's forces and marched to Harrenhal, she witnesses several women taken into the bushes and raped by the guards; when one finally fights back, Gregor beheads her.[18] When Roose Bolton takes Harrenhal, he punishes the people for "aiding and abetting" the Lannisters, and these punishments include having women shaved, stripped, and put in the stocks for the pleasure of his men.[19] When Jaime liberates Harrenhal, he beheads a man who attempts to rape one of those women, and the man is confused by the verdict: "I had her before, a hunnerd times [...] A hunnerd times, m'lord. We all had her."[20] The rape culture of Westeros has not

[15] Martin, *A Clash of Kings*, 467–8.
[16] Ibid., 468.
[17] Gravdal, "Camouflaging Rape," 364, 369.
[18] Martin, *A Clash of Kings*, 417.
[19] Ibid., 886.
[20] Martin, *A Feast for Crows*, 636.

prepared this man to be punished for rape, but to expect that it is not only allowed, but encouraged.[21]

Likewise, in the slavery culture of Essos, rape is prevalent both in outright violence and because most of the prostitutes are actually sex slaves. When Tyrion arrives in Pentos, Magister Illyrio Mopatis tells him that he can take his pick of Illyrio's servingwomen, and "none will dare refuse you." Despite the fact that slavery is technically illegal in the Free Cities, including Pentos, Illyrio indicates that his servants have no choice but to give Tyrion anything he wants, including sex. This part of Tyrion's storyline and character development show him to be in a very dark place, and part of the expression of this darkness is sexual assault. While Tyrion has been liberal with his coin when it comes to prostitutes up to this point, he has always maintained the appearance of consent, though how truly consenting a prostitute can be is another question. However, when one of the servingwomen expresses disgust at his appearance and drunkenness, he orders her to his bed, though if he follows through on his threat and clear intent to rape her, it does not happen on page and is not mentioned again.[22] Later, in Volantis, Tyrion does rape a slave and is aware that it is rape while he is doing it – "*This girl is as good as dead. I have just fucked a corpse.* Even her eyes looked dead. *She does not even have the strength to loathe me*" – which does not stop him from doing so again.[23] This is possibly one of the most disturbing instances of rape in the books, partly because it happens on-page and involves a POV character, and partly because the character involved is a fan- and author-favorite who has, up until this point, been mostly a sympathetic figure. Likewise, the incident involves the abuse of a woman to further the character development of a man. While the incident exists

[21] Emilie Buchwald, Pamela R. Fletcher, and Martha Roth define "rape culture" as "[A] complex of beliefs that encourages male sexual aggression and supports violence against women. It is a society where violence is seen as sexy and sexuality as violent. [...] A rape culture condones physical and emotional terrorism against women *as the norm.* [...] In a rape culture both men and women assume that sexual violence is a fact of life, inevitable as death or taxes" ("Preamble," *Transforming a Rape Culture* [Minneapolis: Milkweed Editions, 1993], vii).

[22] Martin, *A Dance with Dragons*, 23, 28.

[23] Ibid., 325.

to illustrate how far Tyrion has fallen into drunkenness, self-hatred, and misanthropy, and Martin has referred to Tyrion as a villain,[24] it is concerning that a character he repeatedly calls his favorite could engage in such behavior without consequence. However, it certainly further illustrates the plight of slaves in general and sex slaves in particular.

While Tyrion's perception of slavery (which will be discussed in more detail in the next chapter) is informed only by his own interaction and experience with it, Daenerys fights to free slaves. Her crusade against slavery begins with rape: she witnesses women of the Lhazareen being raped and taken into slavery so that Drogo can raise money to hire ships to conquer Westeros in her name. She orders the rape stopped, and several men, including Jorah Mormont and Drogo himself, attempt to explain that these women are now property, that they are less than human, and that they are there for the men of the *khalasar* to do with as they please.[25] All of them are confused and somewhat amused at her refusal to take that for an answer and her insistence on claiming all of the slave women for her own in order to protect them. However, at this stage, her power, like so many women's power, depends on a man – Drogo – and when Drogo is incapacitated, the men of the *khalasar* take the slave women back. One, Eroeh, is gang raped and murdered while Daenerys is recuperating from the death of her child.[26] In this instance, rape is used not only as an expression of ownership and power over a woman, but also as vengeance against Daenerys for denying the men's claim to Eroeh earlier.

The difficulty with rape in *A Song of Ice and Fire* is that commentators have trouble differentiating between authorial endorsement and portrayal. However, Martin's narrative voice, hidden as it is behind the third-person viewpoint with which he writes the series, clearly does not approve of rape or violence in general. In *A Song of Ice and Fire*, men who rape are always shown to be terrible people; even Tyrion, when he rapes the slave at a brothel, is not excused for his state of

[24] "George R.R. Martin Steers a Six-Book Cavalcade," *Cyberhaven.com*, February 10, 1999, https://web.archive.org/web/19991013131915/http://cyberhaven.com/books/sciencefiction/martin.html.

[25] Martin, *A Game of Thrones*, 667–71.

[26] Ibid., 758.

mind. Yet Martin very rarely shows rape on-page, and very few of his POV characters have been raped, which leaves the majority of the perspective on rape to the rapists. Even considering that the rapists are not sympathetic characters and the reader is clearly not supposed to like them, their viewpoint and the ways in which they justify their actions to themselves are given more attention than the reactions of the women who have suffered. This, as well, recalls Chrétien's romances, in which rape is explored exclusively from the male point of view and rarely on-page; rape is always either threatened or has already taken place.[27] Only Cersei and Daenerys provide an internal view of what rape is like for a woman, and in Cersei's case those memories fuel her assault on Taena Merryweather, while Daenerys falls in love with her attacker.[28] Other, non-POV, rape victims are either dismissed or used to further a male character's development and plot. After Lollys is raped during the riot in King's Landing, Shae is disgusted by her inability to cope with the trauma and resulting pregnancy – "All they did was *fuck* her," she complains to Tyrion.[29] Jeyne Poole's rape after her wedding to Ramsay Bolton is part of Theon Greyjoy's development as he regains his identity and becomes strong enough to defy Ramsay.[30] And Tysha's rape at the hands of Tywin's entire garrison and then Tyrion himself is a defining moment in Tyrion's development that follows him through the books and serves as motivation for many of his actions, including killing Tywin.

Examples of men who reject sexual violence are rarer in *A Song of Ice and Fire*, which further complicates the portrayal-versus-endorsement issue. Every character who considers the issue believes that every man is a latent rapist, and that the right set of circumstances will inevitably lead him to brutal acts of violence. This goes beyond Phaedra Starling's theory of "Schrödinger's Rapist," wherein a woman must consider every man she encounters a potential rapist and

[27] Gravdal, *Ravishing Maidens*, 50.

[28] While Daenerys' initial sexual encounter with Drogo is written as consensual, it is problematically so due to her age and the circumstances, and he rapes her every night on the way to Vaes Dothrak.

[29] Martin, *A Clash of Kings*, 780.

[30] Martin, *A Dance with Dragons*, 538–9.

prepare herself accordingly,[31] and into a darker philosophy in which men cannot be expected to control themselves under certain circumstances. The narrative of *A Song of Ice and Fire* does not do much to counter this philosophy, either; in very few instances does a male character put in the position to sexually assault a woman resist doing so. This, presumably, is another thread of the "Barbaric Age" medievalism Martin espouses, and another element he considers necessary to constructing a "realistic" society in Westeros. When one considers his claim to base his fictions on what he sees when he "look[s] around at the real world" and finds it "full of greys," this treatment of sex and violence is also a sad indictment of human nature, and especially of male sexuality.[32] More specifically, it also raises a question regarding nature and nurture: is this tendency toward violence, especially sexual violence, an inherent male trait or the result of socialization?

"A woman needs to be loved": Female Sexuality

Unlike chivalric romance and many contemporary fantasies, Martin avoids portraying women's sexuality as nonexistent, the property of a specific man, or inherently transgressive. Although the culture of Westeros adheres to many of the stereotypes of women's sexuality, Martin's characterization of the women of Westeros and Essos includes nearly as many approaches to sexuality as there are women. While Westerosi culture expects women's sexuality – where it is allowed at all – to be in service to men, women in the novels engage in sexual relations for love, lust, power, and control.

The first sexual encounter in the books is between Ned and Catelyn and takes only part of a sentence, more implied than seen. The results are clear, though; Catelyn muses on the "good ache" between her thighs and hopes that she might become pregnant and give Ned

[31] Phaedra Starling, "Schrödinger's Rapist: Or a Guy's Guide to Approaching Strange Women Without Being Maced," *Shapely Prose*, October 8, 2009, https://kateharding.net/2009/10/08/guest-blogger-starling-schrodinger%E2%80%99s-rapist-or-a-guy%E2%80%99s-guide-to-approaching-strange-women-without-being-maced/.

[32] "From the Book to the Screen."

one more child.[33] Although their marriage was arranged, they have grown to love each other, and their lovemaking is consensual. Yet the arranged nature of the marriage is an example of how women's bodies and sexualities are used as objects of exchange between men. Catelyn was first betrothed to Brandon Stark, Ned's older brother, and on his death, the betrothal passed to Ned. The alliance was the important part of the betrothal, not which son was involved in the bond. Many such marriages, both for alliances and for power-grabs, exist in *A Song of Ice and Fire*, and few of them are as happy as Catelyn's and Ned's. As with much in the early chapters of *A Game of Thrones*, Catelyn and Ned's relationship follows expected neomedieval fantasy tropes, setting up the reader's expectations so they can be overturned and serving as a contrast to the other relationships in the series.

The main contrast has already been hinted at by the time Catelyn and Ned have their encounter: Robert's first act on arriving in Winterfell is to visit the crypts to see the grave of his betrothed, Lyanna, whose kidnapping and death were major causes of Robert's rebellion. In part, then, the rebellion was fought over ownership of a woman and her sexuality, as Rhaegar either stole Lyanna from Robert or Lyanna took control of her own sexuality and ran away with Rhaegar. In a patriarchal system such as that found in Westeros, a woman taking control of her own sexuality and her own place in the exchange between men is demonized and considered transgressive. Yet Robert idolizes Lyanna, and he may believe she was taken against her will because he cannot think of her as anything but a paragon of beauty and maidenly modesty; had she voluntarily run away with Rhaegar and borne his child, she would no longer fit Westerosi society's view of a well-behaved woman. He does not have the same feelings for Cersei, and thus her choice to refuse to have sex with him very often leads him to characterize her as "cold" – "the way she guards her cunt, you'd think she had all the gold of Casterly Rock between her legs."[34] That his only (spoken) complaint about Cersei is that she will not readily have sex with him demonstrates the Westerosi view of women as property of their husbands, obliged to submit to sexual relations,

[33] Martin, *A Game of Thrones*, 58–9.
[34] Ibid., 310.

however unwanted, in order to satisfy their husbands and bear them heirs.

That this is the expectation for married women and that, as discussed above, men cannot be expected to control themselves leads to a troubling scene between Tyrion and Sansa on their wedding night. Sansa is on the cusp of thirteen and Tyrion is close to thirty, but he admits that he "want[s]" her when she undresses.[35] In a rare turn of events for Westeros, Tyrion recognizes that Sansa is too young and too unwilling for him to have sex with, and decides to ignore his father's orders to get Sansa pregnant as soon as possible and forego sex until Sansa is ready. What makes the scene unsettling – beyond the twelve-year-old girl lying naked in bed waiting to be raped, and Tyrion's obvious arousal – is that Tyrion's decision is so unusual in Westeros that it seems to be designed to make him more heroic. Yet his decision seems to be based less on not wanting to rape a twelve-year-old girl and more on refusing to obey his father, who has already ordered him to rape one wife. Similarly, Sansa's question about what will happen if she chooses never to have sex with Tyrion clearly upsets him, as did her refusal to kneel so he could cloak her at the wedding.[36] In both instances, the narrative voice seems to favor Tyrion over Sansa, casting her as the villain in choosing to remain a virgin and deny Tyrion his rights rather than "do her duty." Yet it is necessary for the plot that Sansa remains a virgin so that she can remarry later, as Westerosi society values virginity in their highborn girls more than any other attribute.

The fetishization of virginity shows in Hoster Tully's treatment of his daughter Lysa, who had sex with Petyr Baelish and became pregnant. Hoster forced her to take abortifacient herbs, then married her to Jon Arryn, who was close to sixty. The marriage was partly a punishment – Hoster could not marry Lysa to a more desirable man now that she had been deflowered – and partly a strategic move, as Jon Arryn needed a wife who had been shown to be fertile.[37] The sequence of events makes Lysa paranoid and overly attached to her

[35] Martin, *A Storm of Swords*, 392.
[36] Ibid., 393, 387.
[37] Ibid., 39.

son, Robert Arryn, and her continued love for Petyr leads her to murder Jon Arryn and almost murder Sansa. It is not Lysa's decision to have sex before getting married that drives her nearly mad, as might be the case in a romance, but rather her treatment after the fact – being forced to abort the child of the man she loves, being married off to a man three times her age, and being manipulated into murdering that man. In this way, Martin shows that this sort of treatment of women is damaging to their health, both mental and physical.

On the other side of this situation is Margaery Tyrell, who marries three times and yet remains a virgin. Her first marriage, to Renly Baratheon, is not consummated because Renly is in a relationship with Margaery's brother Loras; her second is not consummated because Joffrey dies at the wedding feast; and her third is not consummated because Tommen is eight years old. Each of her marriages is in service of an alliance, and she is able to move the Tyrell allegiance from Baratheon to Lannister because the first marriage was unconsummated. Margaery's continued maidenhood is a major plot point in *A Feast for Crows*, as Cersei tries to either prove that she is no longer a virgin (and thus either lied about her virginity before marrying Joffrey or has been unfaithful to Tommen, either one an act of treason) or to manipulate Margaery into taking a lover so that she can be proven unfaithful to Tommen. Cersei's own sexual habits come under scrutiny in the process, and she is imprisoned and punished by the Sept. She does not confess to incest or to adultery while Robert was alive, thus sparing herself worse punishments, but is forced to confess to fornication in order to be released from a cell and promised a trial.[38] That nobody seems to be working for the release of the Queen Regent shows how unpopular and inconvenient Cersei has become, partly because of her leadership style and partly because of her sexual choices. Such cloistering or imprisoning of inconvenient women is frequent in literature and history, so leaving Cersei in prison rather than rescuing her is no surprise. In Westeros, women (noblewomen, at least) do not own their sexuality and are not allowed to make their own choices with regard to their partners.

Brienne's virginity is an interesting case because, rather than being

[38] Martin, *A Dance with Dragons*, 790–3.

the usual virginal woman, her character more closely matches the model of a chaste, chivalric knight, Galahad being the prime example. Her belief in honor and insistence on comporting herself as she believes a knight should echo courtly-love traditions, but, in classic Martin fashion, these traditions do not quite fit with the world. As John Cameron puts it, Brienne is not:

> a man in love with an unapproachable maiden but a female knight in love with a king, one who is both married to another and engaged in an affair with his wife's brother. Oblivious to this, Brienne sees Renly – in the best courtly love tradition – as a wholly perfect king and man.[39]

Despite not being a knight, or even a man, Brienne identifies more closely with knighthood than ladyhood; when Catelyn laments the fate of the knights of Renly's camp, calling them the "knights of summer" while "winter is coming," Brienne contradicts her, claiming that their deaths will be made into songs, in which "all knights are gallant, all maids are beautiful, and the sun is always shining."[40] Brienne knows that not all maids are beautiful, being an un-beautiful maid herself, so in order to reconcile the cognitive dissonance of the songs and life, she aligns herself with the knights instead. As a Galahad-figure, Brienne is chaste and even asexual, showing little sign of sexual desire; when she does occasionally have "stirrings," she is confused by them and redirects her thoughts to Renly, who is a safe object of desire due to his preferences and, later, his death.[41] Like Galahad, Brienne is often defined by her virginity, being called "the Maid of Tarth," and by her looks, being called "the Beauty" (albeit not with the seriousness with which Galahad is referred to as "fair"). Yet in Westeros, even a chaste and chivalric almost-knight is threatened with rape, if she is a woman, and Brienne frequently has to defend herself against those who would seek to "put her in her place" by raping her. Brienne is another example of a woman who is not allowed to make her own sexual choice, even when that choice is to abstain. In a way, Brienne's

[39] John H. Cameron, "A New Kind of Hero: *A Song of Ice and Fire*'s Brienne of Tarth," in *Quest of Her Own: Essays on the Female Hero in Modern Fantasy*, edited by Lori M. Campbell (Jefferson: McFarland, 2014), 191.

[40] Martin, *A Clash of Kings*, 350.

[41] Martin, *A Feast for Crows*, 189.

sexuality is the least transgressive thing about her; as a cross-dressing woman acting in a masculine fashion and thus breaking the barriers of Martin's patriarchal world, her status as a chaste woman in love with a man is remarkably normalizing.[42]

Only a few women are allowed to flout the rules and have sex with who they want, and the most prominent of these is Asha Greyjoy. Asha began having sex at sixteen and has lost count of the number of men she has bedded.[43] She makes her own choices about whom she will and will not have sex with and how, going so far as to flee an arranged marriage performed *in absentia*. She rejects romantic notions about marriage and sex, refusing her girlhood sweetheart, Tristifer, who has remained celibate waiting for her to decide to marry him and be his lady. While Asha is able to make her own sexual choices, this ability comes because of the culture of the Iron Islands, in which women are allowed to be reavers alongside men, and because she can use violence to enforce her choices. Rape is less of a threat to Asha than to other women in the novels because she can defend herself using traditionally male tools and attitudes. Perhaps this is why the one sex scene Martin wrote for her is so disturbing – it is a rape fantasy role-play, but that is not evident until the end of the scene. Instead, it appears to be a rape scene, with Asha threatening to kill Quarl, him "forcing" her legs apart, and Asha crying out in in protest.[44] Afterward, she lies in bed with him and thinks about their relationship, which has gone on for years, but this is the first the reader knows about it. Before the "rape," no indication is provided to the reader that Asha and Qarl are anything more than shipmates or passing acquaintances. On its own, the scene might be read as a pair of lovers engaging in rough sex and role-play, but in the larger context of the novels, with the frequency of rape and rape threats, the scene has sinister implications for women and women's sexuality. Asha and Cersei, the two women who have sex frequently and choose their own partners, both engage in violent

[42] Thanks to Alexandra Garner for bringing up this point while reading and responding to this chapter.

[43] Martin, *A Feast for Crows*, 243.

[44] Martin, *A Dance with Dragons*, 366–7.

encounters of questionable consensuality, either being raped by, pretending to be raped by, or indeed raping their partners.

Arianne Martell also has more freedom to choose her partners, but the one sexual encounter she has on-page involves her using sex as a tool to get Arys to help her kidnap and crown Myrcella. Previously, Doran had arranged for her to marry Viserys Targaryen without her input or consent. When that plan fails due to Viserys' death, Arianne is named Doran's heir and informed of his deeper plans. So while she was intended for an alliance marriage, she was not allowed to be involved with the political aspect of Dorne, but once that alliance marriage is no longer tenable, she is allowed to assume a traditionally male role and act as Doran's ambassador. Thus, while she is allowed more sexual freedom than most Westerosi women, she is still expected, initially, to marry to forge an alliance without being informed of the details.

While Martin has chosen to convey his story primarily through the viewpoints of noblemen and -women, and in his construction of the Middle Ages, love matches are rare, the fact that incidences of rape and sexual assault far outnumber consensual love-matches further contributes to his presentation of the Middle Ages as "barbaric." Women in Westeros are allowed three roles, which match the female faces of the Seven: maiden, mother, and crone. Martin's portrayal of women and their reaction to being confined to these three roles, as well as the effect this confinement has on their psyches, shows clear attempts to reject the Madonna/Whore dichotomy and underscore how harmful the patriarchy is to women. However, as with his portrayal of women in general, his depiction of women's sexuality falls into unfortunate patterns that make every woman a victim or potential victim, even those who should be able to protect themselves.

Renly's Rainbow Guard: Queer Sexualities and Encounters

Overt homosexuality and same-sex encounters are not common in neomedieval fantasy and medieval texts. Of course, this is not to say that homosexuality did not exist in the Middle Ages, only that the literature rarely dealt with it, even those texts that prioritize homosocial relationships above heterosexual ones. Critics and historians generally agree that "homosexual" as an identity did not exist in the Middle Ages, but as Mark Jordan puts it, sexuality is constructed, medieval people constructed it for themselves, and "we have to (re) construct their constructions."[45] As usual, however, whether medieval peoples had a concept for homosexuality – or sexuality at all, as we understand the term – is not the main concern when analyzing a neomedieval text. Rather, Martin's ideas about sexuality in the Middle Ages and how they reflect modern ideas are the primary focus.

Martin includes characters who have same-sex preferences and characters who have same-sex encounters without identifying as queer. Renly Baratheon, who puts himself forward as king after his brother Robert's death, has a relationship with Loras Tyrell, his wife's brother; he married Margaery Tyrell after his relationship with Loras began, however, and only to help solidify his position as king. The relationship is strongly implied rather than explicitly shown, and Renly's orientation is revealed only through very subtle clues, most of which must be read through Loras after Renly's death.[46] The subtle hints are too numerous to list here, but the least subtle by far is Jaime Lannister threatening to take Loras' sword away "and shove it up some place even Renly never found."[47] What Martin has constructed through Loras and Renly is a fascinating undermining of stereotypes about homosexual men and the chivalric knight; both Loras and Renly are considered epitomes of manliness and chivalric prowess, and yet they enjoy each other's sexual company. Likewise, their relationship has very little overt impact on the plot; Martin presents it as a reasonable relationship between two men who keep it mostly hidden because of

[45] Mark D. Jordan, "Homosexuality, *Luxuria*, and Textual Abuse," in *Constructing Medieval Sexuality*, edited by Karma Lochrie, Peggy McCracken, and James A. Schultz (Minneapolis: University of Minnesota Press, 1997), 24.

[46] In sharp contrast to Martin's handling of Renly's sexuality in the novels, the HBO series is much more overt; Renly's proclivities are an open secret that men laugh about around their cookfire, Margaery offers to have Loras get Renly "started" so that they can produce an heir, and Renly and Loras are shown pre- and post-coitus on screen. Perhaps the showrunners felt it necessary to be explicitly clear about Renly's sexuality where Martin is more coy, though perhaps the relationship is used, as so many sexual encounters are in HBO shows, as voyeuristic titillation (see Chapter 5).

[47] Martin, *A Storm of Swords*, 848.

the prejudices of society, not a reason why Renly should not be king or a method by which others attempt to delegitimize his potential reign.

Besides Renly and Loras, whose preferences, if not lifestyles, are queer, at least two women in *A Song of Ice and Fire* have same-sex encounters which do not define them as queer. Daenerys' handmaiden, Irri, performs sexual acts on her as a service, though Daenerys tells her that she is no longer a slave and is not required to do such things.[48] Cersei sexually assaults Lady Taena, trying to imitate all the men she has known so she can be a respected ruler.[49] Both of these women appear to prefer sex with men, but circumstances bring them into sexual contact with women. While these scenes are not "gratuitous" in the sense that they add nothing to the narrative, the differences in the way Martin approaches same-sex female relations and same-sex male relations can be difficult to justify.

While the narrative voice in *A Song of Ice and Fire* makes no judgments about characters' sexual choices, the amount of time and detail spent on the various relationships is enlightening. As mentioned already, the one confirmed same-sex relationship in *A Song of Ice and Fire*, between Renly and Loras, is subtle and never shown on-page. Though it is almost an open secret in the kingdom and many people are aware of it, few ever speak of it, except in careful, veiled terms. While Stannis is eager to use Cersei's incestuous infidelity against Joffrey's claim to the throne and to spread that accusation as far and wide as possible, he never uses Renly's relationship against him, and nor does anyone else. Yet whenever people do speak of the relationship, they often use language which denotes disgust or superiority, usually directed at Loras.

Regardless of how Westerosi society views same-sex relations, the different ways in which Martin handles the relationships on-page are problematic. While Renly and Loras are never seen together, every same-sex interaction between women is seen, usually in some detail. Daenerys and Cersei's same-sex interactions seem crafted primarily for a male audience, for the male gaze, and hark back to the age of

[48] Martin, *A Storm of Swords*, 325.
[49] Ibid., 689, 693.

fantasy in which women were present only for the convenience and pleasure of the male characters, and female sexuality was portrayed to titillate adolescent male readers.[50] Cersei's encounter with Lady Taena is violent and detailed; she has just returned from a council meeting, Taena is naked in her bed, and Cersei "wondered what it would feel like to suckle on those breasts, to lay the Myrish woman on her back and push her legs apart and use her as a man would use her, the way Robert would use *her* when the drink was in him."[51] Cersei remembers enjoying sex with Robert only once, on their wedding night, before he called her "Lyanna," the namc of his then-dead sweetheart.[52] After that, she remembers every encounter as rape, with him drunk and "mauling" her breasts, while she lay still and waited for it to be over.[53] Robert always blamed alcohol, refusing to take responsibility for hurting her when she complained. Cersei takes on the role of Robert, drunk and lustful, and begins touching Taena, purposefully hurting her; when Taena complains, Cersei says "It's just the wine. [...] I am the queen. I mean to claim my rights." The language used during the scene is coarse, Taena's body described in intimate detail, "her nipples two black diamonds, her sex slick and steamy," her vaginal area described as a "Myrish swamp." Cersei brings Taena to orgasm with her hand, but "could not feel it, whatever Robert felt on the nights he took her. There was no pleasure in it, not for her."[54] Cersei even elides Robert's death-by-goring with this experience, "let[ting] herself imagine that her fingers were a bore's [*sic*] tusks, ripping the Myrish woman apart from groin to throat."[55] To Cersei, sex is power, and her assault on Taena is an attempt to wield a man's power, but the graphic description adds a discomfiting element of voyeurism. While Cersei frequently uses her sexuality as a weapon, this scene is the only one for which Martin provides so much detail; even an otherwise detailed

[50] See Joanna Russ, "Introduction," *Uranian Worlds: A Guide to Alternative Sexuality in Science Fiction, Fantasy and Horror*, edited by Eric Garber and Lyn Paleo, 2nd edition (Boston: GK Hall, 1990), xxiii–vi.

[51] Martin, *A Feast for Crows*, 685.

[52] Martin, *A Game of Thrones*, 487.

[53] Martin, *A Feast for Crows*, 685.

[54] Ibid., 692.

[55] Ibid., 693.

scene in which Cersei and Jaime have sex in the Great Sept of Baelor does not match this one.

Just as troubling is Daenerys' sexual interaction with her companion Irri. Irri is one of three slave girls presented to Daenerys at her wedding to Khal Drogo; Irri was bought specifically to teach Daenerys how to ride a horse.[56] After Drogo's death, Daenerys is celibate for months as she leads her people through the Red Wastes, to Qarth, and then to Astapor. Her first sexual contact of any kind after Drogo's death occurs when her sworn sword, Jorah, ambushes her while she is dressing and kisses her.[57] Though she does not entirely dislike the kiss, she rebukes him for taking the liberty. Later, she realizes that her sex drive has reawakened; before Jorah's kiss, she had not felt any sexual urges after Drogo's death.[58] However, it is not Jorah she wants, and so she struggles with having no outlet for her feelings. One night Irri wakes to find Daenerys touching herself, and dutifully takes over:

> Wordless, the handmaid put a hand on her breast, then bent to take a nipple in her mouth. Her other hand drifted down across the soft curve of belly, through the mound of fine silvery-gold hair, and went to work between Dany's thighs. [...] Irri never said a thing, only curled back up and went to sleep the instant the thing was done.[59]

Later, Irri offers to "pleasure the *khaleesi*" because Daenerys is sad, but Daenerys turns her down, reminding her that she is not a sex slave.[60] Yet Daenerys takes advantage of Irri's skills and willingness to serve when she has trouble sleeping at least two more times, both times aware that she is trying to replace Drogo and Daario with Irri, with poor results.[61]

Both Daenerys and Cersei replace unavailable men with available women, but their partners, while ostensibly consenting, are in less-powerful positions and thus may have no choice but to consent,

[56] Martin, *A Game of Thrones*, 103.
[57] Martin, *A Storm of Swords*, 120.
[58] Ibid., 324.
[59] Ibid., 325.
[60] Ibid., 328–9.
[61] Ibid., 993; *A Dance with Dragons*, 340.

which places Daenerys and Cersei in the position of rapists, as well. The portrayal of these relationships normalizes and even celebrates non-consensual sexual acts perpetrated against women. Perhaps most contentious, however, is the fact that we see female same-sex interaction on page, but not male. Some allowance can be made for the fact that neither Renly nor Loras is ever a POV character, while Daenerys and Cersei are, but that raises a question of why Martin chose not to cause any of his male POV characters to engage in same-sex interactions.

One possibility is that when Martin began writing *A Song of Ice and Fire* in the 1990s, male same-sex activity in fantasy literature was still not accepted in the mainstream. This may explain why, besides not including a queer POV character, Martin does not have his characters openly discuss Renly and Loras' relationship. Another reason may be his desire to portray a "real" Middle Ages, in which although male same-sex activity existed, the only texts to contain open discussion are religious ones, in which it is condemned. In an interview, Abigail Pritchard asked Martin specifically about the issue of on-page sexuality, and his explanation was that he uses a "very tight third-person viewpoint" with "a handful of characters in a cast of hundreds." He claims that until a sexual encounter "happens to one of my characters on stage, to one of my viewpoint characters," these encounters will remain invisible and rumored only.[62] However, this answer does not explain why he chose not to include POV characters who were queer, and thus does not provide satisfactory closure on this issue.

Along with the problem of the invisibility of male queer sexuality comes the fact that Daenerys and Cersei, though neither of them is lesbian, both engage in lesbian activity when no men are available, whereas men who do not have women available simply abstain. In her analysis of Poe's "Ligea," Valerie Rohy asks, "What is sex between women who don't really want each other? One answer: a straight fantasy."[63] Cersei does not really want Taena; she wants to experience

[62] "Fantastic Forum Interviews George R.R. Martin," *YouTube*, 13:12, posted by "Fantastic Forum," April 11, 2015, https://www.youtube.com/watch?v=jVdj_YVZECE.

[63] Valerie Rohy, "Ahistorical," *GLQ* 12, no. 1 (2006), 75.

the thrill she imagines Robert felt when he drunkenly raped her. Daenerys does not really want Irri; she wants Daario or Drogo, but both are out of reach. Thus, all of these interactions could be classified as "straight fantasy": though they do provide some further insight into the women's inner lives, the level of detail adds an eroticism that goes beyond what is necessary for either character development or plot (particularly in comparison with the authorial handling of male same-sex relations).

Like so many of the themes and trends in *A Song of Ice and Fire*, the portrayals of sex and sexuality are a blend of medievalist and modern. While the culture of Westeros allows readers to examine sexual politics and sexuality from a safe distance, considering issues such as rape, rape culture, toxic masculinity, and women's ability to choose their own partners, Martin's extreme portrayal of these issues and claim that his portrayal is accurate to the historical Middle Ages perpetuate beliefs about the period that can be difficult for readers to see beyond.

4

Postcolonialism, Slavery, and the Great White Hope

MEDIEVALIST FANTASY IS a blend of the modern and the medieval, containing many colonial and postcolonial issues to be parsed. Despite the possibilities offered by the fantastic to explore unfamiliar realms inhabited by creatures that do not exist and humans with magical abilities, writers are still restricted by their own experiences as well as the necessity of communicating their ideas to an audience. Thus, ideas and cultures from the familiar world will still creep in, and for Western writers, this can include an almost subliminal imperialism. Nancy Batty and Robert Markley argue that science fiction is frequently imperialist in its assumption of the "manifest destiny" of human exploration and colonization of space.[1] Fantasy, as Myles Balfe argues, tends to be set in a "moralized neo-medieval Europe," and the plot is often concerned with "the efforts of various (male) heroes to defend 'their' (Good/familiar/known) landscapes from attacks by 'Others', or with the inability of the heroes' emasculated Eastern counterparts to do the same."[2] The people of the "Eastern" lands in these tales, Balfe claims, are in some way evil or corrupt and need the efforts of the Western heroes to save them, as they "cannot redeem their cultures, their selves, let alone [...] protect their landscapes from outside invaders. Indeed, 'their barbarous nature' arguably serves to continually threaten the land-

[1] Nancy Batty and Robert Markley, "Writing Back: Speculative Fiction and the Politics of Postcolonialism," *Ariel* 33, no. 1 (2002), 6.

[2] Myles Balfe, "Incredible Geographies?: Orientalism and Genre Fantasy," *Social and Cultural Geography* 5, no. 1 (2004), 78–9.

scapes and homelands in which they live."[3] Helen Young discusses at length how issues of race, Orientalism, and distrust of the Other are hard-wired into fantasy through Tolkien and Robert Howard, and how these issues have been perpetuated throughout the genre.[4] While Martin does not set up obvious dichotomies between good and evil, black and white, Us and Other, his various peoples experience differing levels of invasion, occupation, colonialism, and postcolonialism, creating a dense tapestry of interaction between the cultures.

Examining a medieval, medievalist, or neomedieval text through a postcolonial lens can be tricky, as postcolonial critics, especially foundational ones such as Edward Said, tend to believe that imperialism is a post-medieval construct and thus no pre-modern history or text can be colonial or postcolonial. However, medieval scholars have argued, at length, that imperialism and colonialism are not restricted to the modern era just because the concept was not defined and explored until the eighteenth century. Barbara Fuchs and David J. Baker argue that "the past is not 'pre-colonial' but is instead marked by multiple, historically specific temporalities that preceded modernity and came to be integral to colonialism as we usually think of it."[5] Not only did imperialism, colonialism, and postcolonialism exist in the Middle Ages, but moreover, the Middle Ages is where much of the foundation for imperialist ideas in the modern era was laid, and the Middle Ages are often used to create nationalist identities that help to justify imperialism and colonialism.[6] Likewise, in many ways, discussions and uses of the Middle Ages are imperialist in their own way, with nationalistic ideologies relying on medievalist views of the Middle Ages that empty the era of its own meaning and "historical agency"

[3] Ibid., 79.

[4] Young, *Race and Popular Fantasy Literature*, 34–66.

[5] Barbara Fuchs and David J. Baker, "The Postcolonial Past," *Modern Language Quarterly* 65, no. 3 (2004), 337.

[6] Kathleen Davis and Nadia Altschul, "Introduction: The Idea of the 'Middle Ages' Outside Europe," in *Medievalisms in the Postcolonial World: The Idea of the "Middle Ages,"* edited by Kathleen Davis and Nadia Altschul (Baltimore: Johns Hopkins University Press, 2009), 1–2.

and instead project meaning backward onto it.[7] Thus, reading *A Song of Ice and Fire* with an eye to the ways in which Martin portrays the various historical imperialist actions, colonial movements, and post-colonial consequences seen in Classical Europe and medieval Britain as adapted for Westeros is certainly possible.

Westeros is not the only culture or continent in *A Song of Ice and Fire*. Essos, to the east, and Southros, to the south, take up the vast majority of the space on what has been referred to by fans as "Planetos." The layers of history Martin has borrowed in order to build the cultures of "Planetos" lead to varying levels of imperialism and postcolonialism in both Westeros and Essos. Perceptions of Essos in Westeros also slide into the realm of what Edward Said has called "Orientalism" – casting the "Other" as barbaric, mystic, or magical. While Westerosi society still shows latent signs of the waves of colonialism in the tension between various populations, Daenerys' invasion of Slavers Bay shows imperialism in action, as well as the tendency for Western cultures to act as "saviors" for Eastern peoples. Martin explores the issues surrounding imperialism and postcolonialism, giving voice to colonized peoples, many of whom have clear antecedents in English history.

While Martin's determination to speak out for colonized peoples and their way of life may be well intentioned, the area is notoriously difficult to negotiate. While Martin can be lauded for including people of color in his novels (especially people of color who are not immediately coded evil, as such inclusions are sadly rare in neomedieval fantasy), his characterization of the non-Westerosi peoples yet drifts toward Orientalism and race essentialism. Likewise, his tendency to idealize Celtic culture and mythology over Mediterranean can be problematic. As Young points out, he continues the "habit of Whiteness" by centering the action of his books in a geography and culture clearly identifiable as Western – European and English.[8] These issues are best examined through the lenses of postcolonialism, as they

[7] John Dagenais and Margaret Greer, "Decolonizing the Middle Ages: Introduction," *Journal of Medieval and Early Modern Studies* 30, no. 3 (2000), 435–6.

[8] Young, *Race and Popular Fantasy Literature*, 67.

involve recovering the voices of those swept aside by imperialist dogma, and race theory.

"Why shouldn't we rule ourselves again?": Postcolonialism in Westeros

Two different approaches to postcolonial ideas are evident in *A Song of Ice and Fire*: exploring a heritage lost to colonialism and witnessing colonialism in action. In Westeros, Martin creates a layered colonial structure that in many ways mirrors medieval England's. According to Winterfell's maester, Luwin, the first inhabitants of Westeros were the Children of the Forest, a non-human race of diminutive people who "lived in the depths of the wood, in caves and crannogs and secret tree towns."[9] Then came the First Men, conquerors from the south who crossed a land-bridge from the continent of Essos, bringing horses and bronze; they nearly wiped out the Children before they reached an agreement and forged peace through the Pact of the Isle of Faces. For four thousand years, the First Men and the Children lived in peace, with the First Men even adopting the Children's gods.[10] The Andals were next, conquering the south of Westeros with steel, while the north held out against the incursion.[11] Roughly three thousand years later, the Targaryens of Valyria invaded with dragons and conquered the entire continent, uniting it into the Seven Kingdoms of the novels. Although there are very few one-to-one historical correlations in Martin's work, the waves of conquerors in *A Song of Ice and Fire* might be read as analogous to the Romans, the Anglo-Saxons, and the Norman conquest and settlement of England.[12] Any correlation between British or English settlers and Martin's peoples is subject to interpretation; as with much of Martin's historicism, the

[9] Martin, *A Game of Thrones*, 737.

[10] Ibid., 738.

[11] Ibid., 739.

[12] For a more detailed comparison between Martin's peoples and their historical antecedents, see my essay "Barbarian Colonizers and Post-Colonialism in Westeros and Britain," in "*Game of Thrones" versus History: Written in Blood*, edited by Brian Pavlac and Elizabeth Lott (Malden, MA: Wiley-Blackwell, 2017), 73–84.

relationship between history and Westeros is not a case of simple allegory. The defining characteristics of the various historical peoples are distributed among the various Westerosi settlers so that the Children of the Forest can be interpreted as analogous to the Picts and the Celts, the First Men as Romans and/or Anglo-Saxons. This, however, connects with a fairly common trope of fantasy writing: the various pre-Roman and pre-Anglo-Saxon tribes of Britain are often conflated in neomedieval fantasy and imbued with special powers or morality, which exacerbates the problems surrounding the way in which those tribes or their analogues are portrayed in novels such as these.

The Children of the Forest, then, seem analogous to the British tribes and are idealized and romanticized due to their presumed extinction. While romanticizing indigenous cultures is a common problem with imperialism, in the case of those who have also been victims of genocide, the native people cannot reject or educate away this romanticization. For all intents and purposes, the Children of the Forest are extinct; they no longer have a palpable presence in Westeros. The godswoods may provide a physical reminder of their previous inhabitance, but this reminder can be read the same way Deane reads early Revival translations of Celtic poetry: "little more than obituary notices in which the poetry of a ruined civilization was accorded a sympathy which had been notably absent when it was alive."[13] While some fantasy narratives, such as Marion Zimmer Bradley's *The Mists of Avalon*,[14] describe the decline of indigenous people and their religion, Martin's occurs thousands of years after the Children have been all but destroyed. However, recorded history in Westeros is muddled, and the Children pre-date the written word. Thus, Maester Luwin's accounts of the lives of the Children of the Forest are questionable at best, especially his insistence that they no longer exist; Osha, a Wildling captive-turned-servant, tells Bran that "North of the Wall [...] that's where the children went, and the giants, and the other old races," but Luwin calls that "folly."[15] Belief in the Children's extinction

[13] Seamus Deane, *Celtic Revivals: Essays in Modern Irish Literature, 1880–1980* (Boston: Faber & Faber, 1985), 34.

[14] Marion Zimmer Bradley, *The Mists of Avalon* (New York: Alfred A. Knopf, 1983).

[15] Martin, *A Game of Thrones*, 738.

allows Luwin to think of them in romantic, nostalgic terms, rather than as a living group who may prove inconvenient were they to reappear in the south.

Several layers of imperialist thought are evident in Martin's construction of the Children of the Forest and the way the rest of Westeros remembers them. Diegetically, he explores the tendency of the colonizer/conqueror to romanticize the now-extinct peoples and cultures that occupied the land before the arrival of the colonizers. In this case, he specifically bases the Children of the Forest, the First Men, and the Andals on the indigenous British and their Roman and Anglo-Saxon conquerors. While the British tribes were primarily pushed to the outer areas of the British Isles – Scotland, Ireland, and Wales – and then subject to imperialist oppression,[16] the Children of the Forest were nearly completely wiped out. Thus, those Westerosi like Luwin who are aware of the history and how the Children were destroyed are able to mourn their treatment without compensating for it, as no one exists with whom to make amends. The Westerosi are also released from guilt because their generation was not the one to destroy the Children of the Forest, nor do they continue their oppression.

At the same time, Martin perpetrates this same romanticization through his characterization of the Children of the Forest, who are clearly supernatural in nature and bear more resemblance to the Sidhe of Irish mythology than to human beings. As is common for a romanticized people, the Children of the Forest are closer to nature, are generally peaceable, and practice magic. Although the Children of the Forest are fictional, Martin's insistence on historical antecedent and the clear parallels between the British tribes and the Children of the Forest contribute to a tendency to idealize the British tribes as they were before the Romans and Anglo-Saxons settled the isles, while the effects of English colonization are still felt among the Scots, Irish, and Welsh.

This treatment of the British tribes or their mythological equivalent is hardly unusual for fantasy literature, of course; critics such as

[16] Barry Cunliffe, *Britain Begins* (Oxford: Oxford University Press, 2013), 423.

C.W. Sullivan have explored how Welsh myth, for example, is used in the genre. Interestingly, this use of Celtic myth is not one of the traditions that can be fully attributed to Tolkien, as Tolkien generally disliked Celtic mythology and the majority of his Celtic influences appear in the *Silmarillion* rather than the vastly more popular *The Hobbit* or *The Lord of the Rings*.[17] Sullivan credits William Morris, Kenneth Morris, and Lloyd Alexander with introducing more direct Celtic influence to the genre.[18] The modern fantasy conception of elves, Druids, and pagan goddesses owes much to these authors, and this conception has clearly influenced Martin even as he has mostly avoided outright magic in *A Song of Ice and Fire*.

When Bran encounters the remnants of the Children, he learns that they are indeed not human, but an elfin race the size of ten-year-old humans. Leaf, the one with whom he interacts most frequently, has dappled brown skin, gold-and-green eyes with a vertically-slit pupil, and brown hair that is full of leaves and vines. Perhaps because of their bond with nature, they are pacifists, fighting only when they must; Bran considers their slow extinction, which Leaf refers to as "our long dwindling," and thinks that "Men would be wroth. Men would hate and swear bloody vengeance. The singers sing sad songs, where men would fight and kill."[19] Bran seems to blame the Children for their own extinction because they do not react in the way he would expect; withdrawing rather than fighting for their lives is a failing in Bran's mind, as he projects his beliefs and experience as a human onto another species. He does not, however, voice these thoughts to Leaf or Brynden, their human greenseer; rather, he accepts their ways and training in order to become their new greenseer. In a way, Martin relieves the conquerors of responsibility for their conquest, instead implying that such conquest is either the natural way of things – the

[17] Argument can be made that Celtic themes and mythology crept into Tolkien's work whether he meant them to or not; see Dimitra Fimi, "'Mad' Elves and 'Elusive Beauty': Some Celtic Strands of Tolkien's Mythology," *Folklore* 117 (2006), 156–70; Marjorie Burns, *Celtic and Norse in Tolkien's Middle-Earth* (Buffalo, NY: University of Toronto Press, 2005).

[18] C.W. Sullivan, "Celtic Myth and English-Language Fantasy Literature: Possible New Directions," *Journal of the Fantastic in the Arts* 10, no. 1 (1998), 91.

[19] Martin, *A Dance with Dragons*, 498.

Children were unable to defend themselves against a greater force and thus were destroyed – or otherwise inevitable. Both implications fall in line with his "Barbaric Age" medievalism and his insistence on historical realism; the first matches the brutality and wanton violence of his medievalism, while the second keeps the history of Westeros on a similar path to that of Britain.

Like the Children, their successors, First Men, are idealized, held up as paragons of honor and virtue, especially in the north. The men of the north are proud of being descendants of the First Men and embrace the Old Ways, including worship of the weirwoods, as the First Men learned from the Children of the Forest. The Old Ways, as the descendants of the First Men practice them, emphasize honor, duty, and loyalty. For example, when Eddard explains to Bran why he executes a deserter from the Night's Watch himself rather than turning him over to a headsman, he attributes the tradition to the First Men: "[O]ur way is the older way. The blood of the First Men still flows in the veins of the Starks, and we hold to the belief that the man who passes the sentence should swing the sword."[20]

Catelyn Stark finds a notable difference between the atmosphere of Winterfell, the seat of House Stark, and her childhood home to the south; in Riverrun, the godswood "was a garden, bright and airy, where tall redwoods spread dappled shadows across tinkling streams, birds sang from hidden nests, and the air was spicy with the scent of flowers." Winterfell's godswood, by contrast, is "a dark, primal place, three acres of old forest untouched for ten thousand years as the gloomy castle rose around it."[21] Despite being dedicated to the same gods, the godswoods of the south and those of the north reflect the differences in culture; the south is of the Andals, while the north is of the First Men. The country is divided and dualistic, united only due to the efforts of the Targaryens, who no longer rule Westeros. By describing the differences in culture between the north and south, Martin sets up the schism that will later lead to the Seven Kingdoms fracturing.

Unlike the Children, the First Men built with stone and thus

[20] Martin, *A Game of Thrones*, 16.
[21] Ibid., 22.

left tangible marks on the world, primarily in the form of barrows and ruins scattered across Westeros, though these are concentrated primarily in the north. While traveling south, Eddard shows King Robert the barrows of the First Men.[22] Later, Catelyn rides into Moat Cailin, an ancient stronghold of the First Men, which now lies mostly in ruins.[23] History weighs heavily on the various ruins and structures of the First Men, as Bran discovers when he reaches the Nightfort, an abandoned castle at the Wall. All of his nurse's stories about the Nightfort return to him, most of them bloody and horrifying. Bran thinks that "[a]ll of that had happened hundreds and thousands of years ago, to be sure, and some maybe never happened at all," but the Nightfort is oppressive both in size and age, keeping Bran in a constant state of anxiety during his stay.[24] The ruins and barrows, along with the tales about them, contribute to a sense of postcolonialism similar to that which Nicholas Howe and Seth Lehrer have identified in Anglo-Saxon literature.[25]

The ruins of the First Men and the godswoods remind the Westerosi of the Children of the Forest and the First Men, standing as visible history as well as adding a particular sense of gloom and fatality to the north. Despite the physical remains, however, the history of the First Men is uncertain, as their written language consisted only of "runes on rocks"; according to Sam Tarly:

[22] Ibid., 111.

[23] Ibid., 596–7.

[24] Martin, *A Storm of Swords*, 756.

[25] Howe reads postcolonial overtones in *The Ruin*, *The Wanderer*, and *The Seafarer*, claiming that "[t]he stones that litter the texts of Gildas, Bede, and the Old English poets can be read as the visible traces of a colonial past" ("Anglo-Saxon England and the Postcolonial Void," in *Postcolonial Approaches to the European Middle* Ages, edited by Ananya Jahanara Kabir and Deanne Williams [Cambridge: Cambridge University Press, 2005], 34). Lehrer finds similar colonial traces in *Beowulf*, pointing to descriptions of architecture that would have been Roman in origin, such as the paved road ("*fagne flor*") of Heorot. He claims that the descriptions of the Roman remains set *Beowulf* in a specific place in history, as well as adding a sense of inevitability of the destruction of a culture ("'On fagne flor': The Postcolonial *Beowulf*, from Heorot to Heaney," in *Postcolonial Approaches to the European Middle* Ages, edited by Ananya Jahanara Kabir and Deanne Williams [Cambridge: Cambridge University Press, 2005], 77–8).

> The oldest histories we have were written after the Andals came to Westeros. The First Men only left us runes on rocks, so everything we think we know about the Age of Heroes and the Dawn Age and the Long Night comes from accounts set down by septons thousands of years later. There are archmaesters at the Citadel who question all of it. Those old histories are full of kings who reign for hundreds of years, and knights riding around a thousand years before there were knights.[26]

Written language, in this case, is power, since written language lasts longer and can be disseminated further than oral histories or carved runes; in this way, Martin creates a power imbalance that highlights the imperialism of the Andals over the First Men and the Children of the Forest. Language is a potent force in colonial endeavors, allowing the colonizer to gain control through renaming and enforcing linguistic changes on the native population.[27] While physical remains give the First Men a greater cultural legacy than the Children of the Forest, their history is still muddy and mostly oral. The Andals have the advantage in this respect and project their own ideas of culture backward onto the era of the First Men. Yet the written history is known to be corrupted and inaccurate, which implies that the oral history of the Children and the First Men may be purer and more honest despite its impermanence; this again romanticizes the colonized cultures.

The various reminders of the past in the north allow the people to retain their heritage as First Men, and they define themselves as an opposing counter to the people of the south. The Andals did not conquer the north; the First Men turned them back at the Neck, at the north–south midpoint of the continent.[28] Until the Targaryens, the final wave of invaders, arrived and united the continent, the north had its own king and an uneasy truce with the south.[29] Yet the memory of

[26] Martin, *A Feast for Crows*, 114.

[27] Bill Ashcroft, Gareth Griffiths, and Helen Tiffin, "Language: Introduction," in *The Postcolonial Studies Reader* (New York: Routledge, 2003), 283–4.

[28] Martin, *A Game of Thrones*, 739.

[29] Martin, *A Storm of Swords*, 147.

their former sovereign status, despite the roughly three hundred years between the Targaryen conquest and the events of *A Song of Ice and Fire*, drives the men of the north to rebel when the succession to the throne of the Seven Kingdoms comes into question and Eddard Stark is executed. Greatjon Umber declares that he will no longer submit to rule from the south:

> Renly Baratheon is nothing to me, nor Stannis neither. Why should they rule over me and mine, from some flowery seat in Highgarden or Dorne? What do they know of the Wall or the wolfswood or the barrows of the First Men? Even their *gods* are wrong. The Others take the Lannisters, too, I've had a bellyful of them. [...] Why shouldn't we rule ourselves again? It was the dragons we married, and the dragons are all dead! [...] *There* sits the only king I mean to bow *my* knee too, m'lords. [...] The King in the North![30]

With every tie that bound the north to the south severed, the men of the north decide they will no longer submit to the various colonial forces that have pressed on them for three hundred years. Their heritage is ten thousand or more years old, and the reminders of the First Men's greatness allow the men of the north to keep that heritage always in mind. In many ways, the descendants of the First Men exemplify the Irish and Welsh attempts to reclaim their heritage from English dominance; the First Men define themselves in opposition to the Andals, and, as Kath Filmer-Davies says of the Welsh Celtic revival, their heritage is used to encourage violence against the "oppressors."[31]

Martin's construction of the First Men is fairly typical of medievalist thought, especially medievalist race theory. Martin has cited Sir Walter Scott's *Ivanhoe* as one of his greatest influences, and Scott was in turn influenced by the modes of thinking of his time.[32] Throughout the sixteenth and seventeenth centuries, interest in the Anglo-Saxons as predecessors of the English rose, and they were "viewed

[30] Martin, *A Game of Thrones*, 796.

[31] Kath Filmer-Davies, *Fantasy Fiction and Welsh Myth: Tales of Belonging* (New York: St. Martin's Press, 1996), 2.

[32] George R.R. Martin, "Reading Recommendations," *Not a Blog*, March 13, 2013, http://grrm.livejournal.com/316785.html.

as a freedom-loving people, enjoying representative institutions and a flourishing primitive democracy."[33] By the eighteenth century, when Romanticism's idealization of the individual, rather than the institutional, was on the rise, Scott portrayed his Anglo-Saxons with "homely, blunt, simple, honest qualities" and emphasized their straightforwardness and love of liberty.[34] Likewise, he portrayed his Anglo-Saxon heroes in opposition to the Norman occupiers, while including reminders that they once were conquerors and continued to be occupiers, as well.[35] Thus, Martin's portrayal of the First Men – freedom-loving, honest, straightforward, yet balanced between conqueror and conquered – shows clear influence from Scott and the Romantic medievalist view of the Anglo-Saxon people as a whole. Yet this ideal is not only illusory – the Karstarks and the Boltons do not hold to the honor system of the Starks, after all – but also a handicap, as it is Ned's strict adherence to the honor system that ultimately leads to his death.

By setting the "present" of his novels thousands of years after the struggle between the Children of the Forest and the First Men, Martin is able to evoke a sense of nostalgia and romantic loss for a time when the inhabitants of Westeros were connected to nature. At the time of the novels, the Children of the Forest, the giants, the shapeshifters, and those who sympathize with them have all been driven north of the Wall, a great structure that protects the world of men from the supernatural threat of the Others. The choice to adhere to a sense of historicity lends inevitability to the disappearance of the Children of the Forest: because other cultures and religions overtook the British Isles and industrialized them, pushing aside the nature-conscious Celtic pagans – as writers such as Marion Zimmer Bradley (*The Mists of Avalon*, 1979) interpret historical events – so must Martin's Andals overtake his Children of the Forest. The Children and the Celts are

[33] Reginald Horsman, "Origins of Anglo-Saxonism in Great Britain Before 1850," *Journal of the History of Ideas* 37, no. 3 (1976), 388.

[34] Ibid., 394.

[35] Louise D'arcens and Chris Jones, "Excavating the Borders of Literary Anglo-Saxonism in Nineteenth-Century Britain and Australia," *Representations* 121, no. 1 (2013), 88.

erased by imperialism, and Martin attempts to restore their voices – at least, what the he imagines those voices would have been.

Slavers and Barbarian Hordes: Essos as "Barbaric Other"

Counter to the romanticization Western cultures, Eastern cultures are often portrayed as lesser or savage, as discussed in Said's *Orientalism*. Said defines Orientalism as an "enormously systematic discipline by which European culture was able to manage – and even produce – the Orient politically, socially, militarily, ideologically, scientifically, and imaginatively."[36] As with many "-isms," however, definitions of the Orient through Orientalism provide more insight into the minds of those practicing it and the dominant culture that produces such definitions than they do about the Orient itself.[37] In *A Song of Ice and Fire*, the eastern cultures, primarily represented by the Dothraki and the cities of Slaver's Bay, are juxtaposed with and unfavorably compared to the cultures of Westeros – a typical Orientalist construction that Said describes as "a collective notion identifying 'us' Europeans against 'those' non-Europeans."[38] Critics often lament the tendency of neomedieval fantasy literature to focus on the European Middle Ages and exclude the Middle East or Asia, so Martin may be credited for including other cultures, but he does not present them in a new or revisionist manner; rather, Martin's non-Western peoples fall prey to Eastern Otherness and Orientalism, and his plotting and characterization show remarkable similarities to other colonialist literature. While Martin's description of Westeros presents a settled postcolonialism, his treatment of Essos, particularly Slaver's Bay, describes colonialism in action.

In Abdul R. JanMohamad's "Manichean allegory," defined as "a field of diverse yet interchangeable options between white and black, good and evil, superiority and inferiority, civilization and savagery, intelligence and emotion, rationality and sensuality, self and Other,

[36] Edward Said, *Orientalism* (New York: Vintage Books, 1978), 3.
[37] Ibid., 22.
[38] Ibid., 7.

subject and object,"[39] colonialism has two phases: the dominant phase, or active colonialism, and the hegemonic phase, during which native people accept the colonizer's culture and values. The hegemonic phase may begin during the dominant phase and continue into the postcolonial phase.[40] In colonialist literature, native people are cast as "savage" and even "evil," used as the butt of jokes if they attempt to imitate and integrate into the colonialist culture, and are generally used to "justify imperial occupation and exploitation" by shifting the reason for colonization from exploiting the natural resources of the area to "civilizing" the "savages." Colonialist literature shows the necessity of staying in the colonized area by "demonstrat[ing] that the barbarism of the native is irrevocable" and thus "the European's attempt to civilize him can continue indefinitely, the exploitation of his resources can proceed without hindrance, and the European can persist in enjoying a position of moral superiority."[41] The Manichean allegory is evident in Martin's construction and portrayal of the peoples of Essos, especially those east of the Free Cities; in many ways, his narrative choices mirror those of colonialist writers such as Rudyard Kipling and Joseph Conrad.

The first introduction the reader has to a non-Westerosi society is early in the first book, through the eyes of Daenerys Targaryen as she is given in marriage to a Dothraki warlord. The wedding celebration provides the first impression of Dothraki society both for the reader and Daenerys; Illyrio tells Daenerys that "[a] Dothraki wedding without at least three deaths is deemed a dull affair."[42] He also tells her that the Dothraki do not have the same conception of shame or privacy as the people of the Free Cities and have sex out in the open, like animals.[43] While these statements can be read as Illyrio's particular view of the Dothraki, colored by his bias against them

[39] Abdul R. JanMohamad, "The Economy of the Manichean Allegory: The Function of Racial Difference in Colonialist Literature," in *"Race," Writing, and Difference*, edited by Henry Louis Gates, Jr. (Chicago: University of Chicago Press, 1985), 82.

[40] Ibid., 80–1.

[41] Ibid., 81.

[42] Martin, *A Game of Thrones*, 103.

[43] Ibid., 103.

as a city-bred man, the described events of the wedding are more objective; while the reader sees the events through Daenerys' point of view and interpretation, the culture itself is presented quite straightforwardly. The women of the *khalasar* dance for Drogo while the men watch, until the men interfere in the dancing: "One of them finally stepped into the circle, grabbed a dancer by the arm, and mounted her right there, as a stallion mounts a mare."[44] Several other warriors join in, until two men fight over a woman, the loser is disemboweled, and the winner finds another woman and has sex with her immediately. As Young puts it, the portrayal of the Dothraki as slavers who engage in public sex and violence "invokes the Orientalist imaginings of Otherness as sexually depraved."[45] Though the wedding scene is likely intended to show Daenerys' plight, thrust into a culture utterly alien to her own with no period of adjustment, it sets the tone for the reader's expectations of the Dothraki. Although Daenerys comes to embrace the Dothraki culture, their practices are still totally unfamiliar to a Western reader. For example, in order to ensure the health of her unborn child, Daenerys must consume an entire raw horse heart:

> The heart of a stallion would make her son strong and swift and fearless, or so the Dothraki believed, but only if the mother could eat it all. If she choked on the blood or retched up the flesh, the omens were less favorable; the child might be stillborn, or come forth weak, deformed, or female.[46]

Though Daenerys has come to accept the warrior culture that would consider "female" as undesirable as "deformed," it is an attitude that a contemporary Western reader will likely find less acceptable, and it codes the Dothraki as savage and barbaric in contrast to Daenerys' civilized attitudes.

Even Daenerys' acceptance has its limits, which she discovers when Drogo begins raiding peaceful villages to gather the wealth needed to invade Westeros. The *khalasar*'s warriors gather women and children

[44] Ibid., 103.
[45] Young, *Race and Popular Fantasy Literature*, 68.
[46] Martin, *A Game of Thrones*, 489–90.

to sell as slaves, and while Daenerys pities their fate, she does not avert it. Only the cries of a young girl stir her to action. She orders her personal bloodriders to stop the rape, which her Westerosi knight Jorah finds perplexing, claiming, "You have a gentle heart, but you do not understand. This is how it has always been. Those men have shed blood for the *khal*. Now they claim their reward."[47] In order to stop the rapes, Daenerys claims all of the female slaves for her own, taking them under her protection. This incident marks the beginning of her rejection of the markers of barbarism that Martin has placed in the text, particularly rape and slavery.

Slavery becomes a central motif for Daenerys' interactions with eastern cultures, and Martin frequently uses slavery as shorthand for barbarism or poor moral character. Jorah Mormont is an exile from Westeros because he engaged in slave trading; he escaped Westeros before Eddard Stark could execute him.[48] This revelation establishes Jorah's lack of trustworthiness early, and his callous disregard for the lives of others – as seen in his words to Daenerys about the rape above – and lack of honor continue through the books. Jorah convinces Daenerys to buy slaves to fight her battle for Westeros, and when Daenerys protests that her brother Rhaegar, whom she strives to emulate, only led free men into battle, Jorah replies that "Rhaegar lost on the Trident. He lost the battle, he lost the war, he lost the kingdom, and he lost his life. [...] Rhaegar fought valiantly, Rhaegar fought nobly, Rhaegar fought honorably. And Rhaegar *died*."[49] Jorah, then, is cast as a civilized man who has come to "sympathize or consort with the natives," a role usually villainous in colonialist literature, and certainly not heroic here.[50] Jorah serves as Daenerys' go-between, explaining Dothraki culture to her because the Dothraki seem incapable of or uninterested in doing so, instead expecting her to assimilate with no explanation beyond "it is known."

Despite the heavy-handed approach to slavery as an immoral act and those who engage in it as immoral people, the condition of slavery

47 Ibid., 666–8.

48 Ibid., 111.

49 Martin, *A Storm of Swords*, 330.

50 JanMohamed, 91.

is often a grey area in the novels. Daenerys agrees to buy a slave army, called the Unsullied, from Astapor in order to facilitate her invasion of Westeros. Jorah convinces her to buy slaves rather than raise a free army partly by telling her how awful war is:

> Your Grace [...] I saw King's Landing after the Sack. Babes were butchered that day as well, and old men, and children at play. More women were raped than you can count. There is a savage beast in every man, and when you hand that man a sword or spear and send him forth to war, the beast stirs. The scent of blood is all it takes to wake him. Yet I have never heard of these Unsullied raping, nor putting a city to the sword, nor even plundering, save at the express command of those who lead them.[51]

Since it is Jorah who convinces Daenerys to buy the slaves, and Jorah's attitudes so often align with those portrayed as typically "Essos," one could argue that Daenerys' agreeing to buy the slaves is a sign that the east, through Jorah, is corrupting her. However, having consented to purchase the Unsullied, she then turns them against the slavers of Astapor. After they sack the city and free the slaves, Daenerys frees the Unsullied from slavery, yet they do not leave her service. Likewise, Missandei, a slave girl included with the Unsullied as a gift, stays with Daenerys after being freed because she has nowhere else to go.[52] Though Daenerys frees all of her slaves, they continue to serve her because they know no other life. Others request the right to return to slavery, much to Daenerys' surprise; Daario explains that these are "well spoken and gently born [...] Such slaves are prized. In the Free Cities they will be tutors, scribes, bed slaves, even healers and priests. They will sleep in soft beds, eat rich foods, and dwell in manses. Here they have lost all, and live in fear and squalor."[53] The lack of personality or character development in most of the former slaves exemplifies Naamen Gobert Tilahun's statement that in colonialist literature, the colonized people "are not allowed to participate in

[51] Martin, *A Storm of Swords*, 328–9.
[52] Ibid., 372.
[53] Ibid., 984.

their own liberation."[54] Daenerys does not seem to respect the slaves of Essos so much as she seeks to assuage her own guilt about and discomfort with slavery by setting them free.

Finally, Martin presents a disturbing theory of slavery through Tyrion Lannister, who thinks that many slaves have better lives than Westerosi peasants: "Slaves were chattels, aye. They could be bought and sold, whipped and branded, used for the carnal pleasure of their owners, bred to make more slaves. In that sense they were no more than dogs or horses. But most lords treated dogs and horses well enough."[55] Besides, Tyrion thinks, there is always a choice: "*There has never been a slave who did not choose to be a slave* [...] *Their choice may be between bondage and death, but the choice is always there.*"[56] Though this attitude characterizes Tyrion's privilege – before being taken into slavery, he was the son of a powerful Westerosi lord, acting Hand of the King, and Master of Coin – it also casts slavery even further into a morally grey area and ventures uncomfortably close to victim-blaming; if a person can choose to die rather than be a slave, then it is ultimately that person's own fault that he or she is a slave, not the slavers'. Tyrion's ideas are reinforced by some of the slaves' request that they be allowed to return to slavery, as they actively choose to be slaves; in their case, the discomfort and possible death by starvation they face as free men and women is less appealing than the softer lives lived in slavery. As the former slaves are left to starve in the street or hired at less-than-living wages by their former masters, the only bearable option they see is to return to slavery. There is also never any mention of Daenerys paying the "freed" slaves who continue to serve her. All of this serves to imply that some people are not meant to be free or take care of themselves, that slavery is their "rightful" or "natural" place, much as the feudal, three-estates structure of Westerosi society insists that people's placement within that society is natural and rightful.

[54] Naamen Gobert Tilahun, "Thoughts on 'Colonialism ... in ... Space!' and on the Ground," in *The Wis-Con Chronicles: Provocative Essays on Feminism, Race, Revolution, and the Future*, vol. 2, edited by L. Timmel Duchamp and Eileen Gunn (Seattle: Aqueduct Press, 2008), 42.

[55] Martin, *A Dance with Dragons*, 952.

[56] Ibid., 952.

Slavery is a difficult topic in *A Song of Ice and Fire*, perhaps because Martin's medievalism and liberalism come into conflict. The hallmark of the former is an insistence on what he sees as historical accuracy, yet today we cannot accept slavery as a normative practice. Thus, the institution of slavery continues to be a marker of immorality, perhaps because point-of-view characters with whom the reader is supposed to agree, such as Ned and Daenerys, see it so. Meereen in particular is cast as a hive of immorality. In her quest to free the slaves of Essos, Daenerys uses her dragons and Unsullied to sack the cities of Slaver's Bay. As they approach Meereen, they discover that not only have the Meereenese lords burned the fields between Yunkai and Meereen, they have also "nailed a slave child up on every milepost along the coast road from Yunkai, nailed them up still living with their entrails hanging out and one arm always outstretched to point the way to Meereen."[57] After Daenerys takes and occupies the city, the former masters begin fighting back, forming the Sons of the Harpy and engaging in guerrilla tactics against her Unsullied as they patrol the streets; Barristan brings her the body of one named Stalwart Shield, who was stabbed at least six times, his body left in the street with a harpy drawn in his own blood near his head and a goat's genitals forced down his throat.[58] The Sons escalate their attacks until one night nine men lie dead in the streets, both Unsullied and former slaves, particularly those former slaves who became too successful in their new professions or too outspoken against their former masters.[59] The masters of the city are not only trying to make Daenerys leave, but they are also punishing those she freed for being and acting free.

Perhaps the clearest mark of barbarism in the city is the fighting pits, which Daenerys agrees to reopen as part of the price of peace in the city. The first fighter to die is a sixteen-year-old boy, whom Daenerys' consort Hizdahr insists is a grown man, fully knowledgeable and consenting to this fate.[60] However, Daenerys draws the line at loosing lions on a pair of dwarven jousters (Tyrion and Penny, though she

[57] Martin, *A Storm of Swords*, 775.
[58] Martin, *A Dance with Dragons*, 41–2.
[59] Ibid., 168.
[60] Ibid., 758.

does not know that), claiming that they cannot consent as the boy did. Hizdahr and the pit master argue that failing to release the lions will disappoint the people and ruin the fun, but Daenerys insists. The people of the city are shown to be a bloodthirsty mob, "scream[ing] its approval" when fighters die, and "hiss[ing] their disapproval" when the dwarves are allowed to leave unscathed.[61] When the noise and blood attracts Drogon, Daenerys' largest and wildest dragon, Hizdahr's reaction to Drogon killing and eating one of the fighters is "a queer look [...] part fear, part lust, part rapture."[62] Hizdahr, as the owner of most of the fighting pits in the city, as well as one of the possible leaders of the Sons of the Harpy, represents the worst of the Meereenese: power-hungry, bloodthirsty, and corrupt. In this way, the people of Essos are shown to be savage, even evil, and ultimately irredeemable, leading to Daenerys' decision to stay and rule Meereen rather than return to Westeros.

Martin includes no Meereenese POV characters to provide a different perspective, just as there are no Dothraki POV characters. Indeed, there are no POV characters who originate from any of Martin's eastern cultures, so the only perspectives provided are Daenerys', Barristan's, Quentyn's, and Tyrion's; all four of these characters are originally from Westeros. Martin thus relegates all things eastern to a subaltern state, failing to allow the east to speak for itself.[63] When asked about the two-dimensionality of the Dothraki, Martin replied, "I haven't had a Dothraki viewpoint character, though," indicating that the internal view of the Dothraki would be different from the external view provided through Daenerys.[64] Yet Martin has no plans to resolve this issue: "I could introduce a Dothraki viewpoint character, but I already have like sixteen viewpoint characters."[65] He also argues

[61] Ibid., 757–9.

[62] Ibid., 761–2.

[63] Gayatri Chakravorty Spivak analyses the idea of the subaltern and the tendency for the privileged classes to speak for a colonized or otherwise subordinated group, in the process essentializing and Othering said group, in her essay "Can the Subaltern Speak?" in *Can the Subaltern Speak? Reflections on the History of an Idea*, edited by Rosalind C. Morris (New York: Columbia University Press, 2010), 21–78.

[64] Anders, n.p.

[65] Ibid., n.p.

that while the Dothraki seem barbaric, they are partly based on the Mongols, who "became very sophisticated at certain points, but they were certainly not sophisticated when they started out, and even at the height of their sophistication they were fond of doing things like giant piles of heads."[66] Though Martin's world is entirely imaginative, his claims to historical realism and attempts to find the "truth" of such issues as chivalry, politics, communication, and labor in the Middle Ages would seem to demand an attempt at such "truth" for the Middle East, as well. Instead, he constructs his eastern city-states much as Said argues the Occident constructed the Orient in the late Middle Ages and early Renaissance.[67] This is perhaps enlightening as regards his authorial practice, as all authors' historical research and accuracy are inevitably bound not only by their own cultural position, but also by that of the historians they read. However, that Martin is content to portray the eastern cultures and characters entirely externally, with no attempt to explain their behavior or traditions from the inside, is troubling, especially when considered in light of Daenerys' character and choices.

"Is there no way to please these people?": Daenerys as White Savior

While Martin makes it clear that the leaders of Slaver's Bay are corrupt, at least from the viewpoint of a Westerosi character or Western reader, Daenerys' choice to take down the slave trade carries many markers of the "white savior" trope or the "white man's burden." Coined by Rudyard Kipling in 1899, the phrase "white man's burden" refers to the tendency of Western people to believe they have a duty to colonize and rule non-Western, non-white peoples for their own betterment.[68] Daenerys believes herself the rightful ruler of Westeros because she is the last living Targaryen, and frequently lays claim to certain virtues because she is "the blood of the dragon." Yet she turns away from her

66 Ibid., n.p.

67 Said, 3–5.

68 Plamen Makariev, "Eurocentrism," in *The Encyclopedia of the Developing World*, volume 1, edited by Thomas M. Leonard (New York: Routledge, 2006), 636.

plan to invade and retake Westeros in order to combat the slave trade in Essos. Her decision to free the slaves of Essos is never explained in the text; the only reason given is her discomfort with the suffering of the people, first the victims of her own *khalasar*, though she only protects the women, and then the people of the cities of Slaver's Bay. After she protects the women of the raided village from rape, she has an overinflated idea of both her own impact and the appreciation of the women. Mirri Maz Duur, the village healing woman, disabuses her of that notion by tricking her into taking place in a ritual that leads to her baby's death; Daenerys tells Mirri "I spoke for you. […] I saved you." Mirri replies:

> Three riders had taken me, not as a man takes a woman, but from behind, as a dog takes a bitch. The fourth was in me when you rode past. How then did you save me? I saw my god's house burn, where I had healed good men beyond counting. My home they burned as well, and in the street I saw piles of heads. […] Tell me again what you saved.[69]

Despite this forthright rejection of Daenerys' idea that her intervention merits appreciation and service in return, Daenerys does not learn the lesson immediately. This failure is partly due to Martin's characterization of the slaves she frees as she moves through Slaver's Bay; when Daenerys' army takes Yunkai, the freed slaves gather around her crying "*mhysa*," which Missandei tells her means "mother."[70] This is the reaction Daenerys expects, both because of her actions in freeing the slaves and because of a vision she was granted of this moment in the House of the Undying.[71] Daenerys thinks of the slaves as her children, partly because she is barren after having miscarried her first child, partly because they call her "mother." She assumes a mother's responsibility for them, refusing to force them to fend for themselves outside Meereen, where there is no food, arguing, "I will not march my people off to die," while thinking, "*My children.*"[72] Tilahun argues

[69] Martin, *A Game of Thrones*, 760.
[70] Martin, *A Storm of Swords*, 588.
[71] Martin, *A Clash of Kings*, 707.
[72] Martin, *A Storm of Swords*, 783.

that the colonized people's lack of agency "marks the culture and its people as needing supervision: in other words, they are in need of colonization and the patriarchal white guiding hand that comes with it. At the same time, the whole culture is set up as nothing more than props for the spiritual advancement of the protagonist."[73] Daenerys' insistence on thinking of the slaves as children, and Martin's choice to enable that line of thinking through the faceless mob of former slaves calling her "mother," disenfranchises the newly freed slaves, denying them responsibility for and ownership of their newfound freedom. Like children, they need guidance, and they immediately turn to Daenerys for want of any other adult figure. Ironically, Daenerys is not much more than a child herself: she is about fifteen years old when she frees the slaves of Essos. Hence, her insistence on acting as a savior may be read as youthful naiveté and exuberance, but the authorial decision to have the slaves worship her is controversial.

Though Mirri's lesson is restated when some of the slaves ask to be allowed to return to slavery, since freedom offers a lower standard of living than that to which they have become accustomed, Daenerys still does not quite learn it. Despite her people urging her to leave Slaver's Bay behind and return to her plan to conquer Westeros, Daenerys decides to stay in Meereen, asking them, "How can I rule seven kingdoms if I cannot rule a single city?"[74] She means to use Meereen as practice, declaring, "[m]y children need time to heal and learn. My dragons need time to grow and test their wings. And I need the same."[75] Thus, Daenerys does not seem to see Meereen as a real place, or its people as real people; rather, they are a group on which she can practice without fear of failure, because she can leave for Westeros at any time. She sees herself as an example of propriety for the Meereenese, a civilizing force. She finds the Meereenese ungrateful for her leadership; they leave a session of court in "sullen silence," making Daenerys think, "*They have what they came for. Is there no way to please these people?*"[76] To Martin's credit, other than the hordes

[73] Tilahun, 42.
[74] Martin, *A Storm of Swords*, 995.
[75] Ibid., 995.
[76] Ibid., 56.

of freed slaves who serve Daenerys and call her "mother," few of the people she thinks she is helping cooperate, indicating that they do not see her as a savior, but rather as an uninvited foreign interloper. However, Daenerys' centrality to the plot of *A Song of Ice and Fire* casts her as a positive protagonist, if not a hero, and the expectation that she will eventually rule Westeros serves to reinforce her role as conqueror, which may lead readers to believe her actions are justified and righteous. Thus, Martin invites the self-congratulatory gaze of the white imperialist by idealizing his white savior and demonizing those who wish to be free from her influence and rule.

Since contemporary writers are, by definition, outsiders to the medieval cultures about which they write, they may struggle to escape assumptions and generalizations that can lead to potentially racist or otherwise oversimplified characterizations of medieval or non-Western people. Even well-intentioned attempts to provide these cultures with a voice may fail when the writer's cultural background does not provide the insight or knowledge necessary to fully characterize a culture outside his or her own. Of course, I am not arguing that Western authors should not include people of color or non-Western cultures in their works, or that contemporary writers should not attempt to recreate past cultures, especially if their aim is to draw attention to the tendency to omit these people from fantasy works, or to give voice to a traditionally silenced group. However, careful consideration must be given to the impact of the portrayal of non-Western peoples, especially if they have contemporary analogues; postcolonial approaches can help to illuminate these impacts. Martin's imperialist depiction of the Middle Ages is hardly new or unique – rather, it continues traditions laid down in the very foundations of fantasy literature – but it does approach the period in interesting ways that bear and invite scrutiny. In many ways, he works to avoid these received habits and the Manichean allegory, but while he frequently succeeds, the construction of non-Western peoples that permeates Western culture and fantasy literature continues to creep in.

5

Adaptation and Reception

WHEN *A SONG of Ice and Fire* began to climb the bestseller charts and *The Lord of the Rings* film franchise was a box-office smash, Hollywood began looking for the next fantasy epic, and naturally lit on Martin's work. Having worked in Hollywood before returning to novel writing, Martin was understandably nervous about entrusting his series, which he claimed was written "with an eye toward unproduceability,"[1] to Hollywood executives. "There's so many cases where they just keep the title and change everything," he commented.[2] Various studios wanted to adapt only part of the story – perhaps one character's storyline – or to commit to just a single film rather than a series. Martin was, fortunately, in a financial position that allowed him to turn down all of these suggestions.[3] He was determined that only HBO, which had pioneered the trend of morally grey antiheroes on television with *The Sopranos*, could do his work justice.[4]

In 2005, David Benioff and D.B. Weiss, having read the books and loved them, met with Martin to pitch their idea for an HBO series. The lunch lasted hours and concluded with Martin asking Benioff and Weiss who Jon Snow's mother was as a litmus test for their interest in the story in the books. "Maybe if we had gotten it

[1] Sam Thielman, "Cabler Rises to Epic Challenge," *Variety*, March 12, 2011, http://variety.com/2011/tv/news/cabler-rises-to-epic-challenge-1118033764/.

[2] "Making *Game of Thrones*," *Game of Thrones: The Complete First Season*, HBO, 2011.

[3] Jack Seale, "George R.R. Martin: Hollywood Would Have Ruined *Game of Thrones*," *The Guardian*, June 10, 2015, https://www.theguardian.com/tv-and-radio/tvandradioblog/2015/jun/10/george-rr-martin-hollywood-would-have-ruined-game-of-thrones.

[4] "Making *Game of Thrones*."

wrong, he would have let us do it anyway," Weiss says. "It was still obvious that we love this, and that we wanted to do it more than anything in the world, and that we would respect it and honor it. I think getting (the answer) right probably helped."[5] Martin, in turn, thought that Benioff and Weiss were "mad"; "It's too big," he recalls telling them, "It's too complicated. It's too expensive. HBO doesn't do fantasy." But Benioff and Weiss' enthusiasm convinced him.[6] Benioff and Weiss took Martin's permission and their pitch to HBO, and in March of 2010, HBO announced that it had greenlit the series for production and a basic cast – Sean Bean, Mark Addy, Peter Dinklage, Lena Headey, and Tamzin Merchant (who would later be replaced by Emilia Clarke).[7] Over the next few months, Martin used his "Not a Blog" Livejournal to pass on casting and production news, turning casting into a game for his fans by giving them clues regarding the actors' identities and letting them guess before officially announcing the casting. Throughout pre-production, Martin was consulted on casting, costume design, and set design, and seemed generally thrilled by the work Benioff and Weiss' team was doing.[8]

For the first four seasons, Martin wrote an episode per season, contributing "The Pointy End" (1.8), "Blackwater" (2.9), "The Bear and the Maiden Fair" (3.7), and "The Lion and the Rose" (4.2). He ceased writing for the show during pre-production for season five, as the show had begun to catch up with the books, and he felt his time needed to be focused on writing *The Winds of Winter*. When it became clear to everyone involved that *The Winds of Winter* would not be released before *Game of Thrones* season five, or even season six, Benioff and Weiss flew to Martin's home in Santa Fe, New Mexico, and spent a week with him, learning his plans for each character and

[5] Debra Birnbaum, "*Game of Thrones* Creators: We Know How it's Going to End," *Variety*, April 15, 2015, http://variety.com/2015/tv/news/game-of-thrones-ending-season-5-producers-interview-1201469516/.

[6] George R.R. Martin, "Preface: From Page to Screen," in *Inside HBO's "Game of Thrones": Seasons One and Two*, edited by Bryan Cogman (San Francisco: Chronicle Books, 2012), 5.

[7] Dave Itzkoff, "HBO will Play *Game of Thrones*," *New York Times*, March 2, 2010, http://artsbeat.blogs.nytimes.com/2010/03/02/hbo-will-play-game-of-thrones/.

[8] "From the Book to Screen."

the end of the books.[9] By season six, despite Martin's best efforts, the show had moved beyond the books and into uncharted territory even for book readers.

This chapter examines the treatment in *Game of Thrones* of the topics hitherto discussed in *A Song of Ice and Fire* and is organized in roughly the same order. It also includes a broader consideration of the challenges and issues that adapting a novel series to television presents, and of how Benioff, Weiss, and their team handle these challenges. Attention will also be paid to how the media and fans react to the adaptation, as well as how the production team presents their work to the media. While ideally the show would be examined on its own merits, such an examination is practically impossible for a critic so familiar with the books. Wherever possible, the internal logic and implications of plot, characterization, and writing of the show alone will be discussed, but comparisons with the books are unavoidable.

"The show is the show": Issues with Adaptation

As with any cinematic adaptation of a prose work, changes must be made to accommodate the new format. For *Game of Thrones*, a few alterations were immediately obvious and necessary: the age of the children had to be raised to prevent issues with the sexual content (particularly in Daenerys' storyline), and the sheer size of the cast needed to be reduced. These differences, while small, amplified as the series went on and as Benioff and Weiss made further changes to the story. Not all of these deviations were necessary for production reasons, but many were logical consequences of earlier, smaller alterations.[10] Martin has referred to these escalating differences as the "butterfly effect" of adaptation, and claimed that "the show is the show, the books are the books; two different tellings of the same

[9] Jim Windolf, "The *Game of Thrones* TV-Show Creators Already Know What Happens at the End of the Book Series," *Vanity Fair*, March 24, 2014, https://www.vanityfair.com/hollywood/2014/03/game-of-thrones-show-creators-know-end-of-books.

[10] For more details on changes and how they play out throughout the show, see my blog series "*Game of Thrones* Rewatch" on the Tales After Tolkien blog: https://talesaftertolkien.blogspot.com.

story."[11] Despite the differences, Benioff and Weiss tend to lean heavily on Martin and the books to explain their narrative choices; as early as 2011, Weiss explained the pervasiveness of rape in the show by claiming that Westeros is "not our world but it's a real world, and it's a violent world, a more brutal world. [...] We felt that shying away from these things would be doing a disservice to the reality and groundedness of George's vision."[12] Occasionally, showrunners, directors, or actors would make claims that gave Martin credit or blame for moments in the show that never actually appeared in the books; in the commentary track for "The Old Gods and the New" (2.6), for instance, Vanessa Taylor ascribes the scene of Sansa's near-rape to Martin, claiming that "he really goes there in the books." Kit Harrington (Jon Snow) agrees that this scene is disturbing when it happens in the books. However, in the corresponding book scene, Sansa is threatened with violence but not rape before being rescued, and the gang-rape happens to a minor character off-page.[13] (Contrarily, in at least one instance, Benioff and Weiss give Taylor credit for a scene that occurs in the books.)[14]

As Benioff and Weiss moved past the books and began to face a backlash for choices such as Shireen's death by burning and Hodor's death while "hold[ing] the door," they continued to claim that these were plot points that Martin had revealed to them as upcoming in the books. Some fans, most notably Linda Antonssen, who co-authored *The World of Ice and Fire* with Elio Garcia and Martin and co-runs the *Westeros.org* fansite, feel that these claims are unfair to the book readers, as they spoil major plot points for the books, whereas

[11] George R.R. Martin, "The Show, the Books," *Not a Blog*, May 18, 2015, http://grrm.livejournal.com/427713.html.

[12] Jace Lacob, "*Game of Thrones*' Sexual Politics," *The Daily Beast*, June 5, 2011, http://www.thedailybeast.com/game-of-thrones-sexual-politics.

[13] "The Old Gods and the New," *Game of Thrones*, written by Vanessa Taylor, directed by David Nutter (HBO, 2012).

[14] Sansa's nightmare of being stabbed in the belly and waking up to find she has started her period occurs in "A Man Without Honor" (2.7) and *A Clash of Kings*: "A Man Without Honor," *Game of Thrones*, written by David Benioff and D.B. Weiss, directed by David Nutter (HBO, 2012); Martin, *A Clash of Kings*, 757–8.

Westeros.org has worked hard to avoid spoilers for the show.[15] This tendency of Benioff and Weiss to "pass the buck" to Martin can be interpreted as a reluctance to take responsibility for their choices or to accept criticism for them.

While dozens of changes from page to screen exist, perhaps the most controversial, and thus one that most encapsulates the difficulty Benioff and Weiss have had with adapting the books, is in their treatment of Sansa and her plotline. Several other differences between screen and page tellings – most notably Theon's torture and Bran's journey north and subsequent training – were attributed to consideration of what would be "cinematic": rather than lose Alfie Allen for a season, they chose to show his torture and breaking on screen, which Martin did not; and rather than follow Bran's long journey north, they dropped that storyline for a season.[16] However, both of these still generally followed the character arcs available in the books. In contrast, Benioff and Weiss veered dramatically away from Sansa's story in the books, instead merging her story with that of Jeyne Poole (a character who appears just once in the show) and bringing her into Theon's plotline. While this is perhaps more "cinematic," it has unfortunate implications for Sansa's character arc and Benioff and Weiss' treatment of female characters in general.

In *A Feast for Crows* and the end of *A Dance with Dragons*, Sansa is at the Eyrie, where Petyr Baelish has brought her, posing as Alayne, his bastard daughter. Only Lysa Arryn, her aunt, is aware of her true identity. The subterfuge is necessary because Sansa is a fugitive, having escaped her marriage, a hostage situation, and accusations that she helped to murder King Joffrey. In this environment, Petyr trains Sansa in the "game of thrones," teaching her to negotiate the careful dance of politics in a situation in which the stakes are lower. He has plans to marry her to Harrold Hardyng, who under certain circumstances will become Lord of the Vale, and reveal her identity at that time in order

[15] Matt Saccaro, "Stop Defending *Game of Thrones*: How HBO Gutted the Stories I Love," *Salon*, June 14, 2015, http://www.salon.com/2015/06/14/stop_defending_game_of_thrones_how_hbo_gutted_the_stories_i_love/.

[16] James Hibberd, "*Game of Thrones* Showrunner Explains Why Bran is Not in Season 5," *Entertainment Weekly*, November 5, 2014, http://www.ew.com/article/2014/11/05/game-of-thrones-why-bran-season-5.

to secure both the vale and the north. The sample chapter for *The Winds of Winter* shows Sansa working to secure Hardyng's affection, practicing her courtesy and flirtation techniques under Petyr's tutelage.[17] Meanwhile, Jeyne Poole, whom Petyr has tortured and trained as a prostitute, is masquerading as Arya Stark and marries Ramsay Bolton so the Boltons can secure their claim to the north.

In season four of *Game of Thrones*, immediately after Lysa Arryn's death, Sansa reveals her true identity to the Lords of the Vale in order to prevent Petyr from being prosecuted for Lysa's death. In season five, Petyr tells Lord Royce he is taking Sansa to his childhood home in the Fingers, but instead takes her to Winterfell, convincing her that marrying Ramsay is the way to reclaim Winterfell for the Starks.[18] Once in Winterfell, Sansa's story follows Jeyne's fairly closely, including a wedding-night rape scene, confinement to her quarters, continuous physical and sexual violence, and an eventual escape with Theon.

While giving Sansa more to "do" for a season makes some sense, the choice to uproot her entire storyline and give her one that, in the books, belongs to a lower-class character who has not appeared since *A Game of Thrones* and does not truly have the Stark name behind her, is deeply problematic. What Benioff, Weiss, and Bryan Cogman, who has also defended the changes, seem not to understand is that Jeyne's story is only internally consistent for a girl like Jeyne. Despite being presented as Arya Stark, everyone knows Jeyne is not Arya; even Jaime, who barely had any interaction with Arya, is aware that she is not Arya. He makes a point of telling Brienne that the "Arya" headed north is not Arya, and not to waste her time following her.[19] The northerners are willing to pretend that Jeyne is Arya to placate the Boltons, but their awareness of her identity is clear in their failure to stop Ramsay's ill-treatment of her. Only "Abel" (Mance Rayder in disguise) and his "washerwomen" show any concern for Jeyne's safety,

[17] George R.R. Martin, "Alayne," sample chapter from *The Winds of Winter*, http://web.archive.org/web/20150604025854/http://www.georgerrmartin.com/excerpt-from-the-winds-of-winter/.

[18] "High Sparrow," *Game of Thrones*, written by David Benioff & D.B. Weiss, directed by Mark Mylod (HBO, 2016).

[19] Martin, *A Storm of Swords*, 999, 1007.

and they have no idea that she is not Arya, having been sent by Jon Snow, who believes that she *is* Arya.[20] Given the feudal politics of Westeros, it is just not plausible that the northern lords would allow such treatment to befall a trueborn daughter of the late Warden of the North and sister of the late King in the North. Likewise, bringing Sansa into this storyline reduces her to a prop for a male character's story; in this case, Martin wrote the Winterfell storyline as Theon's redemption arc. Sansa has her own arc and development outside of Winterfell that the showrunners took away from her; in the process, they undid much of her character development, once again reducing her to a victim and tool for the male characters' political games.

The differences in Sansa's story exemplify a few trends in Benioff and Weiss' adaptation of *Game of Thrones*. Frequently, in order to streamline and simplify the show, they remove or pare down the political aspects of the storylines. Sansa's book arc does not involve much action, even before she leaves King's Landing, but instead involves her learning to navigate court and developing a keen political mind. It begins as a survival mechanism: she learns what exactly to say to keep Joffrey from having her killed. As she continues, she learns to tell the difference between friends and temporary political allies, uses courtesy to gain allies at court, and recognizes her place as a valuable political pawn. Much of Sansa's development is internal; she observes and learns and communicates very little of that internal world to the people around her.

In order to externalize her story, Benioff and Weiss made small changes that sadly curtailed her character development or sent it in an unfortunate direction. Rather than fully isolating Sansa and showing how tenuous court friendships can be, Benioff and Weiss forge a true friendship between Sansa and Margaery Tyrell. Whereas in the books, the Tyrells are interested in Sansa only for her inside information on Joffrey and the possibility of wedding her to the Tyrell heir and claiming Winterfell, in the show, Margaery is genuinely interested in and fond of Sansa. Her isolation in the books is what makes her so willing to trust Dontos (who barely appears in her story in the show) and escape with him after the Purple Wedding. When the Lannisters

[20] Martin, *A Dance with Dragons*, 737.

steal a march on the Tyrells and marry Sansa to Tyrion, the Tyrells abandon her entirely: "Margaery gave her such a sad look, and when the Queen of Thorns tottered in between Left and Right, she never looked at her at all. Elinor, Alla, and Megga seemed determined not to know her. *My friends*, Sansa thought bitterly."[21] In the show, once Sansa's engagement to Tyrion is announced (several days in advance, rather than two minutes before the ceremony), Margaery sympathizes with Sansa and even talks to her about sex and encourages her to be open to the idea of having sex with Tyrion. While it makes sense to externalize her internal development for a visual medium, this could have been accomplished through discussions with Dontos or Shae, which would have kept Sansa's isolation from the noble class of King's Landing intact while still allowing the audience insight into her thoughts and overall situation.

The shift in Sansa's engagement to Tyrion creates another point at which her political development is hindered. Giving Sansa time between engagement and marriage to bond with Tyrion creates a relationship that removes the justification for one of Sansa's few moments of defiance in the books: refusing to kneel to be cloaked. Part of a Westerosi marriage ceremony involves cloaks that symbolically move the bride from one family to another; the father (or, in Sansa's case, Joffrey) removes the "bride cloak" in the bride's family's colors, and the groom replaces it with a cloak in his family's colors. The extreme difference in height between Sansa and Tyrion makes this maneuver difficult for Tyrion, and he tugs at Sansa's skirt to try to get her to kneel so he can reach her shoulders. Sansa refuses:

> She was mortified. It was not supposed to be this way. She had dreamed of her wedding a thousand times, and always she had pictured how her betrothed would stand behind her tall and strong, sweep the cloak of his protection over her shoulders, and tenderly kiss her cheek as he leaned forward to fasten the clasp.
>
> She felt another tug at her skirt, more insistent. *I won't. Why should I spare his feelings, when no one cares about mine?*[22]

[21] Martin, *A Storm of Swords*, 387.
[22] Ibid., 386.

She regrets her pride a moment later, when she sees how embarrassed Tyrion is, as well, but the moment is one of the few times she does not bend to the will of those around her. Likewise, Tyrion's method of "asking" for her to kneel is perfunctory and even rude. However, in the show, many of Tyrion's faults have been smoothed, and rather than tugging at Sansa's skirt, he asks her to kneel, and she complies.[23] In this case, Sansa's agency as a character and a clear sign of her development have been erased in favor of making fan- and author-favorite Tyrion a more sympathetic character. This is also a symptom of the overall misogyny of the series, which tends to erase women's agency or major story beats in favor of the men's.

During Sansa's time at court, she is exposed to Cersei's ideas of rulership, and vehemently (in her own mind) rejects them. She is appalled by Cersei's claim that sexuality is a weapon, and is determined that she will rule with love and kindness rather than with fear. In many ways, Sansa is set up as a foil to Cersei, working diplomatically rather than through brute force. However, when Sansa travels with Petyr to the Eyrie in the show, she seems to discover the idea of weaponized sexuality and realizes that she can use Petyr's obsession with her to control him. After she defends him to the Lords of the Vale, he asks her if she thinks she knows him, and she replies that she knows what he wants; the looks they exchange leave little doubt as to what she means. Later, she emerges from her room in a black dress that reveals her cleavage and a chunky black necklace that resembles a collar and chain. Once again, they exchange looks that make his lust and her awareness of his lust clear.[24] According to Michelle Clapton, the costume designer for seasons one through five, Benioff and Weiss wanted Sansa's new wardrobe to indicate that she is "her own woman rather than this victim," and that the necklace is "a miniature of Arya's sword, Needle, and the idea is that there's a ring that you stitch through and that's her weapon."[25] That being "her own

[23] "Second Sons," *Game of Thrones*, written by David Benioff & D.B. Weiss, directed by Michelle McLaren (HBO, 2014).

[24] "The Mountain and the Viper," *Game of Thrones*, written by David Benioff & D.B. Weiss, directed by Alex Graves (HBO, 2015).

[25] Taylor, 148.

woman" requires her to flaunt her sexuality in order to manipulate a man is unsettling.

This exemplifies another problem Benioff and Weiss have displayed in their adaptation: women who engage with politics primarily do so through their sexuality. Margaery, Cersei, and even Olenna are shown to use or to have used their sexuality to manipulate the men around them into giving them what they want (Cersei, oddly enough, does so less in the show than in the books). While Daenerys does not use her sexuality in her politics, being more likely to use her youth to lure men into underestimating her, her interest in Daario has been brought to the fore in the show. As troubling as the foregrounding of the prominent women's sexuality is, they are all grown women, whereas Sansa is, at most, fifteen in this scene. Her age can be easy to forget, given that Sophie Turner is twenty years old and does not look like a fifteen-year-old, but she tells Tyrion after the wedding that she is fourteen.[26] Thus, her sudden grasp of seduction tactics is deeply unsettling.

Finally, even internally to the show's own story, the politics surrounding marrying Sansa to Ramsay Bolton are not consistent. That Petyr would enter into such an arrangement without having all of the necessary facts, considering how carefully he has played the game up to this point, stretches credulity. That he would not have heard of Ramsay's excesses – which, interestingly, are less than the rumors spread in the books[27] – is likewise difficult to believe. That Roose would endanger his position by defying the very house that gave him said position is slightly more believable, as Roose is power-hungry and recognizes the advantage of having the entire north behind him rather than a single southern house that has lost its most powerful member. However, the mechanics of marriage are ignored in marrying Sansa off while Tyrion is still presumed alive; just because he has been labeled a traitor does not invalidate the marriage – in the novels, Petyr says that the betrothal he has arranged for her "must wait

[26] "The Bear and the Maiden Fair," *Game of Thrones*, written by George R.R. Martin, directed by Michelle MacLaren (HBO, 2014).

[27] Lady Hornwood's marriage to Ramsay and subsequent starving to death are not mentioned, nor is the fact that Ramsay frequently hunts young women with his hounds and then names his hounds after the ones he kills.

until Cersei's done and Sansa's safely widowed."[28] Finally, the structure of the plot clearly mirrors Sansa's earlier marriage to Tyrion: Ramsay stands as Tyrion, the reluctant groom; Roose as Tywin, the patriarch who arranges the marriage; and Myranda as Shae, the mistress who is jealous of Sansa and the marriage. Thus, Sansa's plot in season five is merely a more sinister retreading of a path already followed, moving her character development backward rather than forward.

Besides watering-down the political element of the story, the changes to Sansa's story also display a tendency for the showrunners to defend their choices and provide excuses for scenes or issues that have disturbed viewers. Bryan Cogman, who wrote "Unbowed, Unbent, Unbroken" (5.6), the episode in which Sansa's rape takes place, sought to justify the scene by claiming that Sansa is no longer a "timid little girl," but a "hardened woman making a choice."[29] He also claimed that they gave this storyline to Sansa because the audience was already "invested" in her.[30] However, as mentioned above, Jeyne Poole disappeared for several books before being reintroduced for this role, and readers were still able to empathize with her plight. Jeremy Podeswa, the director of "Unbowed, Unbent, Unbroken," also seems to fail to grasp why viewers, especially book-reading viewers, were upset with this scene; he claims the complaints were about the "notion," not the "execution," and claims that not showing the rape itself on screen lessened the horror and impact of it.[31] However, the choice to instead focus on Theon's face makes him the center of attention, which again places Sansa's storyline in a subordinate position to Theon's. Cogman does not believe that this was the case, claiming that the cinematic choice does not "take Sansa's story away from her" and that they did not "shoehorn" her into "Theon's redemption journey," but he does

[28] Martin, *A Feast for Crows*, 893.

[29] James Hibberd, "*Game of Thrones* Producer Explains Sansa's Wedding Night Horror," *Entertainment Weekly*, May 17, 2015. http://www.ew.com/article/2015/05/17/game-thrones-sansa-ramsay-interview.

[30] James Hibberd, "*Game of Thrones* Producers Explain Changing Sansa's Storyline," *Entertainment Weekly*, April 26, 2015. http://www.ew.com/article/2015/04/26/game-thrones-sansa-ramsay-interview.

[31] Don Groves, "*Game of Thrones* Rape Scene Repercussions Play Out in New Season," *Forbes*, December 18, 2015, https://archive.is/E2Kvh.

acknowledge that some people read it that way and apologizes for the implications.[32]

Cogman is the only one to recognize that perhaps cinematic mistakes were made in *Game of Thrones*, and that those mistakes may have introduced troubling elements. A similar problem arose in season four's "Breaker of Chains" (4.3), in which Jaime and Cersei have sexual relations in the Sept, next to Joffrey's body. The scene caused an uproar because it appeared to show Jaime raping his sister; she says, "not here," "no," and "it isn't right," while he grabs her by the back of the head, forcibly kisses her, pushes her to the floor, and penetrates her, repeating, "I don't care."[33] This scene caused serious backlash in the media and fan communities, not only because it showed the rape of a main character on screen, but because its book antecedent was clearly consensual and in the midst of Jaime's redemption arc.[34] The showrunners' reaction was odd and internally contradictory. Graves gave several interviews the day the episode aired, and in one, he calls the incident "rape" and "forced sex."[35] Yet in another, he claims that the sex "becomes consensual by the end" because Cersei is turned on by the power struggle.[36] In yet another, he claims that Cersei consents because she is attempting to manipulate Jaime into killing Tyrion for her, and that Cersei wrapping her legs around Jaime (which is not

[32] Audio commentary on "Unbowed, Unbent, Unbroken," *Game of Thrones*, written by Bryan Cogman, directed by Jeremy Podeswa (HBO, 2016).

[33] "Breaker of Chains," *Game of Thrones*, written by David Benioff & D.B. Weiss, directed by Alex Graves (HBO, 2015).

[34] See, for example, Erik Kain, "*Game of Thrones* Season 4, Episode 3 Review: Sex and Violence," *Forbes*, April 21, 2014, http://www.forbes.com/sites/erikkain/2014/04/21/game-of-thrones-season-4-episode-3-review-sex-and-violence/#5a19431c1734; Alyssa Rosenberg, "*Game of Thrones* Review: 'Breaker of Chains,' Breakers of Will," *Washington Post*, April 20, 2014, https://www.washingtonpost.com/news/act-four/wp/2014/04/20/game-of-thrones-review-breaker-of-chains-breakers-of-will/?utm_term=.a55018b1a337.

[35] Aaron Couch, "*Game of Thrones* Director on Controversial Scene: Jaime 'Traumatized,' Cersei 'a Wreck' (Q&A)," *Hollywood Reporter*, April 20, 2014. http://www.hollywoodreporter.com/live-feed/game-thrones-director-controversial-scene-697733.

[36] Alan Sepinwall, "Review: *Game of Thrones* – 'Breaker of Chains': Uncle Deadly?" *HitFix*, April 20, 2014. http://www.hitfix.com/whats-alan-watching/review-game-of-thrones-breaker-of-chains-uncle-deadly.

visible in the finished cut) and kissing him indicate that consent.[37] So, according to Graves, either the scene was written as a rape scene and he shot it as written, or it was meant to be consensual, or it was somewhere in between.

Martin responded to the controversy by distancing himself from it; he claimed that while Benioff and Weiss frequently run plot points past him, he did not recall them discussing this particular scene.[38] He pointed out that the context for the scene is entirely different from in the books, with Jaime's time in the Riverlands shortened and his return to King's Landing accelerated. At least twice, he said he wished that Benioff and Weiss had kept some of the book dialogue, which (despite the scene being presented from Jaime's point of view) makes it much clearer that Cersei is consenting to the sex, and that her protests are because of the venue, not because of the sex act itself.[39]

Benioff and Weiss, however, barely acknowledged the issue; in the "Inside the Episode" feature, released soon after the episode aired, Benioff refers to the scene as "horrifying," saying that Cersei is resisting and Jaime is "forcing himself on her."[40] This directly contradicts Graves' claim that the scene was not written as rape, or at least did not end up as rape. Benioff and Weiss were subsequently silent on this issue until March 2015, when directly asked about it in a Q&A forum. Benioff's response was halting and meandering, but repeated the claim that the scene depicted rape and was meant to, that they were aware that it was horrifying, and that they write what the story

[37] Denise Martin, "Breaking Down Jaime and Cersei's Controversial Scene with Last Night's *Game of Thrones* Director," *Vulture*, April 21, 2014, http://www.vulture.com/2014/04/game-of-thrones-director-on-the-rape-sex-scene.html.

[38] George R.R. Martin, Comment on "Author! Author!" *Not a Blog*, August 21, 2014, 8:16 pm, http://grrm.livejournal.com/367116.html?thread=19030284#t19030284.

[39] Ibid., n.p.; Annaliza Savage, "George R.R. Martin on *Game of Thrones*, that Controversial Rape Scene, and His Writing Progress," *The Daily Beast*, September 28, 2014, http://www.thedailybeast.com/articles/2014/07/28/george-r-r-martin-on-game-of-thrones-that-controversial-rape-scene-and-his-writing-progress.html.

[40] "*Game of Thrones* Season 4 – Inside the Episode #3," *YouTube*, 4:35, posted by "HBO", June 17, 2014, https://www.youtube.com/watch?v=kk9UEr74BIg.

calls for without concern for what sort of controversy it might cause.[41] Interestingly, "Breaker of Chains" is the only episode on the season four DVD/BluRay set that does not include a commentary track, which would have given writers, director, and/or actors a chance to discuss the controversy, much as Cogman did in the "Unbowed, Unbent, Unbroken" commentary track. This appears to be the one major controversy (and the show has created many) for which the showrunners do not have a clear and forceful defense, instead remaining mostly silent and allowing the director to bear the brunt of the criticism. That the director's explanation for the differences between show and book contradict Benioff and Weiss' has never been addressed.

While changes are necessary to create a story that can be filmed, many of the changes made by Benioff and Weiss run counter to the themes of the books they are adapting, yet they frequently pass blame for controversial scenes or stories to Martin rather than acknowledging how their own decisions helped to cause the controversy. Story moments are not the only element for which Benioff and Weiss avoid responsibility; they also often pass details of worldbuilding to Martin or the Middle Ages and thus engage in neomedieval thinking.

"It's not our world, but it's a real world": Neomedievalism in the Show

As discussed in the introduction, contemporary fiction is at two levels of remove from the medieval: medievalist, which is based on medieval historical or literary antecedents known to the author, and neomedieval, which is based on those author's portrayals of the Middle Ages rather than on the historically medieval. *A Song of Ice and Fire* is a blend of medievalist and neomedieval, as Martin has studied the history and culture of medieval England but taken some obvious liberties with the material to create his world, and shows clear influence from Tolkien. *Game of Thrones*, on the other hand, is

[41] "*Game of Thrones* at the Oxford Union," *YouTube*, 1:15:14, posted by "Oxford Union", March 20, 2015, https://www.youtube.com/watch?v=TfvVluNxujc.

purely neomedieval, as it is based entirely on Martin's work and the showrunners are not medieval scholars of any sort. Once again, this is not a judgment, and no inherent problems exist with neomedieval texts. The difficulty arises when the showrunners insist on historical authenticity to explain away some of the more controversial issues in the show.

"Authenticity" in historically based TV shows is hardly new; Shannon McSheffrey examines the tendency of showrunners to "invoke the copious amounts of 'historical research' that underpins what appears on the screen."[42] She speculates that this invocation is primarily a marketing tool, but points out that it places the show-runners, publicists, and actors in a "double bind" wherein writers, directors, and actors make "internally contradictory statements: the film or program is 'all true,' but it's a fiction so we've taken liberties; it's accurate, but historians cannot agree anyway and so our interpretation is as good as theirs; it's based on rigorous research but it's only a movie."[43] *Game of Thrones* has more leeway in this regard because it is not based on a specific historical incident, time, or story, but on Martin's blending of many different stories, cultures, incidents, and people. Yet showrunners, directors, and actors still routinely invoke the Middle Ages to explain away the frequent rape, the lack of racial diversity, and the treatment of women, and their discussion of the Middle Ages tends to be broad and vague. Sophie Turner (Sansa Stark) refers to the setting of *Game of Thrones* as "back then" and claims that "women didn't have the power to control kingdoms."[44] Benioff claims that "the world of the show" is based on "medieval reality, where women were often considered the property of their husbands."[45] Both of these claims may be true of specific places and times in the

[42] Shannon McSheffrey, "William Webbe's Wench," in *The Middle Ages on Television: Critical Essays*, edited by Meriem Pagès and Karolyn Kinane (Jefferson: McFarland, 2015), 57.

[43] Ibid., 58.

[44] "Sophie Turner Wants *Game of Thrones* to Kill Sansa Stark," *Wall Street Journal*, March 24, 2016, http://www.wsj.com/video/sophie-turner-wants-game-of-thrones-to-kill-sansa-stark/732EDC17-57F3-4A50-AC88-207E2C1A8361.html.

[45] Mike Fleming, "*Game of Thrones*' David Benioff and D.B. Weiss on Shocking Season 6 Finale," *Deadline*, June 27, 2016, http://deadline.com/2016/06/game-of-thrones-season-6-finale-david-benioff-d-b-weiss-hbo-1201780242/.

Middle Ages, but actress and showrunner generalize these claims to encompass the entire span of its time, nations, cultures, religions, and attitudes, a tendency which has already been shown in this book to be quite common among writers and audiences.

More frequently, the showrunners pass the criticism on to Martin, as discussed above. The implication is that Martin's world is based on the Middle Ages, and that this historical authenticity automatically transfers to the show. On the season five DVDs, the special features include "The Real History Behind *Game of Thrones*," wherein Martin, Dan Jones (author of *The Wars of the Roses*, 2014), and Kelly DeVries (medieval historian at Loyola University) discuss the various medieval antecedents to people and incidents in *A Song of Ice and Fire*, with images from the show providing flavor.[46] The implication, again, is that the influences and antecedents for Martin are, by extension, the influences and antecedents for the show, despite clear differences between the books and the show, and despite the fact that all three – Martin, Jones, and DeVries – are discussing the books and Martin's writing, not the screen adaptation. Even reviewers and critics have a tendency to discuss the historical antecedents for the show in their follow-up articles for individual episodes, especially those with large set-pieces ("Battle of the Bastards" [6.9]) or emotionally shocking moments ("The Rains of Castamere" [3.9]).[47]

However, the ones who are by far the most likely to cite historical authenticity when defending the show are the fans. Comment sections on popular blogs are full of insistences that the show is "historically accurate," as well as assertions that if particular writers (or other commenters) do not like the show, they should stop watching it. Others claim that it is "just" a TV show and not worth the kind of scrutiny it receives. For example, when Lupita Nyong'o told

[46] "The Real History Behind *Game of Thrones.*"

[47] See, for example, "*Game of Thrones* Red Wedding Based on Real Historical Events: Black Dinner and Glencoe Massacre," *Huffington Post*, June 5, 2013, http://www.huffingtonpost.com/2013/06/05/game-of-thrones-red-wedding-black-dinner-real-events_n_3393099.html; Nate Jones, "How Accurate was *Game of Thrones*' Battle of the Bastards?" *Vulture*, June 22, 2016, http://www.vulture.com/2016/06/battle-of-the-bastards-game-of-thrones-historical-accuracy.html.

Vogue she would love to have a cameo on *Game of Thrones*, fansite *Watchers on the Wall* published a piece discussing the lack of racial diversity in the show.[48] Comments on the post included complaints about how the show changed the slaves in Slavers Bay from multi-ethnic to primarily people of color, but also exasperated comments about "PC hysterics."[49] User "Master of Keys" claims that "Westeros is a continent set in medieval times. It does not have to be of whatever racial quota we deem acceptable nowadays," while many others point out the characters who were described as white in the books and cast as non-white in the show.[50] Helen Young's analysis of reader/viewer reactions to race issues on *Westeros.org* shows that fans have a tendency to use deflection techniques to dismiss any implication that there is a problem with Martin's portrayal of people of color.[51] Similar commentary can be found on articles discussing rape, torture, patriarchal social structures, and slavery in the show. Debra Farraday claims that these sorts of comments allow viewers (and, in some cases, the actors) to distance themselves from these problems by relegating them not only to the past, but to the unreal; the show is fiction, and fantasy, and medievalist, after all, and therefore has no true relevance to or impact on modern life.[52] The "only a TV show" defense is used frequently for many shows, of course, but the triple-defense of fiction/fantasy/medievalist may be entirely unique to *Game of Thrones*.

While actors – and, to an extent, directors – can be excused for their neomedieval tendencies when discussing the show, as their job

[48] Petra, "Lupita Nyong'o, *Game of Thrones*, and the Diversity Question," *Watchers on the Wall*, September 22, 2015, http://watchersonthewall.com/lupita-nyongo-game-of-thrones-and-the-diversity-question/.

[49] Brooklyn Ann, comment on "Lupita Nyong'o, *Game of Thrones*, and the Diversity Question," *Watchers on the Wall*, September 22, 2015, 1:37 p.m., http://watchersonthewall.com/lupita-nyongo-game-of-thrones-and-the-diversity-question/#comment-436452.

[50] Master of Keys, comment on "Lupita Nyong'o, *Game of Thrones*, and the Diversity Question," *Watchers on the Wall*, September 22, 2015, 1:44 p.m., http://watchersonthewall.com/lupita-nyongo-game-of-thrones-and-the-diversity-question/#comment-436466.

[51] Helen Young, "Race in Online Fantasy Fandom: Whiteness on *Westeros.org*," *Continuum: Journal of Media and Cultural Studies* 28, no. 5 (2014), 737–47.

[52] Debra Ferreday, "*Game of Thrones*, Rape Culture and Feminist Fandom," *Australian Feminist Studies* 30, no. 83 (2015), 31–2.

is to create what the showrunners have handed them, often Benioff and Weiss' neomedieval tendencies read as a reluctance to own their choices and take responsibility for any controversy that might occur. Again, as discussed in the introduction, Westeros is a fantasy world and is not beholden to any aspect of the historical Middle Ages. The choices made are Martin's, Benioff's, and Weiss', not requirements placed on them by history. Insisting on historical authenticity or realism in a fantasy show is disingenuous at best and deflects issues that arise from the narrative choices of the creators.

"You sound like a bloody woman": Men, Women, and Gender Relations

Following Martin's worldbuilding, show-Westeros is a world of faux chivalry and toxic masculinity, where honor is no shield and nobody is safe from violence, rape, or death. As in *A Song of Ice and Fire*, expectations for gender roles are typical for a patriarchal social structure, but many women defy these roles and find their own identity outside of them. Men, however, are less likely to defy the expectations for men – primarily violence and aggressive sexuality – unless their circumstances prevent them from conforming. However, *Game of Thrones* approaches these issues in a much less nuanced fashion, in a way that appears to celebrate the toxic masculinity rather than deconstructing it, while forcing women to gain power through similar violent means, or removing their power entirely either through death or by relegating that power to the male characters.

As discussed in Chapter 2, Martin focuses on the damage that prowess-focused masculinity does to men raised with these expectations, and how that damage manifests in their treatment of women, treatment of men who do not meet the standard, and their own emotional trauma. Through the lives of Sam, Bran, and Tyrion, he shows how psychologically and physically damaging these expectations are for men and their relationships with others. Often, men find the most fulfillment by rejecting societal demands; Sam enters the Citadel to become a maester, Tyrion is an accomplished politician, Bran trains to become a greenseer, and even Jaime finds enjoyment in non-violently cleaning up the Riverlands after the War of the Five

Kings. Instead, *Game of Thrones* pushes non-conforming characters toward a traditional definition of manhood, even when the definition must be bent slightly to accommodate their particular disabilities or difficulties.

Initially, Sam Tarly's backstory and the effect his father's treatment had on his self-confidence follow the book closely. Sam tells Jon that he joined the Night's Watch because his father gave him a choice between taking the Black or dying in a "hunting accident."[53] After that, Sam only mentions his father twice more, once when explaining given names and surnames to Gilly, when he asks her not to name her baby Randyll, and once when Stannis comes to meet him and ask about killing the White Walker.[54] The show does not provide the same level of detail that the books do regarding Randyll's attempts to make Sam into a man, which lessens Sam's trauma to an extent; while his father's ultimatum is awful, the audience is unaware of the years of abuse that led up to that ultimatum, the abuse that caused Sam's "cowardice" and likely his weight issues. Instead, Sam appears to have failed to be a "man" on his own, and Randyll's reaction, while extreme, is less horrible than the book version.

In later seasons, however, Sam's characterization and writing slide toward a more traditional version of masculinity. Rather than killing a White Walker on the trip south from the Fist of the First Men, with witnesses from the Night's Watch, he slays the Walker on the trip from Craster's Keep to the Wall, with only Gilly as a witness.[55] Thus, rather than his brothers dubbing him "Sam the Slayer" out of admiration, they do so out of mockery because nobody believes he really killed the Walker; rather than being embarrassed by adulation, Sam becomes irritated that nobody believes he has performed an act of bravery and heroism.[56] He even brags that he does not need to train at arms with Jon because he is the only member of the Night's Watch

[53] "Cripples, Bastards, and Broken Things," *Game of Thrones*, written by Bryan Cogman, directed by Brian Kirk (HBO, 2012).

[54] "Second Sons"; "Kill the Boy," *Game of Thrones*, written by Bryan Cogman, directed by Jeremy Podeswa (HBO, 2016).

[55] Martin, *A Storm of Swords*, 252; "Second Sons."

[56] Martin, *A Storm of Swords*, 1052; "Breaker of Chains."

who has killed both a White Walker and a Thenn.[57] Whereas in the books, Sam actually spends very little time with Gilly once they reach the Wall, in the show, he spends nearly all his time with her and is frequently condescending. His relationship with Gilly is used to push him further into the tropes of masculinity, as he has to constantly defend her presence to the other men, and finally to defend her bodily from two men who attempt to rape her (he, again, reminds the men, Gilly, and the viewer that he has killed a White Walker and a Thenn in the process). This incident leads to Gilly nursing his wounds and having sex with him.[58] Whereas the book version of their first love-making presents it as mutual comfort – for Gilly leaving her baby at the Wall and for Sam losing Maester Aemon[59] – this seems more a reward for Sam's conforming to traditional ideas of masculinity by protecting "his" woman.

Finally, Sam's plan to take Gilly to Horn Hill, while only a plan in *A Feast for Crows*, yet to be carried out as of the end of *A Dance with Dragons* (in which Sam appears only in Jon's chapters), Benioff and Weiss move it up so that Sam and Gilly stop at Horn Hill before traveling to the Citadel. This change marks the first time Randyll has appeared in the show, as he was not included in Renly's army in season two and Brienne's plot changed so that she never encounters him. The Tarly family is a study in contradictions: Randyll is just as racist, ableist, and patriarchally minded as described, yet his wife and daughter show no qualms about criticizing, contradicting, and even chastising him. When Randyll explodes at Sam about being less than a man, Meleesa attempts to argue that Sam has his own sort of manhood – "Being maester of the Night's Watch is a great honor!" However, Gilly steps up to place Sam back within the definition of traditional masculinity by informing Randyll and Dickon that Sam has killed a White Walker and a Thenn, claiming that Sam is a greater

57 "The Wars to Come," *Game of Thrones*, written by David Benioff and D.B. Weiss, directed by Michael Slovis (HBO, 2016).

58 "The Gift," *Game of Thrones*, written by David Benioff and D.B. Weiss, directed by Miguel Sapochnik (HBO, 2016).

59 Martin, *A Feast for Crows*, 748–9.

warrior than either of the other men.[60] While this defense makes sense in the immediate context – Randyll and Dickon are unlikely to accept that Sam can be an intellectual and a man, and Gilly can use Sam's physical accomplishments to defend him – the continued reminders throughout these two seasons that Sam has entered the realm of masculine prowess by killing moves this beyond a woman defending her lover the only way his father will understand and into continually celebrating violence as the only true way to be a man.

This issue also arises with the portrayal of Bran and his warging abilities. As in the book, Jojen teaches Bran some of what he needs to know in order to consciously control warging into Summer, rather than only doing so in his dreams. Jojen is aware that, since he is not a warg, he does not have the skill to teach Bran what he needs to know for the coming winter. Jojen's quest, then, is to escort Bran north, past the Wall, to meet with the three-eyed crow. One incident in particular breaks with the tone of the books in a manner that celebrates rather than problematizes Bran's capacity to do violence. While taking shelter from a rainstorm in a tower, they spot a group of men on the shore (Jon and the Wildlings, unbeknownst to Bran). Hodor, upset by the storm, begins yelling, and in his desperation to quiet him, Bran wargs into him. In the books, Bran does not tell anyone about what he did, and the others are too concerned about being discovered to ask questions. Clearly, however, Bran knows that warging into Hodor is wrong, and the newfound ability scares him.[61] The language used to describe Bran's warging is strongly reminiscent of rape, indicating that Bran, the narrative voice, and likely Martin are all aware that what Bran is doing is a violation:

> It was not like sliding into Summer. That was so easy now that Bran hardly thought about it. This was harder, like trying to pull a left boot onto your right foot. It fit all wrong, and the boot was *scared* too, the boot didn't know what was happening, the boot was pushing the foot away. He tasted vomit in the back of *Hodor's* throat and that was

[60] "Blood of My Blood," *Game of Thrones*, written by Bryan Cogman, directed by Jack Bender (HBO, 2016).

[61] Martin, *A Storm of Swords*, 554.

> almost enough to make him flee. Instead he squirmed and shoved, sat up, gathered his legs under him – his huge, strong legs – and rose.[62]

Although Bran continues to use Hodor for greater mobility through *A Dance with Dragons*, he is aware that it is wrong, attempts to justify it to himself, and never tells anyone that he is doing it.

Conversely, in "The Rains of Castamere" (3.9), rather than attempting to calm Hodor, Jojen's reaction to his yelling raises the intensity of the scene, building the tension until Bran wargs into Hodor and puts him to sleep. Everyone realizes immediately what has happened, and once the danger has passed, Jojen and Bran discuss it. Jojen is impressed that Bran can warg into another human being, claiming that not even the Wildlings have wargs that can do that (though there is at least one in the books). Jojen's reaction is disquieting, because it positively reinforces Bran mentally overpowering a disabled man to force him to do Bran's will. Nobody suggests that such domination is troubling or in any way problematic.[63] Instead, Hodor is treated as a tool for Bran's use whenever he needs brute force, rather than as a person. Bran uses Hodor in this manner several more times, and at least once forces Hodor to kill a man. When Bran returns control to Hodor, Hodor looks in shock at the dead body and the blood on his hands. Bran immediately starts yelling for Hodor to cut him loose from his bonds, not noticing (or not caring) that Hodor is deeply upset.[64]

The tendency to treat Hodor as a tool rather than a person is what leads to his death. In order to escape the Night King, Meera orders Hodor to "hold the door," and to enforce that order, Bran wargs into him from the past, where he has been watching the previous generation's Stark children at Winterfell. Not only does Bran force Hodor to remain behind and secure their escape, he does so in a manner that causes a feedback loop, causing Wylis, the Starks' stableboy, to see his own future death and fall into a seizure, shouting "Hold the door,"

[62] Ibid., 767.

[63] "The Rains of Castamere," *Game of Thrones*, written by David Benioff & D.B. Weiss, directed by David Nutter (HBO, 2013).

[64] "First of His Name," *Game of Thrones*, written by David Benioff & D.B. Weiss, directed by Michelle MacLaren (HBO, 2014).

which slowly reduces to "Hodor."[65] Ultimately, Bran's continued mental domination of Hodor, encouraged by Jojen and Meera, viewed as a positive and helpful ability rather than a violation of Hodor's mental and bodily autonomy, is the cause of his disability and death. Yet the tone of the show does not seem to indicate that Bran should be blamed for any of this, only that Hodor's fate is sad, another in a long line of unfortunate deaths in *Game of Thrones*. The show and characters spend no time unpacking the fact that Bran has shown entitlement toward the body of another human and has violently forced him to do Bran's bidding, even unto his own death.

Contrarily, Jaime's disability is treated as an inconvenience rather than a massive change in his life. Much like Sansa, Jaime's political storyline (and, by extension, his redemption arc) was strongly reduced in the show in favor of more action. His time in the Riverlands, first as a captive of Robb Stark and then as a hostage on his way to be exchanged, is shortened so that he reaches King's Landing in time for the Purple Wedding rather than just after it. This is primarily a difference of pacing; *Game of Thrones* hits all of Jaime's major character moments from *A Storm of Swords*, but structures the episodes in such a way that his travel time is greatly reduced. Thus, the dynamic of his relationship with Cersei changes dramatically; rather than hearing about Joffrey's death on the road and going straight to the Sept, where he and Cersei have reunion sex, he attempts to rekindle his relationship with Cersei over several weeks and is continuously rebuffed. As Martin mentioned, this means the context for their scene in the Sept is completely changed, and the miscalculations (whether those were on the part of writer, director, or editor) contribute to a situation that undoes Jaime's introspective development and pushes him back into toxic masculinity, taking what he wants by force regardless of whom it hurts.

Jaime's moment with Tyrion after releasing him from prison further shifts his character arc, as Benioff and Weiss decided that, rather than telling the Tysha story again and allowing Tyrion to reveal Cersei's depredations, they would allow Tyrion and Jaime to

[65] "The Door," *Game of Thrones*, written by David Benioff & D.B. Weiss, directed by Jack Bender (HBO, 2016).

part on good terms.[66] Thus, rather than further introspection that drives him away from Cersei and into the Riverlands to begin raising the remaining sieges of the War of the Five Kings, Jaime attempts to atone for his sin of releasing Tyrion from his cell by traveling to Dorne to rescue Myrcella, where the golden prosthetic hand is used for comedic value during a fight. While he does finally go to Riverrun to end the siege and enforce the decree that gave the castle to Walder Frey, the bulk of his travels – using political methods of ending the last of the war and not, incidentally, keeping his vow to Catelyn Stark to never raise his hand against Stark or Tully again – are removed. His major arc, which includes ending his relationship with Cersei, learning to handle problems without violence, and discovering what kind of man he is besides a good fighter, disappears in the show and is replaced with an absurd season in Dorne (more on that later in the chapter) and a deeper and more sinister relationship with Cersei.

Theon's story likewise combines toxic masculinity with ableism, especially after he is castrated. Theon spends season two desperately trying to live up to his father's expectations despite having been raised by the Starks. He consistently chooses the path he thinks is the most Ironborn-like, even when he is aware that that path leads to ruin. In both show and books, he is captured by Ramsay Snow/Bolton and systematically broken down through mental and physical abuse, then must try to build himself back up. Several significant changes from books to show create a similar problem with lauding toxic masculinity in Theon's storyline as is seen in Bran's. Moving the torture from off-page to on-screen required more specific details than are provided in the books, which is likely what led to the writers' choice to remove Theon's genitals rather than just flay him or take off fingers and toes. Ramsay refers to Theon's penis as his "favorite toy" and "most precious possession," which he must take away from Theon as punishment.[67] When Balon Greyjoy learns that Theon has been thus mutilated, he

[66] Audio commentary on "The Children," *Game of Thrones*, written by David Benioff & D.B. Weiss, directed by Alex Graves (HBO, 2015).

[67] "The Bear and the Maiden Fair."

disowns him, claiming that he can no longer be his heir, as he is not even a man anymore.[68]

In order to be a victim, it seems, Theon must be feminized; toxic masculinity does not allow for men to be the object of abuse. Therefore, Theon's on-screen torture involves an attempted rape, a (faux) rescue during which he admits his sins and cries, and the removal of his genitals. After Theon rescues himself and returns to the Iron Islands, he suffers from post-traumatic stress disorder, leading him to dismiss the very idea that he should be king of the Islands. While Yara seems sympathetic and concerned, she quickly becomes callous about his disabilities, taking the fleet to a Volantene brothel ("some of us still like it") and telling Theon that she is "tired of watching [him] cower like a beat dog." She chides him for still being upset about "a few bad years" and says that if he is "so broken that there's no coming back, take a knife, cut your wrists. End it."[69] While her intentions seem good – she wants Theon to be better, to be strong, to be like he was before – her approach is informed entirely by the toxic masculinity of Westeros in general and the Iron Islands in particular, wherein if he cannot live up to her idea of a man, he should simply kill himself. Now that he is no longer a captive, a victim, he is expected to return to the Westerosi ideal of manhood, which does not admit trauma. This could be an astute commentary on the treatment of men – especially veterans – with post-traumatic stress disorder, but while depiction is not always the same as endorsement, there is no sense from the narrative that Yara is wrong, but rather that her straight-talk was what Theon needed to shake himself out of his self-pity and be the strong brother she demands again.

Men are not the only ones who fall victim to the show's celebration of violence and toxic masculinity. Because the show does not deconstruct traditional masculinity the way the novels do, violence is the only true way to power, and women are also caught up in this requirement. In *Game of Thrones*, women who work solely through

[68] "Mhysa," *Game of Thrones*, written by David Benioff & D.B. Weiss, directed by David Nutter (HBO, 2014).

[69] "The Broken Man," *Game of Thrones*, written by Bryan Cogman, directed by Mark Mylod (HBO, 2016).

political means die, while those who are willing to engage in violence thrive. Those women who, in the books, primarily use their political knowledge are either nonexistent in the show (Galazza Galare, Genna Frey, Adrianne Martell) or have their political power reduced and resort to violence – or die (Cersei, Daenerys, Catelyn). Women who were added or had their roles expanded for the show (Ros, Olenna) fail to successfully negotiate the politics of King's Landing and die. The handling of Ellaria and the Sand Snakes, whose roles were both expanded and made more violent, also introduces racial problems which will be discussed further below. While all of the politics have been radically simplified for the show, and only two political players – Tyrion and Varys – are fully successful, the troubling fact is that none of the women whose roles are entirely political, even as advisors rather than active players in the game of thrones, is successful (or included in the show). Even Brienne, who, in the books, engages in regular violence, is made even more violent in the show. Daenerys is the only female character who retains any political ability and survives through season six, but even her storyline's adaptation is disappointing at times, primarily in how responsibility for her ideas and actions in the books has been passed to men in the show.

In the books, Brienne avoids conflict; for the first several books, her pseudo-knighthood is performative. She fights in Renly's tourney, which does not involve actual bloodshed and death. She swears her sword to Catelyn, who does not ask her to fight or enter into dangerous situations that would require Brienne's physical protection. She fights Jaime because he attacks her, but does not harm him. She prefers to avoid conflict rather than actively seeking it out, and even wonders if she has what it takes to kill a man; her father's master-at-arms did not think she did because she is a woman. Brienne does not kill until *A Feast for Crows*, when she is ambushed by some of the Bloody Mummers, and then she kills in self-defense.[70] In the show, Brienne kills early, slaying Renly's guards who attack her after his death.[71] Not only does this lessen the impact of Brienne taking a life,

[70] Martin, *A Feast for Crows*, 419–22.

[71] "The Ghost of Harrenhal," *Game of Thrones*, written by David Benioff & D.B. Weiss, directed by David Petrarca (HBO, 2013).

it reduces Catelyn's political power too; in the books, she is able to convince Robar Royce and Emmon Cuy that black magic killed Renly, not Brienne, and they allow the women to leave.[72]

Brienne kills again while escorting Jaime to King's Landing, when they come upon several hanged women and the men who hanged them. While she fights in defense of herself and Jaime, she also purposefully makes the death of the last man slow in vengeance for a remark he made about two of the hanged women being given quick deaths (the implication being that the third was not).[73] This is the sort of behavior that book-Brienne would have decried as the act of "no true knight," as she did the hanging.[74] In the fifth season, Brienne abandons her post watching for Sansa's signal for help to find and kill Stannis, prioritizing her own need for vengeance in the name of a dead man over her vow to protect a living woman.[75] While it is narratively satisfying and provides a rare moment of closure for a character in the series, Brienne killing Stannis compounds the issue that women must be man-like in order to have power and independence. The Brienne of the books, while acting in a manner coded masculine, is actually shy, even timid, and much more like Sansa in her belief in the ideals of knighthood than the headstrong fighter of the show.

While shifting Brienne toward the violent tendencies of masculinity in the show is, taken in isolation, a potentially understandable change, when taken along with the changes in political capital and increase in violence in other women, it shows a troubling tendency to disempower women unless they accept – even embrace – the toxic masculinity of Westeros and take on male-coded power. Sansa feeds Ramsay to his dogs, imitating his own tendency to torture women with the hounds.[76] Cersei arranges for all of her political opponents

[72] Martin, *A Clash of Kings*, 503.

[73] "Valar Morghulis," *Game of Thrones*, written by David Benioff & D.B. Weiss, directed by Alan Taylor (HBO, 2013).

[74] Martin, *A Storm of Swords*, 25.

[75] "Mother's Mercy," *Game of Thrones*, written by David Benioff & D.B. Weiss, directed by David Nutter (HBO, 2016).

[76] "Battle of the Bastards," *Game of Thrones*, written by David Benioff & D.B. Weiss, directed by Miguel Sapochnik (HBO, 2016).

to be in the Sept and destroys it with wildfire.[77] Daenerys burns down the Temple of the *Dosh Khaleen*, killing all the *khals* of the Dothraki and taking on the role of *khal* herself; Frankel notes that Daenerys (in both books and show) is a male-coded leader while among the Dothraki, dressing in a vest like Drogo's, claiming bloodriders like a *khal*, and attempting to imitate her late brother Rhaegar.[78] However, the sixth season of the show takes this male-coded leadership tendency even further, casting Daenerys as a conqueror, not a politician or even a particularly successful leader. She is not even the main instigator of her own storyline; much of her agency has been removed and is instead credited to men, primarily Tyrion and Daario. The political choices she makes on her own are ineffective and make little sense with regard to the overall storyline.

Throughout her time in Meereen, Daenerys is advised by a group of men – Jorah, Barristan, Grey Worm, Hizdahr zo Loraq, and Mossador. As previously mentioned, Galazza Galare, high priestess of the Temple of the Graces, is absent from the show. Aside from asking for Missandei's advice once, Daenerys has no female advice. During this time, Daenerys frequently needs to be reminded not to act rashly – specifically, not to act like her father – and changes her mind on several issues at the advice of Jorah and Barristan. While these incidents may be intended to show that Daenerys is willing to listen to the advice of her counselors, that Barristan has to explain to her why a fair trial is better than outright execution, or Jorah why diplomacy with Yunkai would be better than burning it to the ground, removes much of Daenerys' innate intelligence and diplomatic abilities. Rather than simply showing her struggling to overcome the Targaryen tendency toward madness and excess, it also sets her up as the puppet of her advisors rather than a strong ruler in her own right.

By mid-season five, Daenerys has locked up her dragons, banished Jorah, and lost Barristan to the Sons of the Harpy. Without guidance, she engages in a series of actions that do not seem to logically follow each other. She threatens the leaders of the great houses, actually

[77] "The Winds of Winter," *Game of Thrones*, written by David Benioff & D.B. Weiss, directed by Miguel Sapochnik (HBO, 2016).

[78] Frankel, 154.

feeding one of the men to the dragons and nearly doing the same to Hizdahr. After a conversation with Missandei about whether she is a good leader, Daenerys decides to marry Hizdahr, declaring her intention to him while he is in prison, on his knees, begging for his life.[79] In the books, this decision is set up over several chapters, with Hizdahr attending every court session to request permission to reopen the fighting pits and Galazza advising Daenerys to marry Hizdahr because his lineage is strong enough to satisfy the people of the city of the right of their children to rule.[80] Daenerys agrees to marry him if he can keep the city violence-free for three months; he does, and they are married. Thus, Daenerys secures peace and security in the city and the end of the guerilla warfare perpetrated by the Sons of the Harpy through her marriage to Hizdahr. In the show, however, no such trade is made, and the Sons of the Harpy attack the celebratory fights at Daznak's Pit, slaying Hizdahr.[81] Therefore, Daenerys' marriage to Hizdahr accomplishes nothing, and her flight with Drogon becomes an escape – one which leaves her advisors and friends behind – rather than her choice to reclaim her identity and birthright as a Targaryen and shed the "floppy ears" she had donned in order to rule Meereen.[82]

Daenerys' season six storyline completely passes the books, which end with Daenerys in the Dothraki Sea, filthy and half-clothed, with Drogon beside her when Khal Jhaqo and his *khalasar* discover her.[83] Her capture by Khal Moro in the show once again removes her agency, as she does not face down the *khalasar* with a dragon at her back, but is captured, tied, forced to walk as slaves are, threatened with rape, and eventually brought to the *Dosh Khaleen*. She puts up with this treatment and does not escape until she is reunited with Daario and Jorah, who have come to rescue her. Daenerys rescues herself, but she does so by murdering all of the *khals* and destroying the Temple, again choosing violence – in this case, a very typically Targaryen violence

[79] "Kill the Boy."

[80] Martin, *A Dance with Dragons*, 323–4.

[81] "The Dance of Dragons," *Game of Thrones*, written by David Benioff & D.B. Weiss, directed by David Nutter (HBO, 2016).

[82] Martin, *A Dance with Dragons*, 764–6.

[83] Ibid., 1033.

– over diplomacy, subtlety, or politics. Daario tells her that she is a conqueror, not a governor, which inspires her to retrieve Drogon and declare every one of the Dothraki following her to be a bloodrider.[84] This action, too, is senseless, as it goes against Dothraki custom – in the books, Drogo's bloodriders refuse to serve her because she is a woman – and since a bloodrider's duty is to die for his *khal* or with him,[85] she has essentially condemned the entire Dothraki nation to either death or dishonor if she should die in battle.

They return to Meereen, where she discovers the city besieged and threatens to reduce Astapor, Yunkai, and Volantis to ash; once again, she is stopped by a man, this time Tyrion, who urges her not to be like her father. When Yara arrives to offer her fleet to Daenerys, the scene is nominally about two women making a pact, but both Yara and Daenerys look for the approval of the men advising them – Theon and Tyrion, respectively – before finalizing the agreement.[86] Overall, Daenerys' characterization has been shifted from an inexperienced but well-intentioned young woman who listens to her advisors but makes her own decisions to an irrational, bloodthirsty woman who is easily swayed by her male counsel.

In general, in fact, the women who have been successful, primarily through violent means, are still directed or overshadowed by men. Only Cersei ends season six with sovereign power, and it seems clear that she will not keep it for long, as Daenerys is sailing across the Narrow Sea. Destroying the Sept and all those in it is at least partly a result of her feeling trapped by the patriarchy; she is constantly told that she is "just" a woman and denied the power she believes to be her birthright. Competent lords, like her uncle Kevan, refuse to work with her.[87] Tommen tries to send her away at Margaery's suggestion. Margaery and her ladies mock Cersei to her face.[88] Cersei unwisely turns to the High Sparrow, hoping to use him to take down her enemies, only to be caught in her own trap. After her walk of

[84] "Blood of My Blood."

[85] Martin, *A Game of Thrones*, 391.

[86] "Battle of the Bastards."

[87] "The House of Black and White," *Game of Thrones*, written by David Benioff & D.B. Weiss, directed by Michael Slovis (HBO, 2016).

[88] "High Sparrow."

atonement, she is shut out of the inner workings of the government entirely.[89] When Tommen becomes strongly devout and outlaws trial by combat – the only way that Cersei will be able to show her innocence – she is left with no options if she wishes to remain free (the punishment for her sins should she be found guilty is never made clear). Prejudice against women and sexualized punishment prevent Cersei from wielding the power she wishes to have, a specifically masculine power, so she finds a different way to wield a man's power, using the wildfire left under the Great Sept of Baelor by Aerys the Mad King to destroy her enemies.[90]

Cersei is the only woman to stand entirely on her own as a political power, and she is a villain. Sansa, the last (known) living Stark heir, must rely on Petyr to ally her with the Boltons, Theon to save her from Ramsay, Petyr again to provide the army to fight Ramsay, and she allows Jon Snow to take the title King in the North without a protest, despite his status as bastard and hers as Stark.[91] Daenerys, as has already been mentioned, requires the help and advice of Jorah, Barristan, Tyrion, Varys, and Daario. Yara seeks to take the throne of the Iron Islands, but also requires the assistance and approval of Theon. Even Melisandre, the powerful witch-woman who can raise the dead and see the future in the flames, constantly attaches herself to men until Jon sends her away.[92] While much of this can be attributed to the patriarchal culture of Westeros, that culture is applied so inconsistently (see, for example, Talisa's tendency to talk back to a king and attend to men on a battlefield without an escort despite her birth status) that it becomes less of a factor in the worldbuilding and characterization and more of a neomedieval excuse to sideline women.

[89] "Oathbreaker," *Game of Thrones*, written by David Benioff & D.B. Weiss, directed by Daniel Sackheim (HBO, 2016).

[90] "The Winds of Winter."

[91] "High Sparrow"; "Mother's Mercy"; "The Battle of the Bastards"; "The Winds of Winter."

[92] "The Winds of Winter."

"Women on top": Sex and Sexuality

The promotional run for the sixth season of *Game of Thrones*, as exemplified in *Entertainment Weekly*, was titled "Dame of Thrones," with the follow-on "Women on Top," with cover variations depicting Sophie Turner (Sansa), Maisie Williams (Arya), Lena Headey (Cersei), Emilia Clarke (Daenerys), Gwendoline Christie (Brienne), and Natalie Dormer (Margaery) in versions of their costumes.[93] While probably intending to offset the frequent complaints and negative press regarding the treatment of women in the show, this advertising, coupled with the events of season six, is still problematic. The tagline "women on top" suggests a sexual position rather than political power, and three of the six covers have a focal point of the actresses' cleavage (Turner's, Dormer's, and Clarke's). In particular, Turner's outfit is the black feathered dress with the collar-and-chain necklace that she wears in "The Mountain and the Viper," which carries all of the connotations of Sansa's sexuality discussed above. While these covers are paratexts[94] rather than part of the text itself, they are inescapable representations of the expectations HBO sets up for *Game of Thrones* and the ways in which the producers attempt to maintain or increase the show's audience, as well as the way the show treats its women and their sexuality.

Much debate has ensued over the role of sex in the series and whether the show contains more sex, more explicit sex, or more exploitative sex than the books. Benioff and Weiss do not think this is the case, and often claim they have actually toned down the sexual content, especially as it applies to the younger characters. However, the shift in context of much of the sexual content, as well as the introduction of "sexposition" during the first season, creates different, often sinister, overtones. Martin has defended the amount of sex in the novels as a part of life and, frequently, politics, and has claimed

[93] Mark Hom and Jonathan Schubert, cover of *Entertainment Weekly*, April 1, 2016, https://backissues.ew.com/storefront/2016/dame-of-thrones-sophie-turner-as-sansa-stark/prodEW20160401D.html.

[94] Defined by Gerard Genette as the productions that surround a text in order to present it to an audience (*Paratexts: Thresholds of Interpretation* [Cambridge: Cambridge University Press, 1997], 1).

that one person's idea of gratuitousness is not necessarily another's. For the most part, sex in the books is plot- or character-relevant and is set up by characters' personalities and choices, though the prose may often be awkward in these scenes. Sex in the show tends much more toward the exploitative, put in place as spectacles rather than plot-driving incidents. Broadly speaking, sexual encounters on the show are framed for the male gaze, with women as objects rather than active, consenting participants.

The most obvious examples of this tendency are in the numerous scenes with prostitutes. As early as episode one, naked prostitutes are a frequent sight. Most often, the women (only two male prostitutes have appeared, only one of them named) are naked while the men are fully or partially clothed or, if naked, hidden by clever camera angles. In season one, only three fully unclothed men appear, and only one in a sexual context.[95] Meanwhile, roughly eighteen unclothed women appear, twelve of them prostitutes. Season one is the home of one of the most controversial scenes in the show, wherein a fully clothed Petyr directs Ros and Armeca in more convincingly feigning pleasure and orgasm.[96] In this and many other scenes, nude women are treated as backdrops to or decorations for the main action. This tendency led Myles McNutt to coin the term "sexposition" to refer to the scenes in which male characters discuss their plans, history, ideas, or other expositional information with women (usually prostitutes) with whom they are having sex.[97] Many of the scenes that take place in brothels in the show do not exist in the books, or take place elsewhere, or the information provided during the "sexposition" is given another way. Thus, the frequency of naked female bodies appears exploitative, taking advantage of the HBO context rather than appearing for narrative necessity.

[95] "The Wolf and the Lion," *Game of Thrones*, written by David Benioff & D.B. Weiss, directed by Brian Kirk (HBO, 2012); "You Win or You Die," *Game of Thrones*, written by David Benioff & D.B. Weiss, directed by Daniel Minahan (HBO, 2012); "The Pointy End," *Game of Thrones*, written by George R.R. Martin, directed by Daniel Minahan (HBO, 2012).

[96] "You Win or You Die."

[97] Myles McNutt, "*Game of Thrones* – 'You Win or You Die,'" *Cultural Learnings*, May 29, 2011, https://cultural-learnings.com/2011/05/29/game-of-thrones-you-win-or-you-die/.

In particular, Ros' death is narratively and visually distressing; she is turned over to Joffrey as a plaything – his first kill – by Petyr as a punishment for spying on him for Varys. In this way, her death reduces her to an object, a piece in the game between Petyr and Varys, as well as a living target for Joffrey's crossbow bolts. When her fate is revealed, she is tied by the wrists to the upper crossbar of Joffrey's bed, her weight hanging from her wrists, her bottom resting against the mattress, one leg stretched out and the other knee bent. She has been penetrated by bolts in four places – her arm, her chest, her thigh, and her lower belly. The placement of these bolts is clearly sexual in nature; Joffrey has been unable to relate to women in any way besides terrorizing them, and showed actual fear when Ros tried to touch him in a previous episode. Joffrey has used the bolts, already phallic symbols, as replacements for the sexual contact he is too afraid to have.[98]

While the narrative reasons for her death are disturbing enough – Joffrey's inability to relate to people and his desire to hurt them have already been well established before this point, and her death is unnecessary to enforce them – the cinematography joins in the horror, also treating Ros as an object to be looked at, even in death. The camera begins on Joffrey, who gets up from his seat and crosses in front of the shot, which follows him to Ros before he passes out of frame. Ros' body becomes the center of the shot. The camera pushes in, then cuts to a pan-up across her body from her waist to just above her head, allowing the viewer to take in the details of her broken body. The way she is positioned and then shot continues the tendency of making Ros into what Frankel calls a "posable doll" – from her "sexposition" scene with Armeca, to her torture scene with Daisy, to her death.[99] Ros has always been an object for the male gaze, and is no less so in death than she was in life.

The portrayal of prostitution and sex slavery is generally inconsistent and in many cases troubling. For the most part, prostitutes in Westeros seem quite content, safe, clean, and happy to be doing their jobs. Only when someone besides a client comes into the brothel – the

[98] Frankel, 119.
[99] Ibid., 119.

Gold Cloaks, the Faith Militant – or the prostitute leaves the brothel – Ros – do things get complicated for them. Occasionally, incidents occur that show that prostitution is not quite the carefree profession it appears; for example, Petyr tells Ros that if she does not immediately stop crying about the murdered bastard baby, he will have no further use for her, and will dispose of her in some particularly unpleasant manner.[100] Petyr's speech, in combination with his turning Ros over to Joffrey for killing, show that he sees the prostitutes in his brothel as his property, just as if he owned a Volantene brothel. Yet when this attitude is inconvenient for a particular story point, it is merely erased, as when the prostitutes Tyrion hires to reward Podrick for his valor return the money he left to pay them for their services.[101] In the next episode, Ros reveals to Varys that Petyr has not even noticed that the money is missing.[102] Despite Petyr having been established as a person who is quite aware of what happens in his brothels and is not careless with money, the narrative ignores this characterization when it is inconvenient for a comedic moment – one that, incidentally, reinforces the idea that men need both sex and violence; Tyrion rewards Podrick for saving his life at the Battle of the Blackwater with three particularly flexible prostitutes.

The established horror of slavery also slips when Tyrion visits a Volantene brothel. Tyrion encounters a sex slave who appears depressed because all the men want one of the others, who wears a blonde wig and a blue dress like Daenerys' (but with the back open up to the waist). While the sadness might be an act to draw in a customer, she recognizes that Tyrion has no money and, after a brief conversation, decides to have sex with him anyway.[103] As a sex slave, it is highly unlikely that she would be able to get away with giving away her master's property in this way. However, the writers want to show that Tyrion has changed – he does not take the slave up on her

[100] "The Night Lands," *Game of Thrones*, written by David Benioff & D.B. Weiss, directed by Alan Taylor (HBO, 2012).

[101] "Walk of Punishment," *Game of Thrones*, written by David Benioff & D.B. Weiss, directed by David Benioff (HBO, 2014).

[102] "And Now His Watch is Ended," *Game of Thrones*, written by David Benioff & D.B. Weiss, directed by Alex Graves (HBO, 2014).

[103] "High Sparrow."

offer, nor does he rape her as he does in the books – so the rules are momentarily lifted and ignored in a manner that strains credulity. If sex slaves are given this kind of freedom, and seem to truly enjoy their work, why do they need Daenerys to liberate them? Benioff and Weiss passed up a good chance to show the difference between voluntary prostitution and sex slavery, or to make the point that they are equally awful, and instead further elevated Tyrion and erased one of his major character flaws.

Also troubling is the increase in the amount of rape; again, numerically, the books may have more, but at least two major sexual incidents from the books were changed from consensual to non-consensual for the show. Jaime and Cersei's encounter in the Sept has already been discussed, and while the book version of the scene is not straightforward, with Cersei's initial resistance calling into question the nature of her consent moments later, the show version of the scene is undeniably rape. Likewise, Drogo and Daenerys' wedding-night scene changed from (quasi-)consensual to outright rape, which shifts the dynamic of their relationship from Daenerys finding freedom in her marriage to Drogo – "he has given me the wind" – to simply being traded into another abusive relationship.[104] In the commentary on the episode, Benioff and Weiss claim that while they initially wrote the scene as consensual, the actors had too much trouble taking the turn from non-consensual to consensual, and so they rewrote it to be entirely non-consensual.[105] Rapes or near-rapes that happen off-page in the books are moved to on-screen, such as Lollys Stokeworth's gang-rape in *A Clash of Kings* being a near-rape of Sansa in "The Old Gods and the New."[106] Sansa's wedding-night rape, discussed above, happened to another character in the books, and the rape itself did not appear on-page.[107] The treatment of Craster's wives at the hands of the Night's Watch mutineers totals two sentences in the books,

[104] Martin, *A Game of Thrones*, 106.

[105] Commentary on "Winter is Coming," *Game of Thrones*, written by David Benioff & D.B. Weiss, directed by Tim van Patten (HBO, 2012).

[106] Martin, *A Clash of Kings*, 600; "The Old Gods and the New."

[107] Martin, *A Dance with Dragons*, 550.

whereas in the show, rape becomes a backdrop to Karl's ranting, and Meera is tied up and also threatened with rape.[108]

In the show, rape becomes casual shorthand to show how bad the rapist is (Karl, the mutineers, Ramsay, Meryn Trant) or how bad the situation is (Daenerys, Sansa), while rarely having consequences. Jaime's rape of Cersei is never mentioned again and does not appear to affect their relationship. Daenerys falls in love with Drogo. Karl and the mutineers are killed to prevent them from telling Mance Rayder the true strength of the Night's Watch, not because of their treatment of the women. Meryn Trant is killed because of his involvement with Syrio Forel's death, not because of his fetish for hitting and raping young girls; indeed, Arya uses this fetish to get close to him in order to kill him.[109] Other opportunities to punish rapists and reinforce that rape is wrong are abandoned; Jaime's time cleaning up the Riverlands, during which he executes a man for rape, for example, does not appear. Rather than using the realities of rape and abuse of women to explore societal issues that give rise to and result from this sort of behavior, Benioff and Weiss fall into clichés about rape and sexual assault, using it to create drama and tension rather than acknowledging it as a horrifying act and a deeply traumatic experience for the victim.

Violence against or exploitation of women is not the only problem with the portrayal of sex and sexuality in the show. Homosexuality is also reduced to its most clichéd, as is most apparent in the treatment of Loras Tyrell. Loras and Renly's relationship is mostly subtext in the books, but the difference in medium and viewpoint for the show allowed Benioff and Weiss to make the relationship clear and explicit, showing Loras and Renly in bed together and making clear Margaery's knowledge both of her brother's sexuality and his relationship with her husband.[110] Initially, this difference provides more insight into the inner workings of Renly's court and a positive portrayal of homosexual men. Some changes in Renly's character

[108] Martin, *A Storm of Swords*, 458–9; "Oathkeeper," *Game of Thrones*, written by Bryan Cogman, directed by Michelle MacLaren (HBO, 2015).

[109] "Mother's Mercy."

[110] "What is Dead May Never Die," *Game of Thrones*, written by Bryan Cogman, directed by Alik Sakharov (HBO, 2013).

creep in, however; he is portrayed as delicate, despising the fighting, hunting, and outdoorsmanship of his brother Robert. He hates the sight of blood, and Loras nicks him while shaving to make the point that he must be stronger if he hopes to become king.[111] This is a sharp difference from his characterization in the books, where he enjoys tournaments and hunting; he fights in the Tourney of the Hand rather than sitting in the stands watching. In both show and books, he has the charisma to inspire people to follow him. The show characterization of Renly pushes away from the subversive one that Martin constructed – despite his preferences, he is still very masculine – and toward a more stereotypical, effeminate personality who is afraid of violence, blood, and the idea of sex with women. The writers even turn the relationship into a punchline, having several Lannister soldiers joking about Loras "stabbing" Renly.[112]

With Renly's death, Loras is left bereft of his lover and his lord. He sits next to Renly's bier, mourning the loss of both, and he and Margaery accept Petyr's suggestion that they ally with the Lannisters in order to take revenge on Stannis (having concluded that his death was Stannis' doing, not Brienne's).[113] He is next seen with Tywin's forces when they break Stannis' siege at the Battle of the Blackwater. His characterization up to this point is that of a fierce warrior, loyal to Renly and his family, and mindful of duty, though he does show a jealous streak, complaining to Renly about Brienne beating him in the melee and being appointed to the Kingsguard.[114] In season three and beyond, Loras' characterization becomes more crude. Book-Loras continues to believe in chivalric masculinity and values, essentially taking a vow of celibacy after Renly's death; he joins the Kingsguard both to protect Margaery and to avoid being forced to marry. He speaks eloquently of Renly and his own celibacy, claiming that "when the sun has set, no candle can replace it."[115] Jaime sees him as arrogant, reckless, and proud, which is exemplified when he

[111] "The Wolf and the Lion."

[112] "Garden of Bones," *Game of Thrones*, written by Vanessa Taylor, directed by David Petrarca (HBO, 2013).

[113] "The Ghost of Harrenhal."

[114] "What is Dead May Never Die."

[115] Martin, *A Storm of Swords*, 168.

insists on being the one to break the siege at Dragonstone so the fleet is available to fight the Ironborn raiding the Reach.[116] Loras valiantly leads the charge and is severely wounded; as of *A Dance with Dragons*, he is still injured and possibly dying.[117]

The show version of Loras, on the other hand, does not remain faithful to the memory of Renly or join the Kingsguard. His brothers are erased from the narrative, leaving him as the sole male heir to Highgarden, and thus unable to join the Kingsguard as he must marry to carry on the family line. While this is technically a minor change to the story, as Willas never appears on page and Garlan is a minor character, so amalgamating all three characters helps to streamline the narrative, Benioff and Weiss combined this with a radical change in Loras' characterization, one which conforms to some of the worst stereotypes of homosexual men. This Loras is courteous and somewhat chivalrous, agreeing to the marriage to Sansa and treating her with respect, though the one long conversation he has with her is awkward and involves him correcting her on the difference between "pin" and "brooch," and waxing poetic about his dream wedding with the bride as an afterthought in a scene clearly meant to provide comic relief.[118] This Loras falls into bed with Olyvar without a second thought, and never mentions Renly again.[119] This Loras is the main target of the High Septon's attack on the nobility and is captured (with barely a fight, despite being armed and armored), charged with and tortured into confessing to "buggery," perjury, depravity, and profligacy, and finally killed with his family in Cersei's destruction of the Sept.[120] Benioff and Weiss' treatment of Loras, rather than subverting and countering traditional stereotypes of homosexual men, reinforces them. Post-Renly, Loras is effeminate, obsessed with clothing, promiscuous, and subject to the trope referred to as "Bury Your Gays"

[116] Martin, *A Storm of Swords*, 923; *A Feast for Crows*, 680.

[117] Martin, *A Feast for Crows*, 755–6.

[118] "The Climb," *Game of Thrones*, written by David Benioff & D.B. Weiss, directed by Alik Sakharov (HBO, 2014).

[119] "Kissed by Fire," *Game of Thrones*, written by Bryan Cogman, directed by Alex Graves (HBO, 2014).

[120] "Unbowed, Unbent, Unbroken"; "Sons of the Harpy," *Game of Thrones*, written by Dave Hill, directed by Mark Mylod (HBO, 2016); "The Winds of Winter."

by *TV Tropes*, in which homosexual characters are not allowed to have happy endings, and usually die.[121] While the last can be justified by the nature of the show and the nature of the death, taken together with the rest of the issues, it compounds the show's uneasy portrayal of same-sex relations in general and Loras as a gay man in particular.

Benioff and Weiss have, of course, frequently been asked to talk about the amount and type of sex on the show. Again, they frequently gesture back to the books or the Middle Ages as justification for both the sex and the sexual violence. As mentioned above, Weiss claims that reducing either would have done a "disservice to the reality and groundedness of George's vision."[122] Both showrunners claim that the books have more gratuitous sex than the show, though both times they have claimed this, they have pointed to the same single scene in the books – where the Qartheen ambassador treats Daenerys to a show by their most talented troupe of dancers, which involves nudity and sex – as an example of a scene they could not film. However, this does not make the point that there is more, or more gratuitous, sex in the book, just that this single scene is too explicit for them to have filmed.[123] In another interview, they joke about it, with Weiss claiming that "gratuitous" is subjective, saying, "There will always be those who want to see less sex, and those who want to see more sex, and those who want to see sex in big tubs of pudding. You just can't please everyone. This year, we're going to focus on the pudding people."[124] They disagree with the term "sexposition," claiming that sex is actually counterproductive for exposition as it tends to distract

[121] "Bury Your Gays," *TV Tropes*, n.d., http://tvtropes.org/pmwiki/pmwiki.php/Main/BuryYourGays.

[122] Lacob, "*Game of Thrones*' Sexual Politics," n.p.

[123] Michael Mechanic, "*Game of Thrones* has Succeeded Beyond its Creators' Wildest Dreams," *Mother Jones*, March/April 2013, http://www.motherjones.com/media/2013/03/hbo-game-thrones-season-3-interview-david-benioff-dan-weiss; Kate Aurthur, "9 Ways *Game of Thrones* is Actually Feminist," *Buzzfeed*, April 17, 2013, https://www.buzzfeed.com/kateaurthur/9-ways-game-of-thrones-is-actually-feminist?utm_term=.roxO7AO1pa#.gtZZY5ZpWL.

[124] Jace Lacob, "*Game of Thrones*' Creative Gurus," *The Daily Beast*, August 29, 2011, http://www.thedailybeast.com/articles/2011/08/29/david-benioff-d-b-weiss-discuss-game-of-thrones-season-2-more.html.

the audience from what is being said: "Once it has their attention, it tends not to let go of it."[125]

However, when the controversy over "Breaker of Chains" erupted and interviewers attempted to discuss the scene and the controversy with Benioff and Weiss, they declined to be interviewed and were largely silent on the issue (as discussed above).[126] Generally speaking, Benioff and Weiss (and occasionally the other writers and directors) appear to think that the audience is overreacting when it objects to the manner in which they portray sex and sexual violence, and they seem to have no intention of doing anything any differently. However, the amount of nudity – exploitative or otherwise – and the number of sex scenes dropped dramatically in season six when compared to season one, with roughly a quarter of the number of sex scenes, just under half the number of nude scenes, and no rape. Benioff and Weiss, however, claim that this is not in response to criticism (as will be discussed in more detail below).[127]

"The Dornish are crazy": Race and Imperialism

Game of Thrones has inherited its share of issues with race, imperialism, and colonialism from *A Song of Ice and Fire*, as well as the ingrained (but erroneous) belief that medieval Europe was entirely populated by white people. Yet, as with the above-discussed topics, the show also creates and constructs new problems that do not appear in the books, some of which Martin seemed to take great pains to

[125] Mechanic, n.p.

[126] Dave Itzkoff, "For *Game of Thrones*, Rising Unease over Rape's Recurring Role," *New York Times*, May 3, 2014, http://www.nytimes.com/2014/05/03/arts/television/for-game-of-thrones-rising-unease-over-rapes-recurring-role.html?_r=0; Denise Martin, n.p.

[127] Interestingly, the other writers have a tendency, especially on commentary tracks, to deny responsibility for "sexposition" or otherwise unnecessary sex scenes, claiming that Benioff and Weiss either moved the scene from an episode they wrote or added it to the episode on their own. Bryan Cogman denies responsibility for Viserys' scene in the bath with Doreah in "Cripples, Bastards, and Broken Things" (1.4), while Martin claims to have had "absolutely nothing to do" – in the book or the script – with Myranda and Violet's seduction of Theon ahead of his castration in "The Bear and the Maiden Fair" (3.7).

avoid. In some cases, the show further exacerbates problems seen in the books, such as the portrayal of the Dothraki as barbarians obsessed with sex and violence. These issues are most clearly seen in the portrayal of Dorne, the peoples of Slavers Bay, and the general handling of slavery and prostitution.

The Dornish are a late arrival to both books and show, with Oberyn Martell arriving in season four and *A Storm of Swords*, and the land of Dorne not appearing until season five and *A Feast for Crows*. Martin claims Dorne was inspired by Moorish Spain, Palestine, and Wales, having a different culture from the country with which it shares a landmass.[128] Dorne is more diverse than most of the Seven Kingdoms; in *The World of Ice and Fire*, Daeron I Targaryen catalogued the Dornish into three types – stony, salty, and sandy – each with their own customs and distinct features.[129] Women in Dorne have more rights, especially with regard to inheritance, and sexuality is more permissive. Unfortunately, the showrunners fixated on permissive sexuality and fighting women for their portrayal of Dorne, which also suffered from their paring-down of the cast through killing off or failing to introduce major characters.

On the way to rescue Myrcella from Sunspear, Bronn comments that "the Dornish are crazy. All they want to do is fight and fuck, fuck and fight."[130] Ironically, this is all Bronn is interested in, as well, but when a group he considers "other" shows similar appetites, he labels them as "crazy." While this statement alone can be read as a simple sellsword's somewhat racist view of an unfamiliar culture, the narrative does not refute or even complicate this view, but reinforces it. The Sand Snakes, Oberyn's bastard daughters, as well as Ellaria, are bloodthirsty and irrational, demanding revenge for Oberyn's death and fighting with Doran because he will not declare war on the Lannisters. The three Sand Snakes included in the show – Nymeria, Obara, and Tyene – fight among themselves and refer to each other

[128] "Historical Influences for Dorne," *The Citadel: So Spake Martin*, February 29, 2000, http://www.westeros.org/Citadel/SSM/Entry/Historical_Influences_for_Dorne/.

[129] Martin, Garcia, and Antonsson, 236.

[130] "Sons of the Harpy."

as "greedy bitch" and "slut."[131] Tyene poisons Bronn and forces him to admit that she is the most beautiful woman in the world while she strips nearly naked before giving him the antidote.[132] Refusing to bow to Doran's more measured, long-view approach to relations with the rest of the Seven Kingdoms, Ellaria and the Sand Snakes kill Myrcella, Doran, Trystane, and Aero Hotah, claiming that "weak men will never rule Dorne again."[133] The characterization of these women falls into unfortunately stereotypical, hypersexualized portrayals that so often plague female characters of color. Non-white bodies are frequently portrayed as "oversexualized and 'animalistic'" in contrast to white women, who are "sexually pure" and need protection.[134] In this case, Myrcella fills this role; during her time in Dorne, she has begun to dress provocatively and fallen in love with Trystane, her betrothed. Jaime appears to rescue her from the threat to her life, but Ellaria kills her by coating her lips with poison and kissing Myrcella. The implication is that Myrcella has been hopelessly corrupted by the Dornish, adopting their mores and manner of dress, and the fact it is a same-sex kiss that kills her further problematizes the depiction.

The introduction of Oberyn Martell suffers from similar issues. Whereas in the books, Oberyn meets Tyrion and they share a fairly straightforward political conversation on the way into the city, in the show, Oberyn skips straight to the brothel, and the audience first sees him picking out one of Petyr's prostitutes for Ellaria. Moments later, some Lannister soldiers in another room begin singing "The Rains of Castamere," and Oberyn flies into a rage, attacking them before Tyrion arrives to calm him down.[135] Oberyn falls into the non-white-male stereotype of sex and violence, and his characterization throughout the season lies in little more than enjoying sex and hating Lannisters.

While Ellaria's coup in Dorne is meant to be part of the "women on

[131] "The Red Woman," *Game of Thrones*, written by David Benioff & D.B. Weiss, directed by Jeremy Podeswa (HBO, 2016); "The Dance of Dragons."

[132] "The Dance of Dragons."

[133] "The Red Woman."

[134] Amanda Moras, "Race and Sexuality," in *The Wiley Blackwell Encyclopedia of Family Studies*, edited by Constance L. Shehan, vol. IV (Malden: John Wiley & Sons, 2016), 1645.

[135] "Two Swords," *Game of Thrones*, written by David Benioff & D.B. Weiss, directed by D.B. Weiss (HBO, 2015).

top" storyline, wherein women seize power and take revenge on those who have harmed them, the plot does not make sense in terms of its internal consistency. The show establishes that women have the same right to rule as men in Dorne, but does not establish that bastards have any more rights of inheritance than they do in the rest of the Seven Kingdoms (Jon Snow becoming King in the North notwithstanding). Even if they can, Ellaria has no claim to the throne, being Oberyn's paramour, not his wife. At best, the eldest Sand Snake should take power if bastards are indeed allowed to inherit. Likewise, Ellaria and Tyene murder Doran and Aero in front of several other guards, and yet not only do the guards not kill them, they allow the women to take power without a fight. The storytelling here has several plot holes that are not satisfactorily explained within the narrative.

Besides rewriting and replacing Martin's storyline for Dorne, this version also abandons nuanced views of the Dornish, their customs, their sexual mores, and their politics. It derides men who think, plan, and refuse to fight as "weak," and it turns the Sand Snakes, who in the books listen to Doran's plan and join in rather than insisting on violence, into hypersexualized stereotypes.

Daenerys' storyline in Slavers Bay and Vaes Dothrak has a different set of tensions surrounding race and portrayals of non-white cultures. In many ways, these echo but amplify the issues already discussed in Chapter 4. Perhaps the most notorious instance of racial portrayal is in "Mhysa" (3.10), when Daenerys is lifted above the crowd of primarily non-white former slaves in celebration. While this can be (and has been) dismissed as a quirk of casting extras in Morocco, with the "white savior" overtones already present in the narrative, this caused much controversy.[136] In the books, the slavery system is not racial, but based on conquest and poverty; people of all races and skin colors appear in the slave pens, fighting pits, brothels, and slave-owning households of Slavers Bay and Pentos. In the show, the slavers are primarily lighter-skinned, whereas the slaves are primarily darker-skinned, and although there is no diegetic explanation for this

[136] George R.R. Martin, comment on "Back from L.A.," *Not a Blog*, June 13, 2013, 9:03 p.m., http://grrm.livejournal.com/325946.html?thread=17814842#t17814842.

tendency, it creates a troubling visual effect and carries connotations of the sort of racially based slavery that existed in the West from the sixteenth to the nineteenth centuries.

When Daenerys escapes Meereen on Drogon's back and encounters the Dothraki again, their portrayal veers away from that of the first season and picks up several offensive stereotypes. The *khalasar* surrounds Daenerys, riding in circles and whooping like Native Americans in a Western. The men make lewd comments about her body as they take her to the *khal*, and when they make camp and she is brought before the *khal*, the bloodriders' conversation is Monty-Pythonesque, with hints of the 1982 film *Conan the Barbarian*:

> KHAL MORO: Seeing a beautiful woman naked for the first time – what is better than that?
> BLOODRIDER #1: Killing another *khal*?
> KHAL MORO: Yes, killing another *khal*.
> BLOODRIDER #2: Conquering a city and taking her people as slaves, and taking her idols back to Vaes Dothrak.
> BLOODRIDER #1: Breaking a wild horse, forcing it to submit to your will.
> KHAL MORO (irritated): Seeing a beautiful woman naked for the first time is among the five best things in life.[137]

Khal Moro's wives want him to kill Daenerys, calling her a witch because of the color of her hair, further emphasizing the superstitious nature of the Dothraki, especially the women. But Moro takes her back to the *Dosh Khaleen*, where she discovers that they are not the powerful group of wisewomen they were in the first season (or in the books), but that even they are subject to the rule of the *Khalar Vezhven*, the council of the *khals*.[138] The *Khalar Vezhven* rules that she will not become one of the *Dosh Khaleen*, but instead be raped to death. Daenerys escapes this fate by burning the Temple down around them, escaping unscathed but, once again, naked. A group who have just seen their temple destroyed and their leadership wiped out might be expected to react with anger and violence, but instead the

137 "The Red Woman."
138 "Oathbreaker."

Dothraki drop to their knees before Daenerys and pledge themselves to her service.[139] This echoes several previous plot points – Daenerys hatching her dragons, freeing the slaves, accepting the adulation of the slaves – in ways that problematize the portrayal of the Dothraki as superstitious, easily led, and lecherous.

Non-white tribal peoples are not the only groups subject to shifts in the narrative that cause issues with portrayal. The Thenns are also changed dramatically from the books in a way that draws upon stereotypes of tribal barbarians, especially northern European and Celtic tribes. In the books, the Thenns illustrate that the Wildlings are not all lawless barbarians: they have a sophisticated society, mine their own ore, make their own weapons, and believe themselves the last of the First Men.[140] The Thenns are not fluent in the Common Tongue, instead continuing to speak the language of the First Men. Geographically and linguistically, they have resisted the colonial influences of the Andals on Westeros much more successfully than any other group. Jon uses this information to convince Alys Karstark to marry Sigorn, the Magnar of Thenn. Contrarily, in the show, they are unabashed cannibals who practice ritual scarification and terrorize the farmers of the north. Unlike the ice-river clans of the novels, they do not practice cannibalism out of a need to survive, but purely for the fear factor. This shift appears to be designed to make the Wildlings more threatening to the Night's Watch so that they will resist Jon's attempts to bring the tribes south of the Wall, but Martin achieved the same effect without stereotypically barbaric characterization.

"We pick and choose what's from the books": Conclusion

Clearly, *Game of Thrones* struggles as an adaptation and is not entirely successful as an internally consistent, logical story in its own right. Several possible reasons for this arise when the production of the show and the creators' statements are examined in some detail. The lack of diversity in the writers' room and among directors is a major

[139] "Book of the Stranger," *Game of Thrones*, written by David Benioff & D.B. Weiss, directed by Daniel Sackheim (HBO, 2016).

[140] Martin, *Storm of Swords*, 362; Dance *with Dragons*, 719.

factor, as is the creators' stated refusal to heed criticism or controversy. They also have a tendency to approach the series as fanfiction of the books rather than an adaptation, and appear fundamentally to misunderstand several central themes of the novels; at one point, Benioff told an interviewer that "themes are for eighth-grade book reports," rejecting the idea that the seasons have overarching arcs, but also rejecting a good deal of the appeal of *A Song of Ice and Fire*.[141]

Throughout its to-date six-season run, *Game of Thrones* has had sixty episodes at ten episodes a season. Six different writers (or sets of writers, as Benioff and Weiss always share writing credit) have penned episodes for the show, and only two of those, Jane Espenson and Vanessa Taylor, are women. Espenson shares a writing credit with Benioff and Weiss for the single episode she wrote ("A Golden Crown" [1.6]), rather than taking full credit. Taylor is the only female staff writer for the show, and she only contributed to two seasons before leaving; *Game of Thrones* has not had a female writer on staff since the end of the third season. The other writers – Bryan Cogman, Dave Hill, and George R.R. Martin – are all white men. Thus, for six seasons, *Game of Thrones* has had two women writers (33.3%) who wrote a combined total of four episodes (6.7%). Further, Benioff and Weiss have written forty-one of the sixty episodes (68.3%), and likely revised most of them. Similarly, of the eighteen people who have directed episodes, only one (5.9%) – Michelle MacLaren – is a woman, and she also only stayed for two seasons. MacLaren directed four episodes (6.7%). The ratio of people of color in the writers' room or director's chair is even worse: none of the writers or directors is non-white. Sixteen of them (69.6%) are American-born, three (13%) are Canadian-born, three are from the United Kingdom, and one (4.3%) is from the former USSR (currently Uzbekistan) but has spent most of his life in America.[142] Thus, the writers and front-line production team

[141] Andy Greenwald, "Winter is Here," *Grantland*, March 27, 2013, http://grantland.com/features/the-return-hbo-game-thrones/; it is difficult to know whether Benioff was joking, as both showrunners frequently do, but Greenwald characterized Benioff's tone as a "sneer."

[142] Alik Sakaharov is Eastern European, and the construction of Whiteness is often complicated there, but he has lived in America for most of his life and "reads" as white.

for *Game of Thrones* form a strongly homogeneous group, with no people of color and very few women in any position to point out that perhaps some plot points, portrayals, or other writing choices might be offensive or problematic.

Benioff and Weiss have also stated a refusal to heed criticism or adjust their writing based on the concerns of critics or the public. In 2014, they claimed that they do not look at online comments or message boards, so as to avoid being influenced by or pointlessly arguing with strangers; Weiss says even positive comments can be damaging because "it gives you a little pleasure-hit each time you click on a comment and before you know it you're like a coke-addicted lab monkey clicking-clicking-clicking."[143] This is a fair assessment, and as comment threads and message boards can sometimes be described as "cesspools," choosing not to visit them is not something for which they should be chided.

However, they choose not to pay attention to *any* of the commentary or criticism, regardless of the source. At the Oxford Union, when asked about the Jaime–Cersei rape scene and what (if anything) they would do to avoid this sort of controversy in the future, Benioff said that the controversy does not affect the writing at all, and that they write what the show calls for, regardless of the reaction it might cause. He expressed amazement that "a fictional interaction between two fictional characters" was covered on the front page of the *New York Times*, reaching subtly back to the "it's just a show" defense that is heard so often from fans (there is also a hint of the idea that if the controversy gets the show major press coverage, it cannot be entirely bad).[144] When Podeswa claimed that Benioff and Weiss were "receptive" to criticism after the Sansa rape scene and planned some changes to the way they approached sexual violence on the show, they responded by saying that it was "not a factual statement." Weiss says, "I can literally say that not one word of the scripts this season have [*sic*] been changed in any way, shape or form by what people said

[143] James Hibberd, "Why *Game of Thrones* Producers Ignore the Internet: 'It Completely Confounds the Normal Creative Process,'" *Entertainment Weekly*, May 4, 2014, http://www.ew.com/article/2014/05/04/game-of-thrones-ignore-internet.

[144] "*Game of Thrones* at the Oxford Union."

on the Internet, or elsewhere."[145] However, as has been mentioned, the amount of sex, sexual violence, and nudity on the show dropped precipitously in season six, so it is possible that, despite their claims, they have listened to the critics.

Finally, the showrunners – not just Benioff and Weiss, but also Cogman – have a habit of talking about the source material as a jumping-off point rather than a guideline for the show, despite their frequent claims that they are being faithful to Martin's vision. As the show has gone on and diverged further from the books, these statements have increased in frequency. During season two, Benioff and Weiss said that they loved creating scenes between characters whose discussions are not seen on page in the books, such as Robb and Jaime.[146] By season five, Cogman admits to "pick[ing] and choos[ing] what's from the books" and moving plot moments around to achieve the character arcs they want to create for each season.[147] As they prepared for season six, Benioff and Weiss admitted that the show had now diverged so far from the books that the show would not spoil the books even as the narrative progressed past *A Dance with Dragons*, yet, as mentioned above, they continued to claim that certain controversial scenes were present because Martin had told them that was where the narrative was headed.[148] While the show is entirely their responsibility and they are "under no contractual restrictions with regards to the storytelling," their continued claims that they are somehow telling the same story as Martin are not reflected in the show itself. Benioff argues that they are adapting the books according

[145] Groves; James Hibberd, "*Game of Thrones* Producers: 'Not One Word' Changed Due to Criticism," *Entertainment Weekly*, April 1, 2016, http://www.ew.com/article/2016/04/01/game-thrones-season-6.

[146] "HBO Releases New Promo Images and Q&A with Benioff and Weiss," *Winter is Coming*, March 23, 2012, http://winteriscoming.net/2012/03/23/hbo-releases-new-promo-images-and-qa-with-benioff-weiss/.

[147] Jennifer Vineyard, "*Game of Thrones* Showrunners on Changes from the Books, the Butterfly Effect, and Arya's Arc," *Vulture*, April 27, 2015, http://www.vulture.com/2015/04/game-of-thrones-showrunners-on-changes-from-the-books.html.

[148] James Hibberd, "*Game of Thrones* Showrunners: Season 6 Won't Spoil the Books," *Entertainment Weekly*, March 23, 2016, http://www.ew.com/article/2016/03/23/game-thrones-season-6-wont-spoil-books.

to "our notion of justice – which won't mesh with the fundamentalist book fans' notions. Which is fine with us, because if the fundamentalists were running the show, there wouldn't be a show."[149] However, there is a difference between expecting the show to adhere to every letter of Martin's novels and expecting it to keep their spirit and basic shape, which *Game of Thrones* has not done since season four.

Game of Thrones, even more than *A Song of Ice and Fire*, relies on "Barbaric Age" or "gothic" medievalism, as well as Kaufman's "muscular medievalism," to lay claim to historical and social authenticity. Rape, violence, abuse of women and children, and slavery are considered necessary plot points because they are somehow required for Benioff, Weiss, and Martin's version of the Middle Ages to "feel" real. While Martin attempts, with mixed success, to unpack, critique, and problematize these aspects of his Middle Ages – even while claiming that including them in the first place is necessary to keep his Middle Ages "authentic" – Benioff and Weiss instead glorify toxic masculinity, use rape and casual female nudity as backdrops to the action, and oversimplify the condition and structures of slavery, all while arguing that the realities of history and Martin's novels have forced them to portray these horrors on screen. Again, these claims are circular – they influence the imaginations and medievalist thought patterns of the fans, who then argue that the Middle Ages was a time of gritty violence, which then influences popular culture to further use violence and rape as "markers of medieval authenticity."[150] Such claims also allow the writers to avoid taking responsibility for the choices they make about the show and to continue without examining the reasons why they find violence, rape, and abuse just as important in creating a Middle Ages as are the tropes of feudalism, armor and weapons.

[149] Mechanic, n.p.
[150] Kaufman, "Muscular Medievalism," 57.

Afterword: "Fantasy for people who hate fantasy"

As a genre, medievalist fantasy is often not taken seriously, at least in part because of its blend of medievalism and fantasy; neither has been particularly well regarded by the academy or those parts of the public that frown on "escapism" and genre literature. Medievalism itself suffers from its association both with the medieval – often used as shorthand for barbaric, backwards, stupid, and infantile – and with inaccuracies and bad history. Medievalism studies are frequently seen as the lesser cousin of medieval studies, the consolation prize for scholars in countries that do not have a medieval history as it is typically understood in Europe. Fantasy, likewise, has been derided as escapist, childish, even psychologically dangerous, and has its own connections to the medieval, particularly through romance, that further keep it from being treated seriously. Thus, it is no real surprise that Martin so vocally rejects the usual tropes of medievalist fantasy and strives for realism and a grounding in medieval history; historical precedent and a lack of traditional fantasy elements might lead to his work gaining more respect than that of other fantasy writers. That attempting to make medievalist fantasy more palatable to those who traditionally frown on such things requires a "grimdark" approach and insistence on the worst parts of the human condition – violence, rape, slavery – being foregrounded is unfortunate. While a medievalist and/or fantastic setting may allow readers and writers to examine modern issues at a comfortable remove, it can also reinforce the stereotypical understanding of the Middle Ages as the "Barbaric Age" – dirty, violent, brutal, patriarchal, sexually deviant – while allowing readers and writers to gloss over the fact that modern life has many of these same issues, to believe in the myth of progressive history and relegate inequality and savagery to the distant past.

The insistence on a realist medievalism also invites criticism on grounds of accuracy and authenticity, shifting the focus from traditional literary analysis to whether Martin got the Middle Ages "right." While examinations of Martin's source materials can be valuable and interesting (see, for example, Carolyne Larrington's *Winter is Coming* [2016]), especially as a gateway to history for those interested in such things, it is important to keep in mind that *A Song of Ice and Fire* is, ultimately, high fantasy, not set in any approximation of the historical Middle Ages.[1] Likewise, as many scholars of medievalism have demonstrated, it is impossible to truly know the Middle Ages and thus to judge the authenticity of any medievalist text. As David Matthews argues, all postmedieval versions of the Middle Ages are invented, and the line between medieval studies and medievalism is often fluid and blurred.[2] While it can be very easy to fall into a right/wrong, true/false exploration of specific incidents, cultures, tendencies, or attitudes in *A Song of Ice and Fire* as compared to their (apparent) medieval antecedents, this approach ignores much deeper questions of why Martin made these choices and why he believes they create a "real" Middle Ages in the world of Westeros, as well as how his portrayal affects the beliefs of those who read his work.

A Song of Ice and Fire shows very clear influences from a myriad of genres – medieval romance, history, Victorian medievalist romance, modern medievalist or neomedieval fantasy, and horror, for example – even when Martin actively works against their familiar tropes. Martin's claim that his work is a more honest and accurate portrayal of the history, sociology, and psychology of the Middle Ages is clearly erroneous, as the sort of accuracy he strives for is impossible, but that does not mean that *A Song of Ice and Fire* is a failure. In reaching for realism, Martin has created compelling characters, complex plots and subplots, and a masterpiece of worldbuilding. The hundreds of years' worth of influence from various genres, authors, and historical

[1] Carolyne Larrington, *Winter is Coming: The Medieval World of "Game of Thrones"* (New York: I.B. Tauris, 2016).

[2] Matthews, 168.

people and incidents make for a delightfully intertextual narrative, with much to unpack for readers who recognize these influences, without leaving behind those who might not.

Martin's bids to avoid or subvert the traditions of medievalist fantasy led to some remarkable thematic similarities with medieval romance, particularly the anxieties of the nobility regarding behavioral expectations, identity, and dynastic succession. While Martin examines the lives of the common people in much more detail than most romances, the central focus is still very much on the upper classes and their rises, falls, politics, and wars. Despite these parallels, the narrative takes a dim view of romance and song, treating stories as unrealistic models and actively dangerous for a young person's development, perhaps reflecting Martin's own perspective on escapism.

The idea and codes of chivalry take the most criticism, and since one of the foundations of chivalry is the protection of women, the women in *A Song of Ice and Fire* are subject to horrible treatment – rape, sexual assault, physical assault – all in the name of "realism," as Martin actively refuses the idea that a code of conduct can protect even noble ladies from the worst treatment men can subject them to. Likewise, Martin's portrayal of these women frequently falls clearly into several archetypes from romance, fantasy, and horror, and these genres also have tendencies to treat women badly, either through action – murder, rape, abuse – or portrayal – the witch, the whore, the bad mother. That women are much more likely to fall into archetypes than the men is a limitation of Martin's writing, and that they are much more likely to be raped or assaulted is common for Kaufman's "muscular medievalism."[3]

Unfortunately, this creates the impression that most men are unable to control themselves and thus that this treatment is inevitable, an approach that reduces men to animal instincts held in check by a barely enforced social code and places women entirely at their mercy. While Martin sets up his medieval patriarchy as fettered by the ultimate in toxic masculinity, and uses his main male characters to show how terrible the expectations of this society are for men to attempt to live up to, many of his secondary male characters appear

[3] Kaufman, "Muscular Medievalism," 56.

to exist in this world with no difficulties, even reveling in the violence and sexual assault that is expected of them. While none of these men are portrayed in a positive light, they far outnumber the "good" ones, and nearly every female character encounters one such man and is assaulted or threatened with assault. By contrast, only one of Martin's male characters is ever threatened with sexual assault, and it does not appear to be a serious threat.[4] This creates the impression that men can never be the victims of sexual assault, which further entrenches the overly masculine version of the Middle Ages that Martin creates.

Martin does manage to avoid the idea that homosexuality did not exist in the Middle Ages, but his writing still falls into the trap of reducing same-sex interactions between women to male voyeurism, whereas the one major male homosexual relationship is framed using traditional romance language. Overall, Martin's portrayal of sexuality of all kinds falls into the deviant or transgressive sexuality of "Barbaric Age" medievalism, including incest, child marriage, and rape, with a paucity of healthy, mutually beneficial sexual relationships portrayed.

In Essos, Martin has created literal barbarians and barbaric societies disguised as polite ones, all of which must apparently be rescued or destroyed by a colonizing force. For these, as well, he leans on historical realism, invoking the Huns and Mongols, Roman-era slavery, and the excesses of Roman emperors. However, the lack of POV characters from these cultures to counterbalance Daenerys, Tyrion, Barristan, and Quentyn makes it all too easy to see the Essos cultures as Other, which further perpetuates a Eurocentric image of the Middle Ages. Likewise, that Daenerys, a white girl with white-blond hair and purple eyes, is the only one able or willing to undo the barbarism of the Dothraki and Slavers Bay invokes worrying ideas of white saviorism and the White Man's Burden.[5] Of course these interpretations are not what Martin intended, so their latency within his text indicates the pervasiveness of such attitudes toward men,

[4] Jaime tells Loras he'll take his sword and "shove it someplace even Renly never found."

[5] In a blog comment, Martin claims that, had he thought of it when he began writing *A Song of Ice and Fire*, he might have made the Valyrians black, which he admits "that choice would have brought its own perils" (Comment on "We're Number One…," *Not a Blog*, July 6, 2013, 10:57 p.m., http://grrm.livejournal.com/326474.html?thread=17888842#t17888842.

women, sex, sexuality, race, and imperialism – and the intersection of all of these things with perceptions of the medieval – in popular American culture and thought.

Meanwhile, *Game of Thrones* exacerbates these issues, reintroduces tropes Martin worked to avoid or subvert, and reduces the themes and characters to shallow copies of their book counterparts. The show celebrates toxic masculinity rather than exploring the psychological impact of its expectations on men, turning trauma into a punchline and basing a man's worth on his ability to dominate others. Rape and female nudity are used for shock value, backdrops, titillation, and shortcuts to character growth. Communities of women and female power are further sidelined, traditional outlets for women's power or contributions reduced to frivolous pastimes for "stupid" girls. "Barbaric" cultures such as the Dothraki and the Wildlings are even more violent and savage than in the books, and issues of race in the casting arise frequently. Yet the showrunners consistently fail to take responsibility for their choices, instead falling back on their "realistic" portrayal of the Middle Ages or Martin's narrative, regardless of how accurate either claim is.

While the approach to the various issues in *A Song of Ice and Fire* and *Game of Thrones* was fragmented in this book, these issues in many ways intersect, and thus there remains room for more focused analysis of settings, people, and themes in both the books and show. Other articles and books could draw out far greater nuance and detail than there was space for here. For example, how does Martin's portrayal of women of color differ from his portrayal of white women, and how do his stated beliefs about the Middle Ages influence these portrayals? How does his use of legend and history to inform and influence the present of the novels mirror or differ from our own medievalism, and what does it mean for his or his readers' view of "real" history? Why does Martin ignore or gloss over the fact that men can also be victims of sexual assault? Class issues, while touched on in this book, have not been subject to intense and isolated examination. Likewise, there remains much room for a film-theory approach to *Game of Thrones*, as this book's approach was primarily literary; costuming, settings, *mis en scene*, casting, and music, for example, have not been covered in any great detail.

Overall, Martin's approach to the Middle Ages, both in the text of

A Song of Ice and Fire and in his interviews, provides an interesting look at beliefs about the Middle Ages and how modern people glorify, demonize, or otherwise Other the era and the people who lived there and then. As with so many things, Martin's claims about the Middle Ages and fantasy reveal much more about his own political and social ideologies, and, by extension, those of the fans who agree with him and modern American society at large, than about the historical reality of the Middle Ages. Likewise, the continued insistence on "realism" in *Game of Thrones* provides insights into Benioff and Weiss' beliefs about the world, both medieval and modern.

Like Tolkien, Martin is a giant of fantasy literature, a strong influence on not only the genre, but on medievalism and neomedievalism as well. Thousands, if not hundreds of thousands, of people have been, are, or will be influenced by his portrayal of the Middle Ages, and thus the neomedieval beliefs about and views of the period that his work promotes will continue to permeate through the culture. Though many historians may find this frustrating in the extreme, some fans may be led to learn more about the historical Middle Ages by reading *A Song of Ice and Fire*, especially since Martin so frequently mentions the historical influences for incidents in his books – the Wars of the Roses, the Hundred Years War, Hadrian's Wall, etc.[6] Martin's work, as well as *Game of Thrones*, can be (and is being) used in classrooms as an introduction to medieval history and literature, linguistics, cultural studies, film studies, anthropology, and literary criticism.[7] Again like Tolkien, Martin may become a fantasy writer whose work is taken seriously enough to help increase the genre's standing in the academic community and beyond.

[6] For an example of how students might come to medieval studies through medievalist texts, see Amy Kaufman's "Lowering the Drawbridge," *The Year's Work in Medievalism* 28 (2013).

[7] See, for example, "The Man Who Created Dothraki for *Game of Thrones* is Teaching a College Language Course," *Time*, April 28, 2017, http://time.com/4759240/berkeley-dothraki-language-class/; Laura Bradley, "*Game of Thrones* is Becoming a Harvard Class," *Vanity Fair*, June 1, 2017, http://www.vanityfair.com/hollywood/2017/06/game-of-thrones-class-harvard; Amanda Bell, "9 Colleges with Actual *Game of Thrones* Courses," *MTV*, October 27, 2015, http://www.mtv.com/news/2362741/game-of-thrones-college-courses/.

Bibliography

Primary Sources

Anders, Charlie Jane. "George R.R. Martin: The Complete Unedited Interview." *Observation Deck*. September 23, 2013. http://observationdeck.kinja.com/george-r-r-martin-the-complete-unedited-interview-886117845.

"And Now His Watch is Ended." *Game of Thrones: The Complete Third Season*. Written by David Benioff & D.B. Weiss. Directed by Alex Graves. HBO, 2014.

Aurthur, Kate. "9 Ways *Game of Thrones* is Actually Feminist." *Buzzfeed*. April 17, 2013. https://www.buzzfeed.com/kateaurthur/9-ways-game-of-thrones-is-actually-feminist?utm_term=.roxO7AO1pa#.gtZZY5ZpWL.

"Battle of the Bastards." *Game of Thrones: The Complete Sixth Season*. Written by David Benioff & D.B. Weiss. Directed by Miguel Sapochnik. HBO, 2016.

"The Bear and the Maiden Fair." *Game of Thrones: The Complete Third Season*. Written by George R.R. Martin. Directed by Michelle MacLaren. HBO, 2014.

Berwick, Isobel. "Lunch with the FT: George R.R. Martin." *Financial Times*. June 1, 2012. https://www.ft.com/content/bd1e2638-a8b7-11e1-a747-00144feabdc0.

Birnbaum, Debra. "*Game of Thrones* Creators: We Know How it's Going to End." *Variety*. April 15, 2015. http://variety.com/2015/tv/news/game-of-thrones-ending-season-5-producers-interview-1201469516/.

"Blood of My Blood." *Game of Thrones: The Complete Sixth Season*. Written by Bryan Cogman. Directed by Jack Bender. HBO, 2016.

"Book of the Stranger." *Game of Thrones: The Complete Sixth Season*. Written by David Benioff & D.B. Weiss. Directed by Daniel Sackheim. HBO, 2016.

"Breaker of Chains." *Game of Thrones: The Complete Fourth Season*. Written by David Benioff and D.B. Weiss. Directed by Alex Graves. HBO, 2015.

"The Broken Man." *Game of Thrones: The Complete Sixth Season*. Written by Bryan Cogman. Directed by Mark Mylod. HBO, 2016.

"The Children." *Game of Thrones: The Complete Fourth Season*. Written by David Benioff & D.B. Weiss. Directed by Alex Graves. HBO, 2014.

Chrétien de Troyes. *Arthurian Romances*. Translated by William W. Kibler and Carleton W. Carroll. New York: Penguin, 2004.

"The Climb." *Game of Thrones: The Complete Third Season*. Written by David Benioff & D.B. Weiss. Directed by Alik Sakharov. HBO, 2013.

Collins, Sean T. "Exclusive: George R.R. Martin Says *Game of Thrones* Ending will be 'Bittersweet.'" *Observer*. August 11, 2015. http://observer.com/2015/08/george-r-r-martins-ending-for-game-of-thrones-will-not-be-as-brutal-as-you-think/.

Couch, Aaron. "*Game of Thrones* Director on Controversial Scene: Jaime 'Traumatized,' Cersei 'a Wreck' (Q&A)." *Hollywood Reporter*. April 20, 2014. http://www.hollywoodreporter.com/live-feed/game-thrones-director-controversial-scene-697733.

"Cripples, Bastards, and Broken Things." *Game of Thrones: The Complete First Season*. Written by Bryan Cogman. Directed by Brian Kirk. HBO, 2012.

"The Dance of Dragons." *Game of Thrones: The Complete Fifth Season*. Written by David Benioff & D.B. Weiss. Directed by David Nutter. HBO, 2016.

Dent, Grace. "George R.R. Martin Meets Grace Dent." *YouTube*. June 12, 2012. https://www.youtube.com/watch?v=MdSPFJcxCNM.

"The Door." *Game of Thrones: The Complete Sixth Season*. Written by David Benioff & D.B. Weiss. Directed by Jack Bender. HBO, 2016.

"Fantastic Forum Interviews George R.R. Martin." *YouTube*. April 11, 2015. https://www.youtube.com/watch?v=jVdj_YVZECE.

"First of His Name." *Game of Thrones: The Complete Fourth Season*. Written by David Benioff & D.B. Weiss. Directed by Michelle MacLaren. HBO, 2014.

Fleming, Mike. "*Game of Thrones*' David Benioff and D.B. Weiss on Shocking Season 6 Finale." *Deadline*. June 27, 2016. http://deadline.com/2016/06/game-of-thrones-season-6-finale-david-benioff-d-b-weiss-hbo-1201780242/.

"From the Book to Screen." *Game of Thrones: The Complete First Season*. HBO, 2012.

"*Game of Thrones* at the Oxford Union – Full Address." *YouTube*. March 20, 2015. https://www.youtube.com/watch?v=TfvVluNxujc.

"*Game of Thrones* Season 4 – Inside the Episode #3." *YouTube*. June 17, 2014. https://www.youtube.com/watch?v=kk9UEr74BIg.

"Garden of Bones." *Game of Thrones: The Complete Second Season*. Written by Vanessa Taylor. Directed by David Petrarca. HBO, 2013.

"George R.R. Martin and Robin Hobb – Exclusive Event." *YouTube*. August

26, 2014. https://www.youtube.com/watch?v=tXLYSnMIrXM&feature=youtu.be.

"George R.R. Martin: Necessary Lies." *Locus* 45, no. 6 (2000): 6–7, 80.

"George R.R. Martin Steers a Six-Book Cavalcade." *Cyberhaven*. February 10, 1999. https://web.archive.org/web/19991013131915/http://cyberhaven.com/books/sciencefiction/martin.html.

"George R.R. Martin on Strombo: Full Extended Interview." *YouTube*. March 14, 2012. https://www.youtube.com/watch?v=fHfip4DefG4.

"The Gift." *Game of Thrones: The Complete Fifth Season*. Written by David Benioff & D.B. Weiss. Directed by Miguel Sapochnik. HBO, 2016.

"The Ghost of Harrenhal." *Game of Thrones: The Complete Second Season*. Written by David Benioff & D.B. Weiss. Directed by David Petrarca. HBO, 2013.

Greenwald, Andy. "Winter is Here." *Grantland*. March 27, 2013. http://grantland.com/features/the-return-hbo-game-thrones/.

Groves, Don. "*Game of Thrones* Rape Scene Repercussions Play Out in New Season." *Forbes*. December 18, 2015. https://archive.is/E2Kvh.

"HBO Releases New Promo Images and Q&A with Benioff & Weiss." *Winter is Coming*. March 23, 2012. http://winteriscoming.net/2012/03/23/hbo-releases-new-promo-images-and-qa-with-benioff-weiss/.

Hibberd, James. "*Game of Thrones* Producer Explains Sansa's Wedding Night Horror." *Entertainment Weekly*. May 17, 2015. http://www.ew.com/article/2015/05/17/game-thrones-sansa-ramsay-interview.

—— "*Game of Thrones* Producers Explain Changing Sansa's Storyline." *Entertainment Weekly*. April 26, 2015. http://www.ew.com/article/2015/04/26/game-thrones-sansa-ramsay-interview.

—— "*Game of Thrones* Producers: 'Not One Word' Changed Due to Criticism." *Entertainment Weekly*. April 1, 2016. http://www.ew.com/article/2016/04/01/game-thrones-season-6.

—— "*Game of Thrones* Showrunner Explains Why Bran is Not in Season 5." *Entertainment Weekly*. November 5, 2014. http://www.ew.com/article/2014/11/05/game-of-thrones-why-bran-season-5.

—— "*Game of Thrones* Showrunners: Season 6 Won't Spoil the Books." *Entertainment Weekly*. March 23, 2016. http://www.ew.com/article/2016/03/23/game-thrones-season-6-wont-spoil-books.

—— "George R.R. Martin Explains Why there's Violence Against Women on *Game of Thrones*." *Entertainment Weekly*. June 3, 2015. http://www.ew.com/article/2015/06/03/george-rr-martin-thrones-violence-women.

—— "Why *Game of Thrones* Producers Ignore the Internet: 'It Completely Confounds the Normal Creative Process.'" *Entertainment Weekly*. May 4, 2014. http://www.ew.com/article/2014/05/04/game-of-thrones-ignore-internet.

"High Sparrow." *Game of Thrones: The Complete Fifth Season*. Written by David Benioff & D.B. Weiss. Directed by Mark Mylod. HBO, 2016.

"Historical Influences." *The Citadel: So Spake Martin*. January 20, 2001. http://www.westeros.org/Citadel/SSM/Entry/1170.

"Historical Influences for Dorne." *The Citadel: So Spake Martin*. February 29, 2000. http://www.westeros.org/Citadel/SSM/Entry/Historical_Influences_for_Dorne/.

Hodgeman, John. "George R.R. Martin, Author of *A Song of Ice and Fire*." *Bullseye*. September 19, 2011. http://www.maximumfun.org/sound-young-america/george-r-r-martin-author-song-ice-and-fire-series-interview-sound-young-america.

Hogan, Ron. "The Beatrice Interview: George R.R. Martin (2000)." *Ron Hogan's Beatrice*. 2000. http://www.beatrice.com/interviews/martin/.

Hom, Mark and Jonathan Schubert. Cover of *Entertainment Weekly*. April 1, 2016. https://backissues.ew.com/storefront/2016/dame-of-thrones-sophie-turner-as-sansa-stark/prodEW20160401D.html.

"The House of Black and White." *Game of Thrones: The Complete Fifth Season*. Written by David Benioff & D.B. Weiss. Directed by Michael Slovis. HBO, 2016.

"Interaction (Glasgow, Scotland, UK: August 4–8)." *The Citadel: So Spake Martin*. August 4, 2005. http://www.westeros.org/Citadel/SSM/Entry/1348.

Itzkoff, Dave. "For *Game of Thrones*, Rising Unease over Rape's Recurring Role." *New York Times*. May 3, 2014. http://www.nytimes.com/2014/05/03/arts/television/for-game-of-thrones-rising-unease-over-rapes-recurring-role.html?_r=0.

——"His Beautiful, Dark, Twisted Fantasy: George R.R. Martin Talks *Game of Thrones*." *New York Times*. April 1, 2011. http://artsbeat.blogs.nytimes.com/2011/04/01/his-beautiful-dark-twisted-fantasy-george-r-r-martin-talks-game-of-thrones/?_r=0.

Kaveney, Roz. "A Storm is Coming." *Amazon.co.uk*. July 2000. http://www.amazon.co.uk/exec/obidos/tg/feature/-/49161/026-1281322-7450821?tag=westeros-21.

"Kill the Boy." *Game of Thrones: The Complete Fifth Season*. Written by Bryan Cogman. Directed by Jeremy Podeswa. HBO, 2016.

Kirschling, Gregory. "George R.R. Martin Answers Your Questions." *Entertainment Weekly*. November 27, 2007. http://www.ew.com/article/2007/11/27/george-rr-martin-answers-your-questions.

"Kissed by Fire." *Game of Thrones: The Complete Third Season*. Written by Bryan Cogman. Directed by Alex Graves. HBO, 2014.

Lacob, Jace. "*Game of Thrones*' Creative Gurus." *The Daily Beast*. August 29, 2011. http://www.thedailybeast.com/articles/2011/08/29/david-benioff-d-b-weiss-discuss-game-of-thrones-season-2-more.html.

—— "*Game of Thrones*' Sexual Politics." *The Daily Beast*. June 5, 2011. http://www.thedailybeast.com/game-of-thrones-sexual-politics.

Levy, Michael. "George R.R. Martin: Dreamer of Fantastic Worlds." *Publishers Weekly* 243, no. 35 (1996): 70–1.

MacLaurin, Wayne. "A Conversation with George R.R. Martin." *SF Site*. November 2000. https://www.sfsite.com/01a/gm95.htm.

"Making *Game of Thrones*." *Game of Thrones: The Complete First Season*. HBO, 2012.

Malory, Sir Thomas. *Le Morte Darthur*. Edited by Stephen H.A. Shepherd. New York: Norton, 2004.

"A Man Without Honor." *Game of Thrones: The Complete Second Season*. Written by David Benioff & D.B. Weiss. Directed by David Nutter. HBO, 2012.

Martin, Denise. "Breaking Down Jaime and Cersei's Controversial Scene with Last Night's *Game of Thrones* Director." *Vulture*. April 21, 2014. http://www.vulture.com/2014/04/game-of-thrones-director-on-the-rape-sex-scene.html.

Martin, George R.R. *A Game of Thrones*. New York: Bantam Spectra 1996. Mass Market Reissue Edition, 2005.

—— *A Clash of Kings*. New York: Bantam Spectra, 1999. Mass Market Reissue Edition, 2005.

—— *A Storm of Swords*. New York: Bantam Spectra, 2000. Mass Market Reissue Edition, 2005.

—— *A Feast for Crows*. New York: Bantam Spectra, 2005. Mass Market Edition, 2006.

—— *A Dance with Dragons*. New York: Bantam Spectra, 2011. Mass Market Edition, 2013.

—— "Alayne." Sample chapter from *The Winds of Winter*. http://web.archive.org/web/20150604025854/http://www.georgerrmartin.com/excerpt-from-the-winds-of-winter/.

—— Comment on "Author! Author!" *Not a Blog*. August 21, 2014, 8:16 p.m., http://grrm.livejournal.com/367116.html?thread=19030284#t19030284.

—— Comment on "Back from L.A." *Not a Blog*. June 13, 2013, 9:03 p.m., http://grrm.livejournal.com/325946.html?thread=17814842#t17814842.

—— Comment on "We're Number One…" *Not a Blog*. July 6, 2013, 10:57 p.m., http://grrm.livejournal.com/326474.html?thread=17888842#t17888842.

—— "Preface: From Page to Screen." *Inside HBO's "Game of Thrones": Seasons One and Two*. Edited by Bryan Cogman. San Francisco: Chronicle Books, 2012. 4–5.

—— "Reading Recommendations." *Not a Blog*. March 13, 2013. http://grrm.livejournal.com/316785.html.

——"The Show, the Books." *Not a Blog*. May 18, 2015. http://grrm.livejournal.com/427713.html.

Mechanic, Michael. "*Game of Thrones* has Succeeded Beyond its Creators' Wildest Dreams." *Mother Jones*. March/April 2013. http://www.motherjones.com/media/2013/03/hbo-game-thrones-season-3-interview-david-benioff-dan-weiss.

Merlin, or the Early History of King Arthur. Edited by Henry B. Wheatley. Ann Arbor: University of Michigan Early English Text Initiative, 1997.

"Mhysa." *Game of Thrones: The Complete Third Season*. Written by David Benioff & D.B. Weiss. Directed by David Nutter. HBO, 2014.

"Miscon Report." *The Citadel: So Spake Martin*. June 3, 2012. http://www.westeros.org/Citadel/SSM/Month/2012/06.

"Mother's Mercy." *Game of Thrones: The Complete Fifth Season*. Written by David Benioff & D.B. Weiss. Directed by David Nutter. HBO, 2016.

"The Mountain and the Viper." *Game of Thrones: The Complete Fourth Season*. Written by David Benioff & D.B. Weiss. Directed by Alex Graves. HBO, 2015.

"The Night Lands." *Game of Thrones: The Complete Second Season*. Written by David Benioff & D.B. Weiss. Directed by Alan Taylor. HBO, 2012.

"The North Remembers." *Game of Thrones: The Complete Second Season*. Written by David Benioff & D.B. Weiss. Directed by Alan Taylor. HBO, 2012.

"Oathbreaker." *Game of Thrones: The Complete Sixth Season*. Written by David Benioff & D.B. Weiss. Directed by Daniel Sackheim. HBO, 2016.

"Oathkeeper." *Game of Thrones: The Complete Fourth Season*. Written by Bryan Cogman. Directed by Michelle MacLaren. HBO, 2015.

"The Old Gods and the New." *Game of Thrones: The Complete Second Season*. Written by Vanessa Taylor. Directed by David Nutter. HBO, 2012.

"The Pointy End." *Game of Thrones: The Complete First Season*. Written by George R.R. Martin. Directed by Daniel Minahan. HBO, 2012.

Poniewozik, James. "George R.R. Martin Interview, Part 1: *Game of Thrones*, from Book to TV." *Time*. April 15, 2011. http://entertainment.time.com/2011/04/15/george-r-r-martin-on-game-of-thrones-from-book-to-tv/.

"Prose Tristan." *A New and Complete Collection of Interesting Romances and Novels*. Edited and translated by Lewis Porney. London: Alex Hogg, 1780. http://d.lib.rochester.edu/camelot/publication/porney-interesting-romances.

"The Rains of Castamere." *Game of Thrones: The Complete Third Season*. Written by David Benioff & D.B. Weiss. Directed by David Nutter. HBO, 2013.

Radish, Christina. "George R.R. Martin Interview: *Game*

of Thrones." *Collider*. April 20, 2011. http://collider.com/george-r-r-martin-interview-game-of-thrones/.

"Readers and Realism." *The Citadel: So Spake Martin*. June 28, 2001. http://www.westeros.org/Citadel/SSM/Entry/1176.

"The Real History Behind *Game of Thrones*." *Game of Thrones: The Complete Fifth Season*. HBO, 2016.

"The Red Woman." *Game of Thrones: The Complete Sixth Season*. Written by David Benioff & D.B. Weiss. Directed by Jeremy Podeswa. HBO, 2016.

"Religions of Westeros." *Game of Thrones: The Complete Second Season*. HBO, 2012.

Richards, Linda. "January Interview: George R.R. Martin." *January Magazine* (2001). http://www.januarymagazine.com/profiles/grrmartin.html.

Salter, Jessica. "*Game of Thrones*' George R.R. Martin: 'I'm a Feminist at Heart.'" *The Telegraph*. April 1, 2013. http://www.telegraph.co.uk/women/womens-life/9959063/Game-of-Throness-George-RR-Martin-Im-a-feminist.html.

Savage, Annaliza. "George R.R. Martin on *Game of Thrones*, that Controversial Rape Scene, and His Writing Progress." *The Daily Beast*. September 28, 2014. http://www.thedailybeast.com/articles/2014/07/28/george-r-r-martin-on-game-of-thrones-that-controversial-rape-scene-and-his-writing-progress.html.

Schindler, Dorman T. "*PW* Talks with George R.R. Martin: Of Hybrids and Cliches." *Publishers Weekly* 252, no. 33 (2005): 37.

Seale, Jack. "George R.R. Martin: Hollywood Would Have Ruined *Game of Thrones*." *The Guardian*. June 10, 2015. https://www.theguardian.com/tv-and-radio/tvandradioblog/2015/jun/10/george-rr-martin-hollywood-would-have-ruined-game-of-thrones.

"Second Sons." *Game of Thrones: The Complete Third Season*. Written by David Benioff & D.B. Weiss. Directed by Michelle McLaren. HBO, 2014.

Sir Gawain and the Green Knight. Translated by J.R.R. Tolkien. New York: Ballantine, 1975.

"Sir Gowther." *The Middle English Breton Lays*. Edited by Anne Laskaya and Eve Salisbury. Kalamazoo: Medieval Institute Publications, 1995. http://d.lib.rochester.edu/teams/publication/laskaya-and-salisbury-middle-english-breton-lays.

"Sons of the Harpy." *Game of Thrones: The Complete Fifth Season*. Written by Dave Hill. Directed by Mark Mylod. HBO, 2016.

"Sophie Turner Wants *Game of Thrones* to Kill Sansa Stark." *Wall Street Journal*. March 24, 2016. http://www.wsj.com/video/sophie-turner-wants-game-of-thrones-to-kill-sansa-stark/732EDC17-57F3-4A50-AC88-207E2C1A8361.html.

Taylor, C.E. *Inside HBO's "Game of Thrones": Seasons Three and Four*. San Francisco: Chronicle Books, 2014.
Thielman, Sam. "Cabler Rises to Epic Challenge." *Variety*. March 12, 2011. http://variety.com/2011/tv/news/cabler-rises-to-epic-challenge-1118033764/.
"To Be Continued." *The Citadel: So Spake Martin*. May 6, 2005. http://www.westeros.org/Citadel/SSM/Entry/To_Be_Continued_Chicago_IL_May_6_83.
Tolkien, J.R.R. *The Hobbit*. New York: Ballantine, 1965.
—— *The Lord of the Rings: The Two Towers*. New York: Ballantine, 1963.
"Two Swords." *Game of Thrones: The Complete Fourth Season*. Written by David Benioff & D.B. Weiss. Directed by D.B. Weiss. HBO, 2015.
"Unbowed, Unbent, Unbroken." *Game of Thrones: The Complete Fifth Season*. Written by Bryan Cogman. Directed by Jeremy Podeswa. HBO, 2016.
"U.S. Signing Tour (Seattle, WA)." *The Citadel: So Spake Martin*. November 21, 2005. http://www.westeros.org/Citadel/SSM/Entry/1391.
"Valar Morghulis." *Game of Thrones: The Complete Second Season*. Written by David Benioff & D.B. Weiss. Directed by Alan Taylor. HBO, 2013.
Vineyard, Jennifer. "*Game of Thrones* Showrunners on Changes from the Books, the Butterfly Effect, and Arya's Arc." *Vulture*. April 27, 2015. http://www.vulture.com/2015/04/game-of-thrones-showrunners-on-changes-from-the-books.html.
"Walk of Punishment." *Game of Thrones: The Complete Third Season*. Written by David Benioff & D.B. Weiss. Directed by David Benioff. HBO, 2014.
"The Wars to Come." *Game of Thrones: The Complete Fifth Season*. Written by David Benioff & D.B. Weiss. Directed by Michael Slovis. HBO, 2016.
"What is Dead May Never Die." *Game of Thrones: The Complete Second Season*. Written by Bryan Cogman. Directed by Alik Sakharov. HBO, 2013.
Windolf, Jim. "The *Game of Thrones* TV-Show Creators Already Know What Happens at the End of the Book Series." *Vanity Fair*. March 24, 2014. https://www.vanityfair.com/hollywood/2014/03/game-of-thrones-show-creators-know-end-of-books.
"The Winds of Winter." *Game of Thrones: The Complete Sixth Season*. Written by David Benioff & D.B. Weiss. Directed by Miguel Sapochnik. HBO, 2016.
"Winter is Coming." *Game of Thrones: The Complete First Season*. Written by David Benioff & D.B. Weiss. Directed by Tim van Patten. HBO, 2012.
"The Wolf and the Lion." *Game of Thrones: The Complete First Season*. Written by David Benioff & D.B. Weiss. Directed by Brian Kirk. HBO, 2012.

"You Win or You Die." *Game of Thrones: The Complete First Season.* Written by David Benioff & D.B. Weiss. Directed by Daniel Minahan. HBO, 2012.

Secondary Sources

"67th Emmy Awards Nominees and Winners." *Academy of Television Arts and Sciences.* 2015. http://www.emmys.com/awards/nominees-winners?page=2.

"2013 Hugo Awards." *The Hugo Awards.* 2013. http://www.thehugoawards.org/hugo-history/2013-hugo-awards/.

Ashcroft, Bill, Gareth Griffiths, and Helen Tiffin, editors. *The Postcolonial Studies Reader.* New York: Routledge, 2003.

Ashton, Gail. *Medieval English Romance in Context.* London: Continuum, 2010.

"Awards and Honors." *George R.R. Martin.* 2016. http://www.georgerrmartin.com/about-george/awards-honors/.

Balfe, Myles. "Incredible Geographies?: Orientalism and Genre Fantasy." *Social and Cultural Geography* 5, no. 1 (2004): 73–90.

Barron, W.R.J. *English Medieval Romance.* Harlow: Longman, 1987.

Batty, Nancy and Robert Markley. "Writing Back: Speculative Fiction and the Politics of Postcolonialism." *Ariel* 33, no. 1 (2002): 5–14.

Bell, Amanda. "9 Colleges with Actual *Game of Thrones* Courses." *MTV.* October 27, 2015. http://www.mtv.com/news/2362741/game-of-thrones-college-courses/.

Blamires, Alcuin. "The Twin Demons of Aristocratic Society in *Sir Gowther.*" *Pulp Fictions of Medieval England: Essays in Popular Romance.* Edited by Nicola McDonald. Manchester: Manchester University Press, 2004. 45–62.

Błaszkiewicz, Bartołomiej. "George R.R. Martin's *A Song of Ice and Fire* and the Narrative Conventions of the Interlaced Romance." *George R.R. Martin's "A Song of Ice and Fire" and the Medieval Literary Tradition.* Edited by Bartołomiej Błaszkiewicz. Warsaw: University of Warsaw Press, 2014. 15–48.

Bradley, Laura. "*Game of Thrones* is Becoming a Harvard Class." *Vanity Fair.* June 1, 2017. http://www.vanityfair.com/hollywood/2017/06/game-of-thrones-class-harvard.

Braudy, Leo. *From Chivalry to Terrorism: War and the Changing Nature of Masculinity.* New York: Alfred Knopf, 2003.

Brooklyn, Ann. Comment on "Lupita Nyong'o, *Game of Thrones,* and the Diversity Question," September 22, 2015, 1:37 p.m. http://watchersonthewall.com/lupita-nyongo-game-of-thrones-and-the-diversity-question/#comment-436452.

Bruckner, Matilda Tomaryn. "The Shape of Romance in Medieval France." *The Cambridge Companion to Medieval Romance*. Edited by Roberta L. Krueger. Cambridge: Cambridge University Press, 2000. 13–28.

Brumlik, Joan. "The Knight, the Lady, and the Dwarf in Chrétien's *Erec*." *Quondam et Futurus* 2, no. 2 (1992): 54–72.

Brzezińska, Justyna. "Reading Beric Dondarrion in the Light of the Robin Hood Legend." *George R.R. Martin's "A Song of Ice and Fire" and the Medieval Literary Tradition*. Edited by Bartołomiej Błaszkiewicz. Warsaw: University of Warsaw Press, 2014. 231–45.

Buchwald, Emilie, Pamela R. Fletcher, and Martha Roth, editors. *Transforming a Rape Culture*. Minneapolis: Milkweed Editions, 1993.

Burns, Marjorie. *Celtic and Norse in Tolkien's Middle-Earth*. Buffalo, NY: University of Toronto Press, 2005.

"Bury Your Gays." *TV Tropes*. http://tvtropes.org/pmwiki/pmwiki.php/Main/BuryYourGays.

Cameron, John H. "A New Kind of Hero: *A Song of Ice and Fire*'s Brienne of Tarth." *Quest of Her Own: Essays on the Female Hero in Modern Fantasy*. Edited by Lori M. Campbell. Jefferson: McFarland, 2014. 188–205.

Chandler, Alice. *A Dream of Order: The Medieval in Nineteenth-Century English Literature*. Lincoln: University of Nebraska Press, 1970.

Charbonneau, Joanne and Desiree Cromwell. "Gender and Identity in Popular Romance." *A Companion to Medieval Popular Romance*. Edited by Raluca L. Radulescu and Cory James Rushton. Cambridge: D.S. Brewer, 2009. 96–110.

Creed, Barbara. *The Monstrous-Feminine: Film, Television, Psychoanalysis*. New York: Routledge, 1993.

Cunliffe, Barry. *Britain Begins*. Oxford: Oxford University Press, 2013.

Dagenais, John and Margaret R. Greer. "Decolonizing the Middle Ages: Introduction." *Journal of Medieval and Early Modern Studies* 30, no. 3 (2000): 431–48.

D'arcens, Louise, and Chris Jones. "Excavating the Borders of Literary Anglo-Saxonism in Nineteenth-Century Britain and Australia." *Representations* 121, no. 1 (2013): 85–106.

Davis, Kathleen and Nadia Altschul. "Introduction: The Idea of 'the Middle Ages' Outside Europe." *Medievalisms in the Postcolonial World: The Idea of "the Middle Ages" Outside Europe*. Baltimore: Johns Hopkins University Press, 2009. 1–24.

Deane, Seamus. *Celtic Revivals: Essays in Modern Irish Literature, 1880–1980*. Boston: Faber & Faber, 1985.

Doyle, Sady. "Enter Ye Myne Mystic World of Gayng-Raype: What the 'R' in George R.R. Martin Stands For." *Tiger Beatdown*. August 26, 2011. http://tigerbeatdown.com/2011/08/26/enter-ye-myne-mystic-world-of-gayng-raype-what-the-r-stands-for-in-george-r-r-martin/.

Drout, Michael. "The Influence of J.R.R. Tolkien's Masculinist Medievalism." *Medieval Feminist Newsletter* 22 (1996): 26–7.

Eco, Umberto. *Travels in Hyperreality*. Translated by William Weaver. San Diego: Harcourt, 1986.

Emig, Rainer. "Fantasy as Politics: George R.R. Martin's *A Song of Ice and Fire*." *Politics in Fantasy Media: Essays on Ideologies and Gender in Fiction, Television, and Games*, edited by Gerold Sedlmayer and Nicole Waller. Jefferson: McFarland, 2014. 85–96.

Evans, Jonathan D. "Episodes in Analysis of Medieval Narrative." *Style* 20, no. 2 (1986): 126–41.

Faxton, Alicia. "The Pre-Raphaelite Brotherhood as Knights of the Round Table." *Pre-Raphaelitism and Medievalism in the Arts*. Edited by Liana De Girolami Cheney. New York: Edwin Mellen, 1992. 53–74.

Ferreday, Debra. "*Game of Thrones*, Rape Culture and Feminist Fandom." *Australian Feminist Studies* 30, no. 83 (2015): 21–36.

Filmer-Davies, Kath. *Fantasy Fiction and Welsh Myth: Tales of Belonging*. New York: St. Martin's, 1996.

Fimi, Dimitra. "'Mad' Elves and 'Elusive Beauty': Some Celtic Strands of Tolkien's Mythology." *Folklore* 117 (2006): 156–70.

Flieger, Verlyn. "Frodo and Aragorn: The Concept of the Hero." *Understanding "The Lord of the Rings": The Best of Tolkien Criticism*. Edited by Rose A. Zimbardo and Neil D. Isaacs. New York: Houghton Mifflin, 2004. 122–45.

——*A Question of Time: J.R.R. Tolkien's Road to Faerie*. Kent, OH: Kent State University Press, 1997.

——*Splintered Light: Language and Logos in Tolkien's World*. 2nd edition. Kent, OH: Kent State University Press, 2002.

——"'There Would Always be a Fairy-Tale': J.R.R. Tolkien and the Folklore Controversy." *Tolkien the Medievalist*. Edited by Jane Chance. New York: Routledge, 2003. 26–35.

Fowler, Rebekah M. "Sansa's Songs: The Allegory of Medieval Romance in George R.R. Martin's *A Song of Ice and Fire* Series." *George R.R. Martin's "A Song of Ice and Fire" and the Medieval Literary Tradition*. Edited by Bartołomiej Błaszkiewicz. Warsaw: University Press of Warsaw, 2014. 71–93.

Frankel, Valerie Estelle. *Women in "Game of Thrones": Power, Conformity, and Resistance*. Jefferson: McFarland, 2014.

Fuchs, Barbara and David J. Baker. "The Postcolonial Past." *Modern Language Quarterly* 65, no. 3 (2004): 329–40.

"*Game of Thrones* Red Wedding Based on Real Historical Events: Black Dinner and Glencoe Massacre." *Huffington Post*. June 5, 2013. http://www.huffingtonpost.com/2013/06/05/game-of-thrones-red-wedding-black-dinner-real-events_n_3393099.html.

Gaunt, Simon. *Gender and Genre in Medieval French Literature*. Cambridge: Cambridge University Press, 1995.

Genette, Gerard. *Paratexts: Thresholds of Interpretation*. Cambridge: Cambridge University Press, 1997.

Gravdal, Katheryn. "Camouflaging Rape: The Rhetoric of Sexual Violence in the Medieval *Pastourelle*." *Romanic Review* 76, no. 4 (1985): 361–73.

—— *Ravishing Maidens: Writing Rape in Medieval French Literature and Law*. Philadelphia: University of Pennsylvania Press, 1991.

Grossman, Lev. "George R.R. Martin's *A Dance with Dragons*: A Masterpiece Worthy of Tolkien." *Time*. July 7, 2011. http://content.time.com/time/arts/article/0,8599,2081774,00.html.

Harrison, Antony H. *Victorian Poets and the Politics of Culture: Discourse and Ideologies*. Charlottesville: University Press of Virginia, 1998.

Hildebrand, Kristina. "'Open Manslaughter and Bold Bawdry': Male Sexuality as a Cause of Disruption in Malory's Morte Darthur." *Sexual Culture in the Literature of Medieval Britain*. Edited by Amanda Hopkins, Robert Allen Rouse, and Cory James Rushton. Cambridge: D.S. Brewer, 2014. 13–25.

Horsman, Reginald. "Origins of Anglo-Saxonism in Great Britain Before 1850." *Journal of the History of Ideas* 37, no. 3 (1976): 387–410.

Howe, Nicholas. "Anglo-Saxon England and the Postcolonial Void." *Postcolonial Approaches to the European Middle Ages: Translating Cultures*. Edited by Ananya Jahanara Kabir and Deanne Williams. Cambridge: Cambridge University Press, 2005. 25–47.

Huber, Emily Rebekah. "'Delyver Me My Dwarff!': Gareth's Dwarf and Chivalric Identity." *Arthuriana* 16, no. 2 (2006): 49–53.

Huot, Sylvia. *Madness in Medieval French Literature: Identities Found and Lost*. Oxford: Oxford University Press, 2003.

Itzkoff, Dave. "HBO will Play *Game of Thrones*." *New York Times*. March 2, 2010. http://artsbeat.blogs.nytimes.com/2010/03/02/hbo-will-play-game-of-thrones/.

Jameson, Frederic. *The Political Unconscious: Narrative as a Socially Symbolic Act*. Ithaca: Cornell University Press, 1981.

Jamison, Carol. "Reading Westeros: George R.R. Martin's Multi-Layered Medievalisms." *Studies in Medievalism* XXVI (2017): 131–42.

JanMohamed, Abdul R. "The Economy of Manichean Allegory: The Function of Racial Difference in Colonialist Literature." *"Race," Writing, and Difference*. Edited by Henry Louis Gates, Jr. Chicago: University of Chicago Press, 1985. 78–106.

Jenkins, Keith. *On "What is History?": From Carr and Elton to Rorty and White*. New York: Routledge, 1995.

Jones, Nate. "How Accurate was *Game of Thrones*' Battle of the Bastards?"

Vulture. June 22, 2016. http://www.vulture.com/2016/06/battle-of-the-bastards-game-of-thrones-historical-accuracy.html.

Jordan, Mark D. "Homosexuality, *Luxuria*, and Textual Abuse." *Constructing Medieval Sexuality*. Edited by Karma Lochrie, Peggy McCracken, and James A. Schultz. Minneapolis: University of Minnesota Press, 1997. 24–39.

Kain, Eric. "*Game of Thrones* Season 4, Episode 3 Review: Sex and Violence." *Forbes*. April 21, 2014. http://www.forbes.com/sites/erikkain/2014/04/21/game-of-thrones-season4-episode-3-review-sex-and-violence#5a19431c1734.

Kaufman, Amy. "Lowering the Drawbridge." *The Year's Work in Medievalism* 28 (2013): 1–8.

—— "Medieval Unmoored." *Studies in Medievalism* XIX (2010): 1–11.

—— "Muscular Medievalism." *The Year's Work in Medievalism* 31 (2016): 56–66.

Kaueper, Richard. *Chivalry and Violence in Medieval Europe*. Oxford: Oxford University Press, 1999.

—— "The Societal Role of Chivalry in Romance: Northwestern Europe." *The Cambridge Companion to Medieval Romance*. Edited by Roberta L. Krueger. Cambridge: Cambridge University Press, 2000. 97–114.

Knight, Stephen. *Robin Hood: A Mythic Biography*. Ithaca: Cornell University Press, 2003.

Kokot, Joanna. "The Text and the World: Convention and Interlacement in George R.R. Martin's *A Game of Thrones*." *George R.R. Martin's "A Song of Ice and Fire" and the Medieval Literary Tradition*. Edited by Bartołomiej Błaszkiewicz. Warsaw: University of Warsaw Press, 2014. 49–69.

Krueger, Roberta L. "Questions of Gender in Old French Courtly Romance." *The Cambridge Companion to Medieval Romance*. Edited by Roberta L. Krueger. Cambridge: Cambridge University Press, 2000. 132–49.

—— *Women Readers and the Ideology of Gender in Old French Verse Romance*. Cambridge: Cambridge University Press, 1993.

Kudrycz, Walter. *The Historical Present: Medievalism and Modernity*. New York: Continuum, 2011.

Lang, Andrew. *Myth, Ritual, and Religion*. Vol. 1. London: Longmans, Green, and Co., 1899.

Lehrer, Seth. "'On fagne flor': The Postcolonial *Beowulf*, from Heorot to Heaney." *Postcolonial Approaches to the European Middle Ages: Translating Cultures*. Edited by Ananya Jahanara Kabir and Deanne Williams. Cambridge: Cambridge, 2005. 77–108.

"The Man Who Created Dothraki for *Game of Thrones* is Teaching a College Language Course." *Time*. April 28, 2017. http://time.com/4759240/berkeley-dothraki-language-class/.

Makariev, Plamen. "Eurocentrism." *The Encyclopedia of the Developing*

World. Volume 1. Edited by Thomas M. Leonard. New York: Routledge, 2006. 634–6.

Master of Keys. Comment on "Lupita Nyong'o, *Game of Thrones*, and the Diversity Question." September 22, 2015, 1:44 p.m. http://watchersonthewall.com/lupita-nyongo-game-of-thrones-and-the-diversity-question/#comment-436466.

Matthews, Richard. *Fantasy: The Liberation of Imagination*. New York: Twayne, 1997.

McNutt, Myles. "*Game of Thrones* – 'You Win or You Die.'" *Cultural Learnings*. May 29, 2011. https://cultural-learnings.com/2011/05/29/game-of-thrones-you-win-or-you-die/.

McSheffrey, Shannon. "William Webbe's Wench." *The Middle Ages on Television: Critical Essays*. Edited by Meriem Pagès and Karolyn Kinane. Jefferson: McFarland, 2015. 53–77.

Mommsen, Theodore E. "Petrarch's Conception of the 'Dark Ages.'" *Speculum* 17, no. 2 (1942): 226–42.

Moras, Amanda. "Race and Sexuality." *The Wiley Blackwell Encyclopedia of Family Studies*. Edited by Constance L. Shehan. Vol. IV. Malden: John Wiley & Sons, 2016. 1644–8.

Morris, Kevin L. *The Image of the Middle Ages in Romantic and Victorian Literature*. Dover: Croom Helm, 1984.

Müller, Max. *Lectures on the Science of Language*. 5th edition. Oxford: Oxford University Press, 1866.

Oakeshott, Michael. *On History and Other Essays*. Totowa, NJ: Barnes and Noble, 1983.

Ortenberg, Veronica. *In Search of the Holy Grail: The Quest for the Middle Ages*. London: Hambledon Continuum, 2006.

Partner, Nancy F. "No Sex, No Gender." *Speculum* 68, no. 2 (1993): 419–43.

Petra. "Lupita Nyong'o, *Game of Thrones*, and the Diversity Question." *Watchers on the Wall*. September 22, 2015. http://watchersonthewall.com/lupita-nyongo-game-of-thrones-and-the-diversity-question/.

Pierce, Tamora. "Girls Who Kick Butt." *Locus* 48, no. 5 (2002): 6–7, 76–8.

Pugh, Tison, and Susan Aronstein. "Introduction: Disney's Retroprogressive Medievalisms: Where Yesterday is Tomorrow's Today." *The Disney Middle Ages: A Fairy-Tale and Fantasy Past*. Edited by Tison Pugh and Susan Aronstein. New York: Palgrave Macmillan, 2012. 1–20.

Pugh, Tison, and Angela Jane Weisl. *Medievalisms: Making the Past in the Present*. New York: Routledge, 2013.

Rabkin, Eric. "Atavism and Utopia." *Alternative Futures* 1, no. 1 (1972): 71–82.

Rich, Adrienne. *Of Woman Born: Motherhood as Experience and Institution*. 2nd edition. New York: W.W. Norton, 1986.

Rider, Jeff. "The Other Worlds of Romance." *The Cambridge Companion to Medieval Romance*. Edited by Roberta L. Krueger. Cambridge: Cambridge University Press, 2000. 115–31.

Robinson, Carol L. and Pamela Clements. "Living with Neomedievalism." *Studies in Medievalism* XVIII (2009): 55–75.

Rohy, Valerie. "Ahistorical." *GLQ* 12, no. 1 (2006): 61–83.

Rosenberg, Alyssa. "*Game of Thrones* Review: 'Breaker of Chains,' Breakers of Will." *Washington Post*. April 20, 2014. http://www.washingtonpost.com/news/act-four/wp/2014/04/20/game-of-thrones-review-breaker-of-chains-breakers-of-will/?utm_term=.a55018b1a337.

Russ, Joanna. "Introduction." *Uranian Worlds: A Guide to Alternative Sexuality in Science Fiction, Fantasy, and Horror*. Edited by Eric Garber and Lyn Paleo. 2nd edition. Boston: G.K. Hall, 1990. xxiii–xxvi.

Saccaro, Matt. "Stop Defending *Game of Thrones*: How HBO Gutted the Stories I Love." *Salon*. June 14, 2015. http://www.salon.com/2015/06/14/stop_defending_game_of_thrones_how_hbo_gutted_the_stories_i_love/.

Said, Edward. *Orientalism*. New York: Vintage Books, 1978.

Salmonson, Jessica Amanda. "Introduction: Our Amazon Heritage." *Amazons!* Edited by Jessica Amanda Salmonson. New York: DAW, 1979. 1–15.

Salter, David. "'Born to Thralldom and Penance': Wives and Mothers in Middle English Romance." *Writing Gender and Genre in Medieval Literature: Approaches to Old and Middle English Texts*. Edited by Elaine Treharne. Cambridge: D.S. Brewer, 2002. 41–59.

Selling, Kim. "Fantastic Neomedivalism: The Image of the Middle Ages in Popular Fantasy." *Flashes of the Fantastic: Selected Essays from the War of the Worlds Centennial: Nineteenth International Conference on the Fantastic in the Arts*. Edited by David Ketterer. Westport: Praeger, 2004. 211–18.

Sepinwall, Alan. "Review: *Game of Thrones* – 'Breaker of Chains': Uncle Deadly?" *HitFix*. April 20, 2014. http://www.hitfix.com/whats-alan-watching/review-game-of-thrones-breaker-of-chains-uncle-deadly.

Sheriff, Mary. *The Exceptional Woman*. Chicago: University of Chicago Press, 1996.

Spivak, Gayatri Chakravorty. "Can the Subaltern Speak?" *Can the Subaltern Speak? Reflections on the History of an Idea*. Edited by Rosalind C. Morris. New York: Columbia University Press, 2010. 21–78.

Starling, Phaedra. "Schrödinger's Rapist: Or a Guy's Guide to Approaching Strange Women Without Being Maced." *Shapely Prose*. October 8, 2009. https://kateharding.net/2009/10/08/guest-blogger-starling-schrodinger%E2%80%99s-rapist-or-a-guy%E2%80%99s-guide-to-approaching-strange-women-without-being-maced/.

Sullivan, C.W. "Celtic Myth and English-Language Fantasy Literature: Possible New Directions." *Journal of the Fantastic in the Arts* 10, no. 1 (1998): 88–96.

Thompson, Raymond H. "Modern Fantasy and Medieval Romance." *The Aesthetics of Fantasy Literature and Art*. Edited by Roger C. Schlobin. Notre Dame: University of Notre Dame Press, 1982. 211–25.

Tilahun, Naamen Gobert. "Thoughts on 'Colonialism . . . in . . . Space!' and on the Ground." *The Wis-Con Chronicles: Provocative Essays on Feminism, Race, Revolution, and the Future*. Volume 2. Edited by L. Timmel Duchamp and Eileen Gunn. Seattle: Aqueduct Press, 2008. 41–50.

Tolkien, J.R.R. "On Fairy-Stories." 1939. *The Monsters and the Critics and Other Essays*. Edited by Christopher Tolkien. New York: Harper Collins, 2006. 109–61.

Tolmie, Jane. "Medievalism and the Fantasy Heroine." *Journal of Gender Studies* 15, no. 2 (2006): 145–58.

Ussher, Jane M. *Managing the Monstrous Feminine: Regulating the Reproductive Body*. New York: Routledge, 2006.

Vines, Amy N. "Invisible Woman: Rape as a Chivalric Necessity in Medieval Romance." *Sexual Culture in the Literature of Medieval Britain*. Edited by Amanda Hopkins, Robert Allen Rouse, and Cory James Rushton. Cambridge: D.S. Brewer, 2014. 161–80.

Webster, P.J. "Tolkien and Escapist Fantasy Literature." *Amon Hen* 133 (1995): 11–12.

Wilson, Edmund. "Oo, Those Awful Orcs!" *The Nation*. April 14, 1956. http://www.jrrvf.com/sda/critiques/The_Nation.html.

Young, Helen. "Authenticity and *Game of Thrones*." Presentation at the 48th Annual International Congress on Medieval Studies, Kalamazoo, MI, May 10, 2013.

—— "'It's the Middle Ages, Yo!': Race, Neo/medievalisms, and the World of *Dragon Age*." *Year's Work in Medievalism* 27 (2012): 2–9.

—— "The Pleasure of Neo/medievalist Fantasy." Presentation at the International Conference on Medievalism, De Pere, WI, July 2013.

—— *Race and Popular Fantasy Literature: Habits of Whiteness*. New York: Routledge, 2016.

—— "Race in Online Fantasy Fandom: Whiteness on *Westeros.org*." *Continuum: Journal of Media and Cultural Studies* 28, no. 5 (2014): 737–47.

Yuval-Davis, Nira. *Gender and Nation*. Thousand Oaks: Sage Publications, 1997.

Index

Medievalism

I

Anglo-Saxon Culture and the Modern Imagination
edited by David Clark and Nicholas Perkins

II

Medievalist Enlightenment: From Charles Perrault to Jean-Jacques Rousseau
Alicia C. Montoya

III

Memory and Myths of the Norman Conquest
Siobhan Brownlie

IV

Comic Medievalism: Laughing at the Middle Ages
Louise D'Arcens

V

Medievalism: Key Critical Terms
edited by Elizabeth Emery and Richard Utz

VI

Medievalism: A Critical History
David Matthews

VII

Chivalry and the Medieval Past
edited by Katie Stevenson and Barbara Gribling

VIII

Georgian Gothic: Medievalist Architecture, Furniture and Interiors, 1730–1840
Peter N. Lindfield

IX

Petrarch and the Literary Culture of Nineteenth-Century France: Translation, Appropriation, Transformation
Jennifer Rushworth

X

Medievalism, Politics and Mass Media: Appropriating the Middle Ages in the Twenty-First Century
Andrew B.R. Elliott

XI

Translating Early Medieval Poetry: Transformation, Reception, Interpretation
edited by Tom Birkett and Kirsty March-Lyons